THE ENGLISH ARISTOCRACY

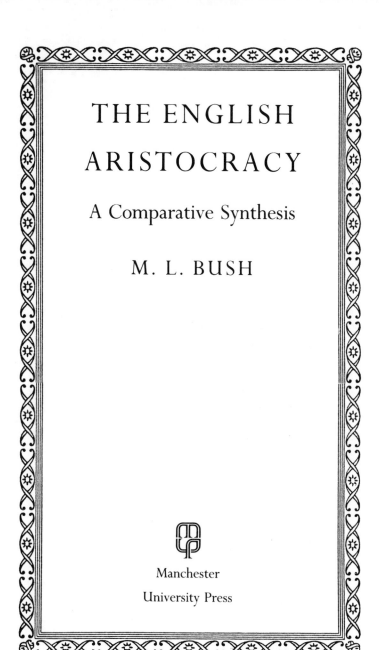

THE ENGLISH
ARISTOCRACY

A Comparative Synthesis

M. L. BUSH

Manchester
University Press

© Michael Bush 1984
First published in 1984 by
Manchester University Press
Oxford Road, Manchester M13 9PL
and 51 Washington Street, Dover
New Hampshire 03820, USA

British Library cataloguing in publication data
Bush, M. L.
The English aristocracy.
1. England – Nobility – History
I. Title
305.5′2′0942   HT653.G7

Library of Congress cataloging in publication data
Bush, M. L.
The English aristocracy.
Bibliography: p. 217
Includes index.
1. England – Nobility – History.
2. England – Gentry – History.
3. Aristocracy. I Title.
HT653.G7B87 1984   305.5′2′0941   84–11261

ISBN 0-7190-1081-0 (cased)

Phototypeset by Wilmaset, Birkenhead, Merseyside
Printed in Great Britain by
Butler & Tanner Ltd, Frome and London

Contents

1. INTRODUCTION   *page*   1

PART ONE: CHARACTER

2. PRIVILEGES   17
   (a) Privileges of rank – 19 (b) The corporate
   privileges – 25 (c) Seigneurial rights – 28

3. COMPOSITION   35
   (a) The peerage – 36 (b) The gentry – 38 (c) Peers and
   gentry – 40 (d) Extinction, promotion and demotion – 43

4. POLITICAL FUNCTION AND POWER   . 48
   (a) Instrument of government – 48 (b) In opposition – 57
   (c) Power – 58

5. WEALTH   61
   (a) The degree of wealth – 61 (b) Landed income – 61
   (c) Non-landed income – 67 (d) Expenditure – 69

6. ETHOS   71
   (a) Changes in mentality – 71 (b) Anti-bourgeois
   attitudes – 73

PART TWO: DEVELOPMENT

7. FORMATION 81
   (a) Pre-Conquest developments – 81 (b) The
   Conquest – 84 (c) Early peculiarities – 85 (d) Feudalism
   and aristocracy – 88 (e) The territorial magnate – 92
   (f) Significance of the fourteenth century – 94

8. ASCENDANCY 99
   (a) The appreciation of the Crown – 99 *(i) The Crown
   and the magnate* – 100 *(ii) The Crown and the gentry* – 109
   (b) Aristocratic revolt – 111 *(i) Medieval revolts* – 113
   (ii) Modern revolts – 118 *(iii) The end of rebellion* – 123
   (c) Aristocratic dominance – 126 (d) Anti-aristocratic
   sentiments – 129 *(i) The tradition of complaint* – 132
   (ii) Complaint in the revolutionary era – 137 *(iii)
   Industrialisation and complaint* – 139 *(iv) Oligarchy and
   complaint* – 141 *(v) Religion and complaint* – 142 *(vi) Political
   revolution and complaint* – 143 *(vii) Industrial versus political
   revolution* – 146 *(viii) Government criticism of aristocracy* – 147

9. DECLINE AND SURVIVAL 150
   (a) The course of survival – 150 (b) The wealth factor –
   154 (c) The failure of revolution – 159 (d) Government
   policy – 163 (e) Aristocratic retirement – 167

PART THREE: IMPACT

10. AGRARIAN CAPITALISM 173
    (a) The Agrarian revolution – 174 (b) The engrossment of
    farms – 175 (c) Enclosing – 179 (d) The development of
    leasehold – 180 (e) The decline of seigneurialism – 183
    (f) The role of a ruling class – 185

11. INDUSTRIALISATION   187
    (a) The aristocratic contribution – 187 (b) The role of
    estate management – 188 *(i) Farming – 188 (ii) Mining –
    189 (iii) Urban development – 190* (c) The contribution of a
    ruling class – 192 *(i) Transport – 192 (ii) Fiscal aid – 194
    (iii) Industry and the state – 194* (d) The contempt for trade
    – 195

12. POLITICAL IMPACT   198
    (a) Representation – 199 (b) State apparatus – 203
    (c) Taxation – 206

13. CONCLUSION   209

    BIBLIOGRAPHY   217

    GLOSSARY   231

    INDEX   233

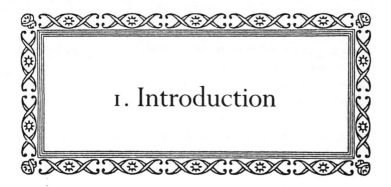

1. Introduction

This book is a reaction against a standard treatment of the English aristocracy. Instead of examining the aristocracy within the narrow confines of a period, it deals with the complete life-span. Instead of separating peerage and gentry, it proposes a gentry–peerage conjunction, presenting the one as a lesser, and the other as a higher, nobility. Instead of assuming that the English aristocracy was a peculiar expression of nobility, the book examines its alleged oddities, concluding that it had much in common with the continental nobilities.

The aim, then, is to examine the English aristocracy as a whole, charting its origins and decline, incorporating the range of aristocratic types, peerage, baronetcy and gentry, and identifying the significant stages, trends and turning points in its development. To counter the normal practice, the book provides an overview. It seeks to establish essentials rather than details. Its subject is the basic features of an order rather than the behaviour of its individual members; its concern is the aristocracy's long-term development rather than its transitory fluctuations.

With one exception, historians of the English aristocracy have operated from within a pre-selected period, usually a narrow one of no more than a century.[1] If more than a century, the chosen period has usually been respectful of medieval and modern, or of early/late medieval and modern, divisions.[2] The periodised approach has its drawbacks.[3] It prevents not only a study in depth of long-term developments but also a proper assessment of the long-term significance of what occurred within the chosen period. With the period approach, the benefits of profound research, facilitated by the selection of a narrow time-span, are outweighed by the problem of linking it to related developments outside the chosen period. Reference to other periods is clearly possible but this tends to create a dubious comparison between what the historian knows well and what he knows only slightly. Thus, modern historians are inclined to make passing reference to the middle ages without studying the latter in depth simply because they see their duty as belonging to modern history, and even early modern historians make reference to the eighteenth and nineteenth centuries without devoting to them the carefulness of study which they show to their own period. Furthermore, to justify the period selected, the historian is driven to invest it with tremendous significance without having the historical perspective necessary for assessing its true importance as a stage of development or turning point. A major aim of this book is to view this periodised research in relationship to the overall history of the English aristocracy in order to assess its value and to relate it to long-term trends. It is therefore a comparative study in a double sense: besides making synchronic comparisons between English and continental nobilities, it offers comparisons of the English aristocracy at different times.

Historians have difficulty in conceiving the English aristocracy as a compound of peerage and gentry, so much so that the term 'aristocracy', like that of 'nobility', is applied exclusively to the peers. Yet this convention sets more problems than it solves. Besides implying that the gentry and baronetcy are of a different order to the peerage, it also deprives them of social definition. Both are deposited in a social limbo from which escape is only possible through promotion to the peerage or demotion to the commonalty. Moreover, by denying the existence in England of a lesser nobility, the convention creates, at a stroke, an implausible distinction between the English aristocracy and the other European nobilities.

Over the centuries commentators were not so scrupulous. Peers and gentry were frequently conceived as parts of the same order. The traditional tripartite distinction between those who fight, those who pray and those who work, coupled with the military origins of barons and knights, proposed that peers and gentry naturally belonged to the same social estate. Accepting this tradition, William Caxton referred to both as 'noble gentlemen' in his translation of Raymond Lull's *Le Libre del Ordre de Cavaylerie* (1484). Edward Dudley in his *Tree of Commonwealth* (1509) regarded them as 'the chivalry'. Thomas Smith in his *De Republica Anglorum* (1562) saw them both as noble, the one major, the other minor. His terminology was used by Thomas Wilson in his *The State of England* (1600) and by Edward Chamberlayne in his *Angliae Notitia* (1669). An alternative term was 'gentlemen': applied to the peerage and gentry in the fifteenth-century *Book of Saint Albans*, in Smith's *De Republica Anglorum*, in William Harrison's *Description of England* (1566–7) and in Gregory King's *Ranks, Degrees, Titles and Qualifications* (1695). When Richard Mulcaster in his *Positions . . . for the Training up of Children* (1581) wrote: 'all the people be either gentlemen or of the commonalty', he was expressing an assumption common to much of the medieval and modern periods. No matter whether they used the term chivalry, nobility or gentility, people firmly believed that peers and gentry were sufficiently alike to belong to the same social category. Moreover, when commentators placed them apart it was usually because of differences in their parliamentary function. Thus, in 1422 Bishop Stafford categorised the peers with the bishops and the knights and esquires with the merchants. Expressed in a sermon delivered before parliament, his view seemed to be a justification of membership in the upper and lower houses rather than an attempt at social stratification.

Over the centuries a number of terms were used to label a social group that contained both peers and gentry. What is the best generic term for this traditional political elite? 'Chivalry' is too arcane, military and medieval in its connotation to be of general use. As all-inclusive terms, both 'nobility' and 'gentry' are unsatisfactory, the former because it does not readily apply to the gentry, the latter because it does not readily apply to the peerage, while 'gentility' is misleading because its normal usage included certain commoners. The point is neatly made by Edward Chamberlayne: having presented the gentry as a lesser nobility he remarked 'all noblemen are gentlemen, though all gentlemen are not noblemen' and elaborated: 'all in England are accounted gentlemen who maintain themselves without manual labour'.[4] The same objection holds for James Caird's term 'the landowners', coined in *The Landed Interest and the Supply of Food* (1878), since in England private landownership was never wholly confined to peers and gentry, even though much of it lay in their hands. Moreover, it would be quite absurd to categorise with the owner of a tenanted estate the owner of a smallholding. In the absence of a more satisfactory term, I have resorted to 'the aristocracy', in spite of the historian's inclination to use it as a synonym for the peerage. (On the subject of terminology and definition, see bibliography, section I(a).)

The subject of the study is three basic groups: the hereditary peerage, the baronetcy and the gentry. Their shared characteristics provide the coherence necessary to justify the inclusion of all three within the same estate. Prior to the twentieth century they were normally landed, with estates large enough to contain a tenantry. In each case, the estate was not simply a source of income but also an expression of lordship, a means of local influence and a mark of social position. Furthermore, besides enjoying advantages conferred by wealth, political licence and popular deference, all three were entitled to juridical privileges. These privileges were normally closed to commoners and secured by elevation into the aristocracy (see ch. 2 (a) and (b)). All three subscribed to roughly the same ideals, the chief of which was to eschew direct involvement in commercial activity, a prejudice which dissuaded aristocrats from farming as well as from practising mercantile and industrial occupations. The three groups were also alike in feeling that they exercised a special political function. They saw themselves as components of the same ruling class with obligations to serve the monarch, to rule the people and to dispense charity and hospitality. Each group esteemed birthright. It readily accepted that its members' social advantages were rightfully imparted by inheritance rather than performance. Landownership, a ruling function, shared ideals and a sense of being socially distinguished from the commonalty made the three groups aware that they belonged to the same social order (see ch. 6). Another bond was kinship, realised by intermarriage and social mobility: before the twentieth century new peers were chiefly recruited from the gentry and baronetcy and new baronets were mainly recruited from the gentry, while the gentry was partially drawn from the sons of peers and baronets whom the rule of primogeniture deprived of their father's rank (see ch. 3).

Distinctions certainly existed between the three, notably in political function, wealth and privilege. For example, lord lieutenants, military commanders and high officers in the royal household tended to be peers. Peers were usually wealthier than baronets and in possession of larger estates, and baronets tended to have more wealth and land than members of the gentry. The peerage held many more privileges than the baronetcy and gentry. Moreover, membership of the house of lords allowed the peerage to acquire a political function by virtue of its privileges. In contrast, the privileges of the baronetcy were simply honorific; as were those of the gentry from the late middle ages after local offices and county seats in the Commons had ceased to be reserved for the knighthood. Most of the gentry's privileges were eventually assumed by commoners. Traditionally, moreover, they were insubstantial. For these reasons, the gentry's aristocratic identity relied heavily upon its members' subscription to the noble ideals, especially rentier landownership. For the peerage and the baronetcy, landownership was not so important as a means of aristocratic identity since the privileges of both remained immune to commoner adoption and clear indicators of noble status (see ch. 2 (a) and (b)). On the other hand, prior to the twentieth century, peers and baronets remained as resolutely landed as fully established members of the gentry. In fact, the differences evident between the three groups did not segregate them into separate classes or estates but merely imposed a hierarchical structure upon one basic social group.

Historians assume and stress the oddity of the English aristocracy. Compared with the other European nobilities, it is characterised as underprivileged, more commercially minded, less closed to newcomers, more flexible in its dealings with the people, less hostile towards political and economic innovations and more independent of the state. Furthermore, these peculiarities are often invested with great significance: historians use them not only to explain the aristocracy's capacity to survive but also to account for certain distinctive political and social developments, notably the abiding constitutionalism of the English state and the long-term commercialism of the English economy (see bibliography I(b)).

Yet, viewed from a broader perspective, the English aristocracy appears less out of the ordinary. If conceived as the ruling elite of an agrarian society and compared with the elites of extra-European agrarian monarchies such as imperial China, Moghul India, the Ottoman empire and the African kingdoms, it becomes a typical European nobility, closely resembling the standard type. In the usual continental manner, hereditary privileges identified and structured its membership; landownership served as the ideal source of wealth and power; a reverence for birthright co-existed with a willingness to admit commoners-born; and trade was dismissed as a proper occupation for noblemen. Moreover, both in England and on the Continent, the aristocracy was regarded as not merely a social elite but a ruling class with a special function in running the state.

The English aristocracy possessed significant peculiarities, but so did every European nobility.

On the Continent, the privileges imparted by noble status normally outnumbered the privileges of noble rank, whereas following the Norman conquest, the status privileges of the English aristocracy were minimal and the rank privileges extensive.[5] Moreover, since the status privileges tended to be inherited by gavelkind and the rank privileges by primogeniture (see glossary), the latter's prominence in England caused primogeniture to prevail in the transmission of privilege. On the Continent, the prominence of status privileges brought gavelkind transmission more to the fore. Furthermore, the few status privileges enjoyed by the English aristocracy tended to lose meaning as a result of their adoption by the commonalty. In England the outcome was a downward movement of individuals within, and even out of, the aristocracy: because the ranks of peer and baronet passed only to the eldest son, the cadet families sank into the gentry, whilst, from the seventeenth century, the younger sons of gentry, their privileges devalued by commoner assumption, sank into the commonalty. Preventing an equivalent downward mobility on the Continent was, prior to the nineteenth century, the substantial existence of status privileges and their inheritance by all of noble birth.

Historians regard the English aristocracy as remarkably underprivileged. The gentry are presented as without, and the peerage as poorly blessed with, juridical privilege. Yet the noble privileges of the peerage were extensive from the fourteenth to the twentieth century, and the gentry was at least privileged even though their noble privileges were few in number, lacking in material and political benefits and eventually reduced by commoner assumption. What is more, although seigneurial rights went into decline at an unusually early date, they remained extensive until the fifteenth century and endured until the twentieth century. In comparison with the continental nobilities, the gentry was underprivileged whilst the peerage was overprivileged.

The English aristocracy's alleged lack of privilege is used to explain its capacity to survive. If such was the case, the gentry and baronetcy should have outlived the peerage. Responsible for the English aristocracy's survival was not the lack of privilege but the absence of certain exacerbating privileges, notably fiscal exemption and reserved office, which in the revolutionary era, incited the people against the nobility.

Another factor was the early decay of the seigneurial system. Both prevented the basic principles of the English aristocracy from being seriously questioned. Terminating nobility on the Continent was not the fact of revolution but the ability of revolutionaries to define injustice as noble privilege rather than wealth, as *égalité* rather than *richesses*. In spite of the peerage's overprivileged nature, in England the task proved less easy to accomplish.

The English aristocracy's abnormal system of privilege affected its social composition. Maintained as nobles by inherited privileges rather than by wealth, poor nobles formed a majority of the noble order in northern Castile, parts of Brittany, Poland, Hungary and Russia. Elsewhere they often formed a substantial proportion. In England, however, the poor aristocrat tended to fall out of his order unless he had a title by which to declare his noble identity (see ch. 3 (d)). Since peers and baronets were inevitably eldest, surviving sons, with the bulk of the family's property conferred upon them along with the title, they were usually very or reasonably affluent. Although it contained huge gradations of wealth, the English aristocracy over the centuries was predominantly rich rather than poor. It was also less variegated in occupation and life-style than the nobilities of many European states. Upheld by a substantial body of status privileges, the continental nobilities contained the whole spectrum of occupations: nobles were found in the professions, and acting as traders, artisans, shopkeepers, peasants, domestic servants, farm labourers and shepherds as well as in the aristocratic mode. In contrast, the lower reaches of the English aristocracy, having minimal privileges to publicise their social status and possessing the necessary resources to avoid ignobility, followed more rigorously the aristocratic way of life. If unable to do so, they tended to cede their aristocratic identity. The system of privilege also encouraged the English aristocracy to preserve its identity as a landowning class. On the Continent a class of landless nobles was formed either from the cadet lines of noble families where primogeniture applied only to the inheritance of land, or by the ennoblement of royal officials who lacked the resources to become landed. Maintaining the landedness of the English aristocracy was partly the strong inclination of peers, baronets and knights to remain landed, partly the government's unwillingness to entitle the landless, and partly the lack of sufficient privileges to prevent landless aristocrats from sinking into the commonalty. Until the twentieth century the English aristocracy possessed a coherence of wealth, occupation and landedness which many continental nobilities had traditionally lacked.

Historians present the English aristocracy as less caste-like than the continental nobilities (see ch. 3 (d)). Accessibility is regarded as its redeeming feature and a main factor in its survival. Upward mobility in England depended upon the Crown's willingness to create titles of peerage, knighthood and baronetcy and to admit new coats of arms, and the state of the land market since entry could follow the acquisition of an estate. On occasions, for example, in the early seventeenth century, large numbers of titles were created, a multitude of coats of arms was dispensed and large numbers of suitable estates came up for sale. Yet, for long periods, few elevations into the peerage and baronetcy occurred; and prior to the 1880s they went, almost invariably, to families which were already aristocratic. The same was true of knighthoods and escutcheons. Moreover, for long periods, the scarcity of estates for sale restricted the basic means by which commoners could gain aristocratic status. The unloading of church and crown land in the sixteenth and early seventeenth centuries provided a flush of opportunity, but thereafter the land market was less obliging. Similarly, in the middle ages, entry to the aristocracy was not easy in view of the lack of land for purchase. Thus, distinguishing the English aristocracy was not only the downward movement of aristocrats into the commonalty but also the very restricted upward movement of commoners into the aristocracy. Because the government only created noble status in association with noble rank, and rarely awarded it to commoners, the latter needed to proceed into the aristocracy by means of an intermediate stage which essentially involved the acquisition of an estate. On the Continent, where the government's patronage normally included the granting of noble status as well as noble titles, access was less complicated and more direct.

Although the nobilities of Europe presented themselves as collections of ancient families fringed with new creations, the families of recent origin usually formed the bulk of the membership: the result of royal reward, the sale of honours and frequent failure of noble families in the male line. Admission tended not to be difficult for wealthy commoners, especially from the sixteenth to the nineteenth centuries, as royal governments bestowed noble status on a massive scale to raise revenue as well as to reward the commoners drawn into the expanding state services. Arguably it was in the republics that the ruling elites were more of a caste than a class. In the monarchies the openness of aristocracy matched the power of the Crown. States in which the nobility dominated the Crown had more exclusive nobilities than states where the Crown was an overriding force. In this respect, royal absolutism threw the gates of entry wide open.

In England the commoner's chances of ennoblement were not greater than on the Continent. In fact, they were probably a good deal less. The difficulties which commoners normally had in gaining entry, coupled with the frequent fall of men of aristocratic birth into the commonalty, created a special social group in English society: the gentility. Socially intermediate between the aristocracy and the people, it recruited its members from both. The existence of gentility helped to dilute the hostility generated by the aristocracy's relative inaccessibility (see chs. 3 (d) and 9 (c)).

Historians tend to assume that the English aristocracy was distinguished by a commercial-mindedness that resulted from its openness, the absence of laws of derogation and the absoluteness of its property rights. Yet over the centuries the English aristocracy was strongly inclined against direct involvement (see chs. 5 and 6). In this respect, its commercial outlook seemed no different from that of the continental nobilities – apart, that is, from the farming nobilities of eastern Europe. In England laws of derogation were unnecessary; customs of derogation acted effectively in their stead. Moreover, the absoluteness of its property rights allowed the English aristocracy to preserve its rentier character. If state rights or tenant rights had got in the way, they might have forced the landlords to become more directly involved in commercial farming and industrial production. Historian's explain the English aristocracy's survival as a consequence of its commercial mindedness. Its capacity to avoid repudiation by popular revolution is attributed to its commercial affiliations. But, in the nineteenth century, its survival depended heavily upon its lack of direct involvement in primary and secondary production. In a world where capitalism created deep conflicts between employer and employee, the aristocracy was removed from the social struggle by its inclination to remain the rentier landlord.

On the other hand, it could not be said that the English aristocracy's relationship with commercial activity was thoroughly typical. The early development of agrarian and industrial capitalism in England produced a relationship between the aristocracy and the economy which, for a time, was highly unusual. By 1750 the landlord–tenant relationship in England was somewhat different from the standard continental pattern: tenants tended to be large-scale commercial farmers subjected to a revisable rent rather than peasants inclined to subsistence farming and subjected to seigneurial exactions. The English aristocracy's early liberation from both the seigneurial system and dependence upon peasant farming did not make it unique but, nonetheless, exceptional. Underway in the sixteenth and seventeenth centuries and finalised in the course of the eighteenth century, these developments produced a society which, in structure and commercial capacity, was decidedly odd by European standards, even before industrialisation made it odder. By restricting the amount of cultivated land tied to subsistence farming and by producing a class of farmers capable of appreciating and applying advanced farming techniques, they transformed agricultural efficiency. By removing one of the major components of revolution, a peasantry incited by seigneurial exactions to take militant action against the landlords, they contributed to the aristocracy's survival (see ch. 8 (d) and 9 (c)).

These agrarian developments did not occur behind the aristocracy's back. Although they tended to avoid farming themselves, English aristocrats had a permissive hand in the development of agrarian capitalism, especially in the way that they managed their estates (see ch. 10).

The same could be said of industrial capitalism (see ch. 11). The specific nature of the English aristocracy's commercialism was its readiness to come to terms with industrial and agrarian capitalism. As landlords leasing out their rights and providing capital, aristocrats made a vital, if indirect, contribution to mining, urban development and transport improvements. Whether or not the English aristocracy was consequently more progressive than continental nobilities, however, is a moot point. Given the opportunity to make profit, landlords on the Continent easily overlooked laws and customs of derogation. The significant feature of its commercialism is that, out of respect for a noble ideal, the English aristocracy tended to desist from directly tapping the profits of capitalism, preferring to receive them in the form of rents and dividends.

In retrospect, the outstanding peculiarity of the English aristocracy is its longevity as a privileged, political elite (see ch. 9 (a)). In spite of industrialisation, it dominated politics until the twentieth century. It retained privileges long after their demise on the Continent. Whereas seigneurial rights on the Continent had been mostly abolished by the mid-nineteenth century, in England they persisted until the statutory conversion of customary tenures to freeholds in the 1920s; and whereas noble privileges on the Continent had largely gone by 1920 – ejected by the revolutions of 1789, 1848 and 1918 – in England they retained political, as well as honorific, value in the late twentieth century, thanks to the durability of the house of lords. Historians partly attribute this survival capacity to the English aristocracy's flexibility, especially its ability to accommodate breaches with tradition and to adapt to the changes of the time. But also evident is a remarkable inflexibility. Commercial farming offered massive profits in the sixteenth century; so did industry in the nineteenth century. And the aristocracy benefited financially from both, but not as a producer. Over the centuries it retained its essential character as a composition of landlords dependent for revenue upon the commercial activities of peasants, tenant farmers, mine operators and property developers. Its landlordism was remarkably obdurate; as were some of its political attitudes. On the Continent, especially in eastern Europe, nobilities demonstrated a remarkable adaptability, first in becoming capitalist farmers and then in accepting royal absolutism. In contrast, the English aristocracy remained stout defenders of constitutional monarchy, stubbornly opposing any increase in the Crown's authority, but also strongly hostile to any increase in the people's authority. Their hostility to the Crown over the centuries upheld and enlarged the powers of parliament and retarded the development of bureaucracy; their hostility to the people in the eighteenth and nineteenth centuries postponed the extension of the parliamentary franchise. The slow realisation of democracy in England – first advocated in the mid-seventeenth century but scoring its first triumph only in 1832 and practically established only in the early twentieth century – expresses not only the effectiveness of the aristocracy's powers of resistance but also the basic inflexibility of its political outlook. Its dominant position in parliament had rendered it a firm believer in representative institutions, but its belief in selection by birth and representation through lordship made it the natural enemy of democracy. Its conceit as a ruling class caused its members to aspire to political office, but its antipathy to royal absolutism made it the enemy of bureaucracy and its attendant professionalisation. As with its acceptance of agrarian and industrial capitalism, the adaptability which it showed towards the establishment of manhood franchise and the extension of a professional bureaucracy revealed no special aptitude for accepting and promoting innovation, only a capacity for complying with the inevitable (see ch. 12 (a) and (b)).

Its survival stemmed from its ability to avoid revolutionary overthrow. The latter rested upon the aristocracy's ability to commit revolution. From the thirteenth to the seventeenth centuries the English aristocracy revealed an outstanding aptitude to resist the Crown's attempts to increase the royal power and authority. Monarchs were overthrown; constitutions were produced restricting the royal prerogative. The long-term outcome of this effective resistance was a form of constitutional monarchy which was developed a stage further by the aristocracy's defeat of royal absolutism in the seventeenth century (see ch. 8 (b)). The defeat of royal absolutism worked against the occurrence of further revolution. Royal absolutism was a major constituent of revolution, making the state autonomous and therefore capable of alienating established elites, and creating a service elite of professional people which became the spearhead of bourgeois opposition to the old regime, notably in the revolutions of 1789–1848. In England the effective opposition to royal absolutism eventually rendered the state the servitor of the landed interest, giving the aristocracy no further cause for complaint, and prevented the creation of a revolutionary bourgeoisie by maintaining the bureaucracy in a primitive condition until, in the course of the nineteenth century, the social problems of industrialisation ordered its modernisation. The belated development of the state safeguarded against the emergence of a discontented professional class (the opportunities for employment and profit in industry and empire worked to the same effect) and preserved for the aristocracy until the late nineteenth century an indispensable role in the administration as unpaid, amateur JPs responsible for local government. Protecting the aristocracy against the charge of redundancy and parasitism, it reduced the likelihood of overthrow. Interlocking with the peculiar development of the state were peculiar developments in English society, notably the emergence of the gentility, the elimination of the peasantry and the creation of large social groups without dependence upon the aristocracy. Between them they allowed the English aristocracy to decline by means of a process of voluntary retirement and *embourgeoisement* rather than as a result of rejection (see chs. 8 (d) and 9).

The English aristocracy had much in common with the range of continental nobilities. Its distinctive features fail to outweigh the basic similarities. Juridically privileged, landed, a ruling class, an hereditary order but with a membership not solely determined by birth, the English aristocracy possessed basic characteristics shared by every European nobility. On the other hand, the inadequacy of its status privileges, the coherence provided by its members' wealth, their landedness and narrow range of occupation, the ease with which aristocrats became commoners and the difficulty with which commoners became aristocrats, its accommodation of agrarian and industrial capitalism, and its ability both to resist the Crown and to withstand popular opposition were highly unusual, if not unique.

Notes to Chapter 1

1. E.g. in the manner of L. Stone's *The Crisis of the Aristocracy, 1558–1641* (Oxford, 1965), G. E. Mingay's *English Landed Society in the Eighteenth Century* (London, 1963), and F. M. L. Thompson's *English Landed Society in the Nineteenth Century* (London, 1963). The exception is G. E. Mingay's *The Gentry, the Rise and Fall of a Ruling Class* (London, 1976).

2. E.g., K. B. McFarlane's *The Nobility of Later Medieval England* (Oxford, 1973), and D. Cannadine's *Lords and Landlords, the Aristocracy and the Towns, 1774–1967* (Leicester, 1980). A fruitful exception is B. Coward's *The Stanleys, Lords Stanley and Earls of Derby, 1385–1672* (Manchester, 1983), although this study perversely chooses a terminal date which long precedes the termination of the developments with which it is preoccupied. J. H. Hexter proposed inter-period study of the aristocracy in his 'A new framework for social history' (*Reappraisals in History* (London, 1961), ch. 2) but with little effect.

3. They are more fully explored in my article 'Place and period in the study of history' (*Times Higher Education Supplement*, September 1980).

4. *Angliae Notitia* (1700 ed.), pp. 295 and 297.

5. See M. L. Bush, *Noble Privilege* (Manchester, 1983) for the privileges of the continental nobilities; and ch. 2 (a) and (b) for the privileges of the English aristocracy.

PART ONE

CHARACTER

2. Privileges

In the continental manner, the English aristocracy enjoyed two types of privilege, the one noble, the other seigneurial. The seigneurial rights were imparted by landownership, the noble privileges by noble status or noble rank. (For basic reference and further reading see bibliography, section II.) Upheld in the law, both rested on a juridical basis. Neither was completely confined to the aristocracy. Since English law never made the ownership of manors a noble monopoly, commoners could gain lawful possession of seigneurial rights, usually by an act of land purchase. It was possible for several noble privileges to be legitimately enjoyed by commoners. By virtue of their appointment, certain state officials, notably JPs, sheriffs and royal heralds, were titled esquire; the peers' right of freedom from arrest in civil causes was enjoyed by all members of parliament during the parliamentary session; before 1711 their immunity from imprisonment for debt was shared by their servants; and the privileges created by the fifteenth- and sixteenth-century statutes restricting apparel and the use of handguns and crossbows admitted certain wealthy commoners to the rights awarded aristocrats (see below, p. 31). This was not unusual: on the Continent commoners were often authorised to enjoy noble privileges, especially fiscal exemption, the right to wear the sword and immunity from the obligation of personal military service.[1] For this reason, the distinction between noble and commoner lay not in the enjoyment of noble privileges but in differences in the way that such privileges were enjoyed. Nobles normally held privileges by hereditary right and claimed the whole range of corporate privileges, that is, the privileges associated with noble status rather than rank. In contrast, only certain of the nobility's corporate privileges were available to commoners and tended to be held for no more than life. Moreover, the privileged noble was the norm whereas the commoner with noble privileges was the exception.

In addition, commoners frequently usurped noble privileges, enjoying them without legal authorisation. Distinguishing the English aristocracy was the fact that eventually the commonalty adopted the bulk of its corporate privileges. By the mid-seventeenth century the designation 'gentleman' and the address form 'mr.', both of them aristocratic privileges in origin, were widely used by men who were not strictly of the aristocracy; and by the nineteenth century members of the bourgeoisie were freely sporting both the title of esquire and coats of arms. The extensiveness of this adoption, however, was due to the paucity of corporate privileges rather than the social aggressiveness and ingenuity of the commonalty.

By special concession and usurpation, commoners in England obtained noble privileges without much difficulty. On the other hand, it was less easy for commoners to secure them through ennoblement. In England noble status was not dispensed. Only noble titles and coats of arms were granted and, over the centuries, the Crown inclined to bestow them on subjects with already acquired aristocratic credentials.

On the Continent privileges served both to stratify and define the noble order. Alongside the nobility's corporate privileges stood the privileges imparted by qualifications indicative of rank, notably a title, ownership of an officially designated noble estate (fief or Rittersgut – see glossary) or a family's long-term possession of noble status. Distinguishing the English aristocracy was the large proportion of privileges conferred by rank. On the Continent fiscal exemption, immunity from certain punishments such as flogging and hanging and from the normal judicial procedures, freedom from compulsory military service and privileges of precedence were often the right of the mere nobility.[2] In England the equivalent privileges tended to be confined to the peerage. On the Continent the privileges imparted by special qualification were easily outnumbered by the corporate rights. In England it was the other way round. Furthermore, in England the rule of primogeniture ensured that most noble privileges passed only to the eldest son, whereas the continental practice transmitted the corporate privileges to every noble offspring. The English system of noble privilege not only denied most noble privileges to the gentry and baronetcy but also withheld from the younger children of aristocratic families many of the privileges enjoyed by their eldest brother.

(a) **Privileges of rank**

Originally, the English peerage was only distinguished from the rest of the aristocracy by its title. As late as the reign of Edward I, the juridical distinction between the peerage and the rest of the aristocracy was no more than an honorific one. Moreover, before the Norman Conquest and in the following two centuries, noble privilege had imparted other than peerage distinctions of rank. The Anglo-Saxon nobility's rank privileges had rested upon royal office and bookland, the tenure of which had qualified nobles to exact a larger wergeld than the nobles without royal office and bookland (see ch. 7 (a) and glossary). Then the Conquest introduced the distinction between tenant-in-chief and sub-tenant, the one distinguished from the other by the exemption of his demesne from the danegeld and his right to advise the king (see ch. 7 (b–d)).

Nonetheless, by the start of the sixteenth century the English aristocracy was basically stratified by the familiar imbalance between the abundant privileges of the peerage and the scant rights of the gentry. This came of a rise of the peerage in the late middle ages. The introduction of the peerage titles between 1337 and 1440 was followed by their generous dispensation. As a result, the peerage was transformed from a small coterie of families, connected with royalty by blood or marriage, into a substantial body of about fifty title-holders (see ch. 3 (a)). Largely associated with the emergence of the house of lords, the peerage acquired several exclusive privileges. At first, membership of the upper house was not confined to the peers and for a long time it was not their hereditary right. A peer only attended because the king's writ had specifically summoned him. However, by the end of the fourteenth century it was normal for all peers, and rare for other laymen, to receive writs of summons.

The upper house was not officially termed the house of lords until the reign of Henry VIII, and the right of peers to receive writs of summons as a permanent, hereditary right was not legally confirmed until 1625; yet by 1500 the upper house was, in practice, the chamber where those with titles of peerage sat by hereditary right, a privilege which until 1911 gave the English peerage an indispensible role in the making of statutory law.

Frequently in the continental diets membership of, or representation in, the noble chamber was not the right of the whole nobility but of nobles specially qualified by title, landownership or lineage. The English system, then, was not that unusual in denying representation in the noble chamber to the bulk of the aristocracy and by allowing it representation only in the house of commons. What rendered the English peerage's parliamentary privileges distinctive was the powers they conferred, a reflection of the authority traditionally exercised by the English parliament and the comparatively limited powers of most continental diets.[3]

English peers enjoyed an impressive range of judicial rights. Except for treason, felony and breaches of the peace, they were immune to arrest, a freedom which prevented a peer from being outlawed in any civil action. Nor could peers be imprisoned for debt. They were exempt from certain writs enforcing appearance in a royal court of law. For example, they could not be served with a subpoena. In certain matters their houses were immune to entry by legal officials unless authorised by a warrant signed by the king and six of his privy council, four of whom needed to be peers. No oath was required of peers; their honour was sufficient. Thus as witnesses, as judges, as subjects ordered to keep the peace, peers, unlike commoners, were not obliged to take the oath. Furthermore, as a party to an action at law, a peer was privileged, until 1751, to have a jury partly composed of knights. This faintly echoed the more important privilege of trial by peerage. Laid down in Magna Carta and given statutory recognition in 1442, it enabled peers to be tried in criminal actions by their fellow peers rather than by a common jury, that is, if parliament had no objection. In case of such an objection, the alternative procedure, yet another privilege because it was not available to the commonalty, was trial in the court of the Lord High Steward. The peer's freedom from the common law courts in matters criminal was complemented by a further privilege granted in 1547 which awarded the peerage benefit of clergy. Thereafter and until 1827, his misdemeanours could escape the common law through the right of trial in an ecclesiastical court, although the right lost much of its value as benefit of clergy was gradually reduced by a process of statutory definition to a small number of offences. In addition, the privilege of *scandalum magnatum* awarded peers a special means of action against slander. Exercised either in the common law courts or in the court of Star Chamber, it resulted in the award of excessive damages to the plaintiff peer. Although it was not abolished until 1887, the privilege ceased operation in the early eighteenth century. Finally, peers sentenced to death could only be decapitated, not hanged, and seemed to enjoy the usual continental exemption from corporal punishment.

The judicial privileges of the English peerage were not as extensive as those of the Polish and Hungarian nobilities, but they were undoubtedly substantial (probably more so than those of the other nobilities of western Europe, Scandinavia and Italy) and very durable.[4] Trial by peerage, the most important of the judicial privileges, was only terminated in 1949. Freedom from imprisonment for debt only ceased to be a noble privilege in the late nineteenth century when the right was awarded the whole citizenry. And freedom from arrest in civil actions remained of value until 1838 when arrest prior to judgement was removed from most civil actions. The value of these judicial privileges is difficult to gauge. They did not excuse sentence and, except in the matter of debt, it could not be said that, as a result of privilege, the peers were more lightly sentenced than commoners. Probably of greater benefit to the peers, and this also applied to the gentry, who enjoyed no judicial privileges whatsoever, was the respect and forbearance habitually shown them by the judiciary.

On the Continent, nobilities frequently enjoyed immunity from state services, originally a consequence of their own special service obligations, although frequently the immunity outlived the obligation. The English peerage was most unusual because one of its privileges excused it from serving in local government. Thus peers were not required to sit on juries or to serve as sheriff and could not be obliged to act as witness in a court of law. Nor could they be commanded by the sheriff to serve in the *posse comitatus*, a traditional measure for suppressing riots and for bringing, through the hue and cry, lawbreakers to justice. Furthermore, following the statute of Marlborough in 1268, peers were freed from the obligation binding every resident of a manor aged between twelve and sixty to attend its court leet. The corollary was exemption from holding the offices in local government which were appointed by the court leet, notably the constables and tithingmen (see glossary). Elsewhere in Europe the nobility's service immunities tended to be corporate rights and the government's dependence upon nobles to staff local government ensured that the privilege was confined to state labour services or postal services. In England it was possible for the privilege to apply to local government because it was enjoyed only by a very small fraction of the aristocracy. In addition, peers enjoyed some indemnity from military service. The Militia Act of 1757 excused their attendance at county musters and enacted that a peer's contribution to the militia could only be assessed by six other peers. This was not unusual. Frequently on the Continent, nobles were exempted from the commonalty's military obligations by virtue of the special military service once required of them.[5]

Fiscal exemption, commonly found as a noble privilege on the Continent, was noticeable by its absence in England.[6] Complete exemption only applied to the early medieval danegeld. Before the Conquest this tax was restricted to holders of bookland and after it to tenants-in-chief. In addition, peers by 1700 were excused duties on a certain amount of imported wine. This was the extent of the English aristocracy's fiscal immunity but not the sum total of its fiscal privileges. For centuries the peers possessed a right of consent to parliamentary taxation. However, in 1678 the Commons' consent was made sufficient for the enactment of money bills. Nowhere else in Europe did this occur: if estates parliaments preserved tax-granting powers, their noble chambers retained a right of approval. Furthermore, in extenuation of its liability to the subsidy, the peerage was granted in 1523 the right to have its wealth assessed by a special commission led by the lord chancellor and the lord treasurer, rather than by the normal machinery. This right, a source of social distinction not of profit, lasted until the establishment of the land tax in 1692.

A peculiar feature of the English aristocracy was not only the early disappearance of its fiscal immunity and the absence of corporately held fiscal privileges but also the early evaporation of its fiscal rights. Whereas the fiscal privileges of the continental nobilities survived until at least the mid-eighteenth century and, in many instances, until the mid-nineteenth century, the English aristocracy's fiscal privileges were erased by 1700; that is, apart from the peerage's right to duty-free wine.

Compensating the English aristocracy for its fiscal liability was the very nature of the tax system, especially its opportunities for tax evasion and the fact that direct taxes were irregular until the late seventeenth century and then, as regular levies, served only to supplement regressive indirect taxes which fell with relative lightness upon the rich. In fact, it seems that the English aristocracy paid no more of its wealth in taxes than the French nobles, even though the *noblesse* retained until the revolution exemption from the government's major source of fiscal revenue, the *taille*.

Further privileges were created by parliamentary statutes which excepted the peerage from what they prohibited. Thus, in 1390 a statute limiting indentured retaining enacted that only peers could lawfully retain. The laws passed in the fifteenth and sixteenth centuries to regulate apparel (e.g. in 1402, 1464, 1483, 1510, 1533 and 1565) allowed the peerage to wear silk, satin, furs, velvet, golden chains and woollen cloth of foreign manufacture; while the Tudor ban on the use of handguns and crossbows granted a special indulgence to peers.

The peerage's crossbow privilege was short-lived: enacted in 1504 it was repealed in 1515. On the other hand, the handgun privilege established in 1548–9 lasted until the 1690s. The peerage's apparel privileges, first established in the mid-fourteenth century and substantiated in Henry VIII's reign, were terminated in 1604. The peer's exclusive right to retain ended in 1628.

The apparel and the handgun/crossbow statutes had not confined immunity to the peerage since they allowed commoners access through achieving a certain degree of wealth. In this respect, the specific nature of the peerage's privilege was to enjoy immunity without fulfilling the wealth qualifications required of commoners. Similar in kind was the peerage's immunity from the game law of 1671 and from the restrictions imposed in the early eighteenth century on those qualified to serve as JPs (enacted in 1732) and MPs (enacted in 1710). In each case a degree of wealth awarded immunity from the statutory prohibition except for peers and their heirs who received immunity by virtue of their aristocratic status. This type of privilege survived until the mid-nineteenth century, when it was extinguished by the Game Law Act of 1831 and the Parliament Act of 1858.

A final group of peerage privileges imparted social distinction rather than material or political benefits. These essentially honorific privileges awarded personal access to the sovereign, the right to graduate at university in three rather than four years, titles, special forms of address and precedence at public gatherings. Most peerage privileges were confined to the holder of the title or his heir and therefore passed by strict primogeniture. But several passed by gavelkind. Thus, all the sons of dukes and marquises are entitled to the appellation 'lord' and all the sons of viscounts and barons can use the prefix 'the Hon.'. The rules of precedence, evident from the late fourteenth century and enacted in 1539, allowed rights of precedence for all the sons of peers. Furthermore, the coats of arms of the peerage were subjected to primogeniture only in their undifferenced state. Appropriately cadenced, they were the inheritance of the younger son.

Although peerage privileges were still undergoing creation in the early eighteenth century, most were well established by 1500. Few of them were ever shared by the gentry or the baronetcy. For this reason, they distinguished the peerage not only from the commonalty but also from the rest of the aristocracy.

Privileges of rank also distinguished baronets from knights, knights from undubbed gentry and esquires from plain gentlemen. Both knights and baronets, for example, enjoyed formal rights of precedence. Yet, as they developed in England, the public rules of precedence made no provision for mere aristocratic status. Baronets and knights, moreover, with their eldest sons shared the peerage privilege of graduating at Oxford in three rather than four years. The laws restricting apparel created privileges for knights as well as for peers. Like the peers, both baronets and knights had the right to confer a more elevated title than plain 'mr.' on their younger sons. In each case it was 'esquire'. For a short while the knights enjoyed the privilege of reserved office: in the twelfth and thirteenth centuries royal officials in local government were expected to be knights. The inadequate supply of knights, however, first produced the royal order of 1247 requiring all freeholders with land worth 40/- p.a. to undergo knighthood and in the fourteenth century caused the privilege to be terminated. A similar reservation was initially placed on county seats in parliament, but was removed in 1440.

An attempt in 1614 to confer upon baronets a range of privileges came to nothing. They were not allowed the proposed exemption from wardship, the right of trial by fellow baronets, the equivalent of trial by peerage, and exemption from holding certain local government offices. Yet special privileges were acquired which imparted definite distinction. Unlike knighthood, the title of baronetcy, with the appellation 'sir', became hereditary; and its other main privilege, the right of the heirs male of baronets to claim a knighthood of the Crown at the age of twenty-one, was not shared by any other aristocratic group.

Whereas baronets and knights transmitted the title of esquire to all their male offspring, esquires transmitted it only to the eldest son, the younger sons receiving the title of 'mr.'. The esquires became a clearly recognised part of the aristocracy in the course of the fourteenth century when they were permitted to acquire their own coats of arms rather than to bear that of their lord. Distinguishing the esquires from the rest of the gentry were not only the privileges confined to the knights but also the privileges denied to the gentry below the rank of esquire. The latter were created by the legislation restricting retaining: the statute of 1390 enacted that only esquires and those of higher degree could be retained. In 1552 esquires, along with the aristocracy of higher rank, were granted the right to wear a hood with tippet at funerals. Further distinction was imparted by the Oxford University statute of 1592 which allowed esquires, as well as knights and peers, to graduate in three rather than four years. However, this privilege was taken from the esquires by a statute of 1636 which restricted the privilege to peers, knights and baronets. A more durable distinction came with the game law of 1671 which banned from the hunting of game all subjects but for those in possession of a freehold worth £100 p.a. or a leasehold worth £150 p.a., and then excepted from this property qualification esquires and persons of higher degree and their heirs. The same act also distinguished between lords of the manor with at least the title of esquire and manorial lords of lesser rank by authorising only the former to appoint gamekeepers with special powers. The game law persisted until 1831; the retaining laws lasted until 1628. Both awarded esquires rights which distinguished them not only from commoners but also from the plain gentleman.

These privileges, however, which made distinctions within the gentry, were too minimal, both in number and import, to destroy the overall stratification determined by the peerage privileges. Peers, baronets, knights, esquires and gentlemen formed a complex hierarchy, but simplifying the aristocracy's structure was the firm, clear-cut distinction which privilege made between peerage and gentry.

(b) The corporate privileges

Besides the privilege of rank were the privileges enjoyed by the aristocracy as an order. By distinguishing it from the commonalty, these corporate privileges imparted a sense of social identity. The chief of them was the right to bear a coat of arms. Although originally an occupational designation, by the close of the fifteenth century, they were firmly recognised as a means of social distinction, a badge of nobility rather than the mark of a military knight. Unlike most of the titles, coats of arms were transmitted by gavelkind, therefore allowing the younger son to inherit aristocratic status. In the course of the late fourteenth and fifteenth centuries the royal heralds received the task of adjudicating upon claims to arms. By the mid-sixteenth century it was fully worked out who was entitled to an escutcheon. The list included not only peers, knights and esquires but also plain gentlemen, the latter achieving admission to the right in the course of the fifteenth century. By the mid-sixteenth century heralds' visitations had been established to scrutinise armigerous claims. These developments gave the aristocracy a corporate privilege, the importance of which was magnified by the scarcity of other corporate rights. The visitations operated periodically until 1689, subjecting membership of the gentry to the formal sanction of the Crown. After that date, new arms required formal authorisation, especially since, in the early eighteenth century, the assumption of a coat of arms by prescription was outlawed; but no machinery existed to prevent the unofficial adoption of coats of arms, a practice encouraged in the nineteenth century by the willingness of Burke's *Landed Gentry*, prior to 1914, to include arms which were not sanctioned by the College of Heralds, and also by the publication of Burke's *General Armoury* which related arms to surnames and generated the impression that sharing a surname entitled the right to share a coat of arms.

Absent in England were the predicates (i.e. the *von*) and the particules (i.e. the *de*) of the continental nobilities, but indicative of aristocratic status was the designation 'gentleman' and the address form of 'mr.'. Both had definite aristocratic significance in 1500 yet had lost it by 1700 thanks to their assumption by commoners. Another corporate privilege was the aristocrat's right to settle disputes of honour by duel and in the court of chivalry. The latter originated in the mid-fourteenth century. It had a sporadic history, sometimes inactive, occasionally revived, until its last sitting in 1737. Furthermore a statute of 1440 made admission to the house of commons as a knight of the shire a corporate right by excluding anyone 'that standeth in the degree of yeoman and beneath' and by admitting, apart from knights, 'such notable squires, gentlemen of birth . . . as be able to be knights'. The legislation on apparel of the fifteenth and sixteenth centuries created another corporate right, distinguishing aristocrat from commoner in the matter of dress. Much of this legislation, it is true, singled out peers and knights, but some of it awarded rights of dress to those of 'the degree of gentleman and above', notably the right to wear foreign furs, enacted in 1510 and terminated in 1532, and the right to wear silk shirts, enacted in 1532 and repealed in 1604. Distinction in dress persisted as a corporate privilege in the statutes of Oxford University until the nineteenth century. Furthermore, the labour statute of 1563 enacted that a gentleman by birth could not be compelled under the terms of the act to serve in husbandry. By the late seventeenth century, Edward Chamberlayne claimed the existence of further corporate rights, notably the ancient custom that an ignoble person found guilty of striking a gentleman should forfeit his hand in punishment, the rule that the child of a gentleman should not be compelled to serve as a chorister in the king's chapel and the gentleman's immunity from having his horses requisitioned to ride post. These privileges may have been few and insubstantial, but their existence was sufficient to give aristocratic status a legal meaning. The plain gentleman resembled the peer not simply because his life-style was in certain respects similar but also because his social status was supported by juridical rights.

The gentry's privileges, however, were few and evanescent. Those that lasted were eventually adopted by the commonalty. Both 'mr.' and 'gentleman' were freely used by the bourgeoisie in 1700. The title of esquire retained its aristocratic identity for much longer but hardly by 1850; and by that date coats of arms had been demeaned by their unlicensed assumption. The narrow range of privileges in the gentry's possession made these designations of noble status tremendously important, but nothing could be done to prevent them from slipping into commoner hands. The English aristocracy avoided popular repudiation but, as a privileged order, it was subjected to something just as damaging: a commoner invasion of its gentry privileges which deprived them of aristocratic signification.

In characterising the English aristocracy, historians present the gentry as unprivileged and the peerage as underprivileged. They also emphasise the importance of primogeniture in the transmission of privilege. Yet, by no reckoning can the peerage be presented as underprivileged. Moreover, since the gentry was privileged, both by rank and status, it is entitled to be regarded as a lesser nobility. The corporate privileges in its possession renders the English aristocracy similar to the continental nobilities. Their paucity only creates a difference of detail. Furthermore, not all the privileges were transmitted by primogeniture. Differenced coats of arms, the address of mr., the titles of esquire and lord, precedence, graduation at Oxford in three years were all cadet rights. 'Mr.' was the right of the sons of plain gentlemen and esquires; 'esq.' was the right of the sons of knights and baronets; 'lord' was the right of the sons of the higher peerage. The younger sons of peers enjoyed rights of precedence and the right of graduation at Oxford in three rather than the normal four years. These gavelkind privileges again liken the English aristocracy to the continental pattern, confirming a difference of extent rather than of kind.

The underprivileged element, the gentlemen and esquires, eventually went under, leaving in the twentieth century an order which, now consisting essentially of peers, baronets and knights, bore little resemblance to the traditional aristocracy.

The survival of noble privilege into the twentieth century then, has to be explained in other terms than its restricted nature. Outstanding contributions were rather made by the absence of privileges prone to incite popular hostility, notably reserved office and fiscal exemption, the confinement of the most important privileges to a very small proportion of the aristocracy, and the ability of commoners to adopt some of the lesser privileges, in this way finding compensation for the fact that, until the twentieth century, the peerage privileges were virtually inaccessible to commoners-born. The survival of monarchy and its readiness to grant honours complemented both the incapacity of the people to mount a revolution which, in the continental manner, could single out juridical privilege as the villain of the piece, and the inability of the government to order the destruction of a clearly anachronistic house of lords.

(c)   Seigneurial rights

As lords of the manor, European nobles held over their tenants rights of jurisdiction and the authority to exact services and dues. Likewise in England, the traditional relationship between landlord and tenant was not based simply upon rent but imparted lordship. By 1300 seigneurial exactions in England were as extensive as anywhere in Europe, although the expansion of royal justice had already curtailed private rights of criminal jurisdiction.[7]

By 1900 seigneurial exactions in England were greater than anywhere on the Continent. However, this was because in most European states revolutionary or conservative governments had dismantled the seigneurial system in order to appease an aggrieved and militant peasantry. In England the seigneurial system survived the revolutionary era because, by the time of the French revolution, seigneurial rights were so limited that they no longer incited the tenantry to take reprisals against the landlords.

By 1550 all seigneurial rights of criminal jurisdiction had disappeared in England, a consequence of the development of royal justice in the twelfth and thirteenth centuries and the Crown's resumption of the franchises in 1536. But having achieved so much and so soon, the state then ceased its encroachments, allowing lords with rights of court leet to retain a jurisdiction in petty offences such as debt, trespass and nuisance as well as to appoint the lowest officers in local government. Only in the nineteenth century was the process of state encroachment revived, when the petty offences were brought within the scope of quarter sessions, and parish councils or JPs acquired the right to appoint the lesser local government officials. By 1900 the public authority of the lord of the manor had been reduced to the making and enforcement of manorial regulations.

Seigneurial rights in England had sometimes included private taxes. This became less common with the decay of serfdom and the abolition of the franchises. However, in the form of river and road tolls and the charges made for the right to trade they lingered on into the twentieth century.

Seigneurial rights in England were diminished not only by state encroachment but also by the development of agrarian capitalism and its impact upon estate management. Pressured by rapid inflation in the sixteenth and early seventeenth centuries, lords incorporated tenures within the demesne and, by doing so, replaced the system of fixed rents and compensatory seigneurial dues by a revisable, economic rent. Their aim in disposing of seigneurial rights, was to uphold the real value of their landed incomes. Earlier, lords had relinquished seigneurial rights in order not to alienate the tenantry. To avoid peasant revolt and to retain or to attract tenants in a period of extreme depopulation seigneurial demands in the late fourteenth and fifteenth centuries were relaxed and reduced. The main outcome was to release the tenantry from the bonds of serfdom. However, in both the late medieval period and the sixteenth century, landlords could react to the economic pressures of depopulation and inflation by intensifying their seigneurial impositions. Thus, in the sixteenth century the raising of entry fines was a frequently used device to counter the effects of inflation upon landed incomes; and in the late fourteenth century lords had sought to offset the fall in incomes that came of a shortage of tenants not only by freeing tenants from serfdom but also by increasing the demands made of the remaining serfs. The latter policy was stopped in its tracks by the peasant revolts of 1381; just as the policy of raising entry fines became less feasible following the revolts in the north of 1536 and in the south of 1549, as well as a host of Tudor disturbances, riots rather than rebellions, in which tenants opposed their landlords usually by removing enclosures, draining fish ponds and exhuming rabbit warrens.

These changes in estate management occurred in conjunction with the rise of the commercial farmer (for the aristocrat's relationship with agrarian capitalism, see ch. 10). In parts of France, notably in the west and the south, a process of demesne expansion abolished the tenures centuries before the French revolution, but failed to sweep away the seigneurial system. All it did was to replace the tenurial smallholdings by demesne smallholdings, many of them leased to share-croppers. In order to compensate for the small return in rent that was exactable from such poor tenants, landlords continued to make seigneurial demands of them. In sharp contrast, in England the process of demesne expansion went hand in hand with the emergence of large-scale commercial farming and the decline of subsistence farming. By reducing the number of farmers, the engrossment of farms made seigneurial dues less profitable, while the success of commercial farming increased the rent which individual farmers could pay for their tenancies. In these circumstances seigneurial dues faded away, largely because they were, quite clearly, not the most effective means of tapping the profits of agrarian capitalism. They lingered on only in certain areas such as the north-west where commercial farming remained limited.

On the other hand, capitalist farming was not necessarily antagonistic to the seigneurial system. When the capitalist was the landowner, operating his demesne by means of labour services rather than by wage labour, or marketing the annexed produce of his tenantry, commercial farming upheld and even extended the seigneurial system. This was the case in much of eastern Europe in the early modern period, but not in England or in other parts of western Europe. In England demesne farming was halted in the late middle ages, a result of the low farm prices and the high labour costs which stemmed from the depopulating effects of recurrent plague. Thereafter, aristocrats farmed only as a sideline or as a hobby, not as an alternative to rent: that is, unless compelled by poverty. The latter had no need of seigneurial rights since they used wage labour, produced profusely and cheaply by the spectacular population growths of the sixteenth and late eighteenth/nineteenth centuries and by the gradual replacement of peasant by capitalist farming.

Needless to say, the early decay of the seigneurial system in England was not unique. It suffered an even earlier collapse in parts of northern Italy and Flanders where it had withered by 1400. However, since it continued to dominate rural society in much of Europe until the late eighteenth and early nineteenth centuries, the early fading of the system rendered the relationship between landlord and tenant in England a highly unconventional one.

The forms of seigneurial imposition in England resembled those on the Continent. Some seigneurial rights were simply sources of income, some were a provision of service and some were a means of tenant control. Through a process of commutation, the services and controls tended to become sources of income as well. Notably lacking in England was the secular tithe: there was no equivalent of the *champart* (see glossary). In England the basic rent was a fixed sum of money, not a fixed proportion of the tenant's crop. Since fixed money rents were less able to hold their value than fixed tithes, English lords were compelled to find either compensation or a substitute for the rent as inflation eroded its value. Apart from private taxes such as tallages and tolls, the other main regular due was the gifts in kind, which at certain times of the year, the tenants presented to the lord.

Besides the regular dues were the casualties. These fell intermittently. Upon the death of a tenant, a heriot was payable, originally in kind and eventually in cash. Upon the succession of the tenant's heir, a relief fell due; and upon the renegotiation of a tenancy, a process involving an alteration in the manorial court roll of its recorded holders and reversioners, an entry fine was owed. Most of these casualties became, in the manner of the rent, fixed by custom. The exception was the entry fine. For this reason it was vigorously exploited by the landlords in periods of rapid inflation. Other casualties were the fines exacted in the manorial court, the profit accruing from the lord's right to the natural resources of the estate, and the fees levied in return for the lord's licence. The latter derived from his right to decide whether a serf should marry, change occupation or migrate, his right of mill and oven and his monopoly of hunting and fishing.

The seigneurial services in England entailed work on the lord's demesne and carrying obligations. The tenants sometimes had to collect fuel and convey it to the lord's house. Service obligations could also concern the transport of building materials. Demesne labour was either boon work or week work, the former falling due at certain times of the year, principally at haymaking and harvest, while the latter was a weekly requirement. With the coincidental collapse of demesne farming and serfdom in the fourteenth and fifteenth centuries, week work largely fell into abeyance; but boon work continued to feature for centuries. So did the carrying services. In the late eighteenth century the earl of Scarborough was using the carrying services of his tenantry to transport coal from his mines to the river Wear.

Tenant control was exercised through the lord's private judicial authority and his right to grant licence. Lords retained rights of jurisdiction until the 1920s, rights which could be highly profitable when populous urban communities fell under their sway. Rights of licence were much reduced by the emancipation of the serf in the late middle ages. As a form of tenant control, the licence rights lost effect when lords came to appreciate them primarily as sources of income, granting permission automatically upon payment of a fee. Tenant control was also weakened as, liberated from serfdom, tenants acquired an equivalent security of tenure to that enjoyed by freehold tenants. The seigneurial system had provided protection for the tenant as well as a means of exploitation for the lord. Its removal, a process which usually substituted a short-term, rack-rent lease for the hereditary, fixed-rent tenure, often placed the tenant more fully under the landlord's control. The opposite happened only when seigneurial rights were terminated by government action through the conversion of tenures into freeholds. This occurred frequently in Europe

between 1789 and 1850, but not in England until the 1920s when the
surviving customary tenures were transformed into freeholds by
parliamentary statute.

The oppressiveness of the seigneurial system was determined not
only by period but also by status. Thus, in the twelfth and thirteenth
centuries it fell lightly upon the freehold tenants since their tenures
were hereditary and their dues were few and fixed. Free from entry
fines, the dues of this type of tenant became notional in the course of
time, bearing little relationship to the rental value of the tenure. On the
other hand, the seigneurial system fell harshly upon the serf. However,
the period in which serfdom was prevalent was limited to the twelfth
and thirteenth centuries and manumission could award the emancipated tenures (customary tenures held by copyhold) the security and
independence of freeholds. Yet these customary tenures were mostly
held for life or several lives. Unlike the freehold they were rarely
perpetual tenancies. Some were protected against raised entry fines but
many were exposed to arbitrary fines which could only be checked by
revolt or the prospect of revolt. In rising against the enlargement of
gressoms (see glossary), the tenantry of the north-west in 1536 and
1537 secured a written promise from their landlords that custom would
be respected and also required the government to place a statutory
restriction upon entry fines, although nothing definite came of these
demands, apart from the fear which they instilled in landlords and its
effect upon their estate management. Certainly by 1700 the seigneurial
system had contracted decisively. But this contraction was far from
being a termination. Because there was no wholesale governmental
abolition of seigneurial right prior to the 1920s, only its piecemeal
removal by individual landlords, the system lived on, occasionally an
irritant between landlord and tenant but no longer seriously disrupting
the relationship. Tenants tolerated it because it was neither onerous nor
interfering and also because it awarded them some security against
eviction and some protection against rack-renting. Landlords tolerated
its existence especially when their dependence upon it was reduced by
the chances of calling upon other sources of income. And, free from
the pressures of popular demand, British governments in the nineteenth
century could allow the survival of something which on the Continent
was swept away by government action.

Notes to Chapter 2

1. See M. L. Bush, *Noble Privilege*, p. 5.
2. *Ibid.*, chs. II and III.
3. *Ibid.*, ch. IV (2).
4. *Ibid.*, ch. III.
5. *Ibid.*
6. *Ibid.*, ch. II (1).
7. *Ibid.*, ch. VI.

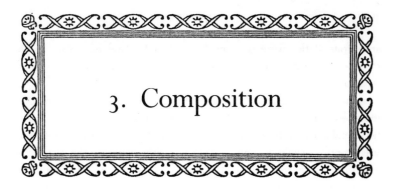

3. Composition

As a European nobility, the English aristocracy was neither populous nor minute. It was certainly small in comparison with the nobilities of Castile, Hungary and Poland which traditionally numbered at least five per cent of the population, yet large when compared with the nobilities of Sweden and the Austrian Territories. In all likelihood, it was no different from the nobility of pre-revolutionary France, comprising at most no more than two per cent of the population.

Structurally, it was less complicated than most continental nobilities (for references and further reading see bibliography, section III). Absent in England was a *noblesse de robe*, the product of royal absolutism: an elite of professional men who were either automatically ennobled by the tenure of public office, as in Russia and France, or ennobled for services rendered in the bureaucracy and army, as in Prussia and the Austrian empire. Also absent before the twentieth century was a high proportion of poor aristocrats or an aristocracy of wide occupational range. On the Continent an extreme heterogeneity of occupation and wealth was encouraged, partly by the system of privilege which preserved the noble identity of aristocrats who could not afford to lead a noble way of life, and partly by the sale of honours, a regular means of raising revenue used, for example, in the early modern period by the Spanish Habsburgs in both their Iberian and Italian territories and by the French monarchy. In England, the paucity of corporate privileges made landownership and life-style of prime importance in the identification of aristocratic status, while the tendency for privileges to pass by primogeniture safeguarded against the mass production of impoverished cadet lines. The younger sons of the English gentry traditionally entered the professions and even trade but not as aristocrats. Titles were occasionally sold in England but, prior to the twentieth century, they went to men who had already attained an aristocratic status.

By the late twentieth century the English aristocracy had acquired a four-tiered structure. It consisted predominantly of a gentry which bore no resemblance to the so-called gentry of eastern Europe since the former was scantily privileged and relatively wealthy whereas the latter was extensively privileged and mostly poor. A second tier was the baronetcy, an innovation of James I. Something of an hereditary knighthood, it formed the upper tier of the gentry. By the mid-twentieth century its membership of 1,500 titles made it twice the size of the hereditary peerage. Prior to the decline of the gentry in the early twentieth century, it never formed more than a minute proportion (never more than five per cent) of the aristocracy as a whole. The upper two tiers of aristocracy consisted of the hereditary and the life peerage. Both were distinguishable from the rest of the aristocracy by their membership of the Lords and the possession of other special privileges. Until the late twentieth century peerages were normally hereditary. The two exceptions were the spiritual peers, the bishops and, until the 1530s, the abbots, and the products of the Appellate Jurisdiction Act of 1876 which authorised the elevation of four, and later nine, judges to the peerage for life. Traditionally, the peerage resembled the baronetcy in forming a small minority within the aristocracy. This never amounted, before the twentieth century, to more than one per cent.

Imparting coherence and integrity to the aristocratic order was not so much privilege as its members' subscription to an aristocratic life-style based upon rentier landownership, a sense of public duty and the lavish display of wealth. These cohesive forces were only destroyed in the course of the twentieth century when the hereditary peers, along with the baronetcy and surviving gentry, reacted to the long-term fall in land values and the profitability of other forms of investment and became more commercial or professional, less landed or even landless, and more modest in their current expenditure. Finally, the profuse creation of life baronies after 1958 turned the peerage into a social ragbag.

(a) The peerage

An hereditary peerage of thirteen families in 1300 had grown to over eight hundred in the mid-twentieth century. The most important stages in this growth occurred in the fourteenth and fifteenth centuries when the peers, having contracted from twenty-two in 1154 to seven in 1327, were increased to sixty. By the mid-fifteenth century the peerage was a substantial group, the result of royal generosity, the establishment of new titles of peerage (before 1337 the earldom was the only peerage title in existence yet by 1440 the complete range, except for the life barony, had emerged), and the Crown's abandonment of its former practice of only awarding peerages to its near kinsmen. The second important period of growth was from 1603 to 1628 when a lavish dispensation of titles by James I and Charles I, frequently for sums of money, doubled the peerage, enlarging it from sixty to 120 titles. The peerage was again dramatically enlarged by the creations of Pitt the Younger: between 1689 and 1784 the size of the English peerage remained roughly constant at between 160 and 170 titles but by 1800 it was composed of three hundred titles. The final significant period of growth occurred between 1886 and the 1960s. By 1911 the peerage consisted of 570 families and by 1956 it exceeded eight hundred. Then, thanks to the creation of the life barony (1958), the peerage numbered about 1,200 individuals in 1980.

Prior to the late nineteenth century, the creation of peerages had little profound effect upon the social composition of the house of lords, only enlarging its membership and increasing the ratio of new to old titles. This was because the recipients of peerage titles were mostly landowners. In sharp contrast, only one quarter of the 246 titles granted between 1886 and 1914 went to landed families, and only a small proportion of the new peers from non-landed backgrounds bothered, in support of their title, to purchase a landed estate. As a result, the house of lords acquired a highly variegated membership which bore no resemblance to its traditional composition.

The government's relative meanness in creating peers, evident for much of the eighteenth and nineteenth centuries, and the long-term tendency to recruit new peers from the baronetcy, the Scottish and Irish peerage and the gentry, suggest that, before the twentieth century, society's acceptance of the peerage did not depend upon its accessibility. Opposition to the peerage, in fact, coincided with periods of openness. The loss of regard for the peerage in the early seventeenth century, strongly expressed in 1649 with the abolition of the house of lords, followed a spectacular inflation of peerage titles. Another phase of decline, this time permanent, accompanied the multiplication of peerage titles in the late nineteenth and early twentieth centuries. At a time when peerage titles were more available to commoners than ever before, the Parliament Act of 1911 severely limited the Lords' constitutional authority. On the other hand, largely responsible for preserving the house of lords in the late twentieth century was the generous bestowal of the life barony.

(b) The gentry

The first important step in the gentry's development occurred in the twelfth century when the professional knight was aristocratised. Instead of providing a specific military service for a salary, he became a landowner who was expected, by virtue of his landownership, to perform a variety of public functions, both civil and military. The transformation of the professional into the aristocratic knight created the beginnings of the gentry. A second important step occurred in the fourteenth and fifteenth centuries when the aristocracy became an armigerous class and first the esquires and then the plain gentlemen landowners were formally admitted to its membership through being allowed to bear coats of arms (see ch. 7 (d) and (f)). The third important step occurred in the sixteenth and early seventeenth centuries, a period which saw a further enlargement of the gentry and a considerable increase in its landownership. In the period the population doubled whilst the aristocracy probably tripled. The gentry's share of landownership increased from something like thirty per cent to fifty per cent, remaining roughly at that level until the twentieth century. This increase in landholding was not at the expense of the peerage whose landed possessions rose in the same period from five per cent to ten per cent. In both cases, the gain was made at the expense of the Crown, the church and the freehold peasantry. However, because the increase in landownership was accompanied by an equivalent enlargement of the aristocracy, it did not make either the gentry or the peerage wealthier *per capita*. The same period also saw a remarkable increase in the number of titled gentry. For this the early Stuarts were largely responsible, not simply through creating the baronetcy but also in generously dispensing the knighthood. Whereas titles of peerage had ceased to be sparingly granted in the reign of Edward III, titles of knighthood continued to be frugally granted until the sixteenth century, so much so that the dubbed knights, a group which required constant renovation as the title of knight was not inheritable, had fallen from 1,200 in 1324 to 375 in 1490. Tudor generosity increased the number to about six hundred on Elizabeth's accession but it had dropped to 550 upon her death. In contrast 3,281 titles of knighthood were created between 1603 and 1641. As with peerages and baronetcies, the early Stuarts awarded knighthoods to raise revenue as well as to create patronage.

In the sixteenth and seventeenth centuries the membership of the gentry came temporarily under Crown control: due to the requirement that gentry families sport a genuine coat of arms and to the county visitations of royal heralds to confirm or admit armorial bearings. Like the peerage and baronetcy, the gentry grew because of the Crown's openhandedness, a liberality forced upon it by a shortage of funds. In the same indebted circumstances the Bourbons and the Spanish Habsburgs acted no differently. However, the gentry's enlargement chiefly sprang from an upsurge of recruitment into the minor gentry from the upper peasantry, the yeomanry. Large numbers of lawyers and merchants also attained gentry status but at least half the recruits were rising yeomen. Accounting for the influx was not only the commoner's deep-seated appreciation of aristocracy but also the opportunities for social promotion provided by a growth in trade and litigation and by a spectacular price rise which especially favoured the farmer. The importance of newly generated wealth in the expansion of the gentry is underlined by the fact that backward Lancashire possessed a gentry which marginally contracted between 1550 and 1650. Since the process of recruitment began with the acquisition of an estate, the influx of commoners into the gentry owed much to a vigorous land market. This was initially generated by the land unloaded not so much by declining aristocratic families as by the church and Crown. Between 1536 and 1660, this unloading, the result of the Crown's annexation of the estates of the monasteries and chantries and its willingness to sell them to subjects, placed between twenty-five to thirty per cent of the country's total landed area on the market. Much of it fell into the hands of the existing aristocracy but some enabled commoners to take the first step towards gentry status, opening up the prospect of social acceptance by the county community, of intermarriage with long-established gentry families and of receiving a knighthood or officially recognised coats of arms.

The third important step in the gentry's development featured a contraction in membership and landownership. Throughout the eighteenth and early nineteenth centuries the proportion of land owned by the gentry marginally increased: from forty-five to fifty per cent (England and Wales) in 1690 to fifty-five per cent (England alone) in 1873. This increase, like the earlier one coincided with one for the peerage: from fifteen to twenty per cent (England and Wales) in 1690 to twenty-four per cent (England alone) in 1873. But then, in the very late nineteenth and the early twentieth centuries, falling rents and land values, high taxation and labour costs caused massive land sales. To survive, gentry families were driven to sell their estates or to farm them. Both measures meant abandoning a way of life upon which their aristocratic identity so much depended. Whereas the titles of peers and baronets enabled them to survive the loss of the estate, the gentry lost their recognised aristocratic status through ceasing to be landowners or through becoming farmers rather than landlords. This contraction, moreover, was absolute and final. In this period the traditional habit of acquiring aristocratic status by purchasing an estate was abandoned. A place in the country remained very much an aspiration of wealthy commoners but, after the first world war, a country cottage normally proved sufficient and even newly established country houses tended to be the hubs of no more than 1000 acre estates. Upholding the gentry over the centuries has been not only the abiding landedness of its members but the willingness of commoners to purchase large estates. Apart from the baronetcy, the gentry was doomed both as old gentry families abandoned their estates and commoners forwent the opportunity to purchase them. Instead of passing to would-be aristocrats, they transferred piecemeal to the tenant farmers, undergoing as a result, an irrevocable fragmentation.

(c) Peers and gentry

The peerage and the gentry were closely related, sharing the same belief in birthright, conceiving themselves as members of the same ruling class and deriving their wealth and local influence from the same landed source. The connexion was confirmed by kinship and recruitment. Gentry rose into the peerage while the younger sons of the peerage descended into the gentry. Intermarriage between peerage and gentry families was common. Furthermore it could not be said that the two had mutually opposed interests: if the one gained an increase in power and wealth it was not necessarily at the other's expense. The two groups were also connected by clientage. The gentry served the great noblemen as vassals in the twelfth century, as employees, tenants, indentured retainers and annuitants in the fifteenth and sixteenth centuries, and as placemen in the parliaments and local government of the eighteenth century.

In all likelihood, the gentry became less dependent upon the peerage in the course of the sixteenth and seventeenth centuries; and the peerage had to become more reliant upon professional people to serve as its leading officials. Certainly the close relationship evident in the early sixteenth century when peers employed gentry by indenture of retainder, as estate officials and household servants and could call upon them as tenants, sometimes to fulfil a feudal obligation, was much altered by the mid-seventeenth century when gentry were much less frequently found in the full-time service of peers and both bastard feudalism (retaining) and feudalism had ceased to be a bond between them. But it is easy to overestimate the gentry's dependence upon the higher nobility in the middle ages and to underestimate it in the modern period. In the late middle ages large numbers of gentry allied themselves with magnates. Faced by a malfunctioning royal government and a growing lawlessness, members of the gentry looked for reward and protection to great subjects rather than to the Crown. This did not make them utterly subservient to the magnates. The careers of the Pastons in Norfolk and the Plumptons in Yorkshire indicate a necessary affiliation with magnates, but also some independence of them. In the mid-fifteenth century John Paston wrote to his brother: 'I have given my lady [of Norfolk] warning that I will do my lord no more service, but 'ere we parted she made me to make her promise that I should let her have knowledge 'ere I fastened myself in any other service; and so I departed'. The gentry of the Wars of the Roses were not bound inextricably to particular lords. Offering their services to magnates out of self-interest, they switched allegiances accordingly, and lordship tended to last only so long as it remained beneficial lordship. Nonetheless, the gentry was orientated towards the magnates for its patronage, protection, justice and employment. Two hundred years later, the relationship was radically changed. A magnate class endured, but its hold over the rest of the aristocracy was much weaker. In the civil war of the 1640s the gentry possessed an independence and political initiative which has been lacking in the Wars of the Roses.

The gentry's independence of the magnates interlocked with the magnates' loss of their former independence of the Crown. Responsible for both developments was the revival of strong royal government under the Yorkists and early Tudors and a massive increase in the Crown's resources of patronage, largely a consequence of the dissolution of the monasteries and chantries in the 1530s and 1540s. The restored effectiveness of royal government restricted the magnate's opportunities to dispense goodlordship in his own name and seriously threatened defecting aristocrats with the prospect of reprisal; while the increase in royal patronage rendered the private patronage of the magnates trifling in comparison. The gentry's independence of the magnate was a repercussion of the process whereby the aristocracy was persuaded to look more to the Crown than to an intermediate magnate for its advancement, satisfaction and protection; and the Crown became the primary patron for peers and gentry alike.

The change in relationship between peers and gentry was already evident by the mid-sixteenth century. Between 1547 and 1549 Thomas Seymour, the brother of Protector Somerset and uncle to Edward VI, sought to impose himself in the manner of a fifteenth-century magnate and failed, it seems, because of the gentry's unreliability. Giving evidence at Seymour's trial, the marquis of Dorset claimed that Seymour 'further willed me that I should not trust too much unto the gentlemen for they had somewhat to lose'. The earl· of Rutland deposed that Seymour had told him to 'make much of the gentlemen in his country', but issued the warning that 'there is no great trust to be to them'. In 1450 a magnate could rely on gentry support even when his cause went counter to that of the Crown, support which had made the political resistance of magnates to the government formidable and sometimes effective. With this support no longer guaranteed in 1550, it seems that the traditional power base of the magnates had been seriously disturbed. Seymour's solution was to cultivate the yeomanry. He advised Dorset to go 'to their houses, now to one, now to another, carrying with you a flaggon or two of wine and a pastry of venison and to use familiarity with them'. But this offered no workable substitute (see also ch. 8 (a)).

The changed relationship between the gentry and the magnates profoundly affected contemporary politics. It helps to explain the Tudors' success both in retaining a usurped crown, in spite of the problems created by religious schism and the succession to the throne of a minor and two queens, and in centralising the political system especially as the latter was accomplished through the centrifugal force of the Court rather than the cohesive machinery of an extensive bureaucracy. But the gentry's independence of the magnates was arguably shortlived. By the eighteenth century the gentry, it seems, had again succumbed to magnate leadership both at Westminster and in local government. Its independence in the sixteenth and early seventeenth centuries was evidently an isolated episode in its history, occurring only in the time that the higher nobility took to adapt to the changing nature of the state and to recover its political ascendancy. By the close of the seventeenth century strong, effective monarchy was an impossibility in England. In its place emerged ministerial rule by magnates who, having taken charge of the Crown's patronage, manipulated it to uphold their governments. Gone was the independent political force traditionally embodied in the Crown to which ambitious gentry could attach themselves as an alternative form of allegiance to that of the magnates. For many gentry the choice now was which magnate interest to serve, a throwback to the political world of the fifteenth century. Yet there were differences between the politics of the two periods, the result of the emergence of party political ideologies, the decline of the aristocracy's ability to wage private war and also the preservation, throughout the eighteenth century, of an independent gentry which formed roughly half the membership of the house of commons. This independent element remained a force in politics because governments needed to enlist its support or, at least, to avoid its opposition, and therefore pursued a policy broadly amenable to its interests. The task of controlling this maverick element eventually eased with the development of party organisations in the early nineteenth century.

(d) Extinction, promotion and demotion

Like most other nobilities in Europe, the English aristocracy was composed largely of recent elevations: the result of the extinction of dynasties, the promotion of commoners into the aristocracy and the demotion of aristocratic offspring into the commonalty. Since their survival as separate dynasties depended on producing male heirs, and was handicapped by the practice of monogamy, aristocratic families were easily terminated, either becoming totally extinct or more often merging through the marriage of an heiress or through collateral descent with other dynasties. The failure rate was spectacularly and constantly high. This is evident in McFarlane's sample of 357 families that received writs of summons to parliament between 1300 and 1500. Not all were peers. Twenty-seven per cent of the families became extinct in the direct male line every twenty-five years. In the modern period the extinction rate remained very high. Thus, of the 204 baronetcies created by James I only ninety-seven survived after 140 years; and by 1800 667 of the 946 baronetcies created before 1701 were extinct. Thirty-three per cent of the peerages existent in 1485 had failed to produce male heirs by 1547, and of the sixty-three peerages existent in 1559 only twenty-two had survived by direct descent in 1641, twenty failing in the direct male line and passing by collateral descent and twenty-one failing completely in the male line. To take a local example: in the 1770s there were twelve peers in Essex. None was of medieval creation and five were elevations of the eighteenth century. Of the twelve, six had become extinct in the direct male line by 1800.

In the middle ages the Crown frequently forfeited estates and titles. But extinction was rarely the outcome, largely because forfeiture was usually followed by a pardon and restoration of the estate and title. Forfeiture tended only to terminate a family's membership of the aristocracy when its coincidence with the absence of a direct male heir left no one to make a strong case for restoration (see ch. 8 (a)).

Gentry families more easily survived the failure to produce a male heir than peerage and baronetcy families since they could maintain their continuity through the marriage of an heiress to a commoner. In contrast, baronetcy and many peerage titles were legally restricted to descent in the male line. Moreover, the peerage titles which were transmissable on the female side tended to become the possession of other aristocratic families since the heiresses of peers usually married peers or their eldest sons. On the other hand, gentry families were more easily terminated by indebtedness. Upheld by distinctive privileges, the aristocratic status of peerage and baronetcy families was less dependent upon wealth and landedness.

Countering the failure of families to survive was the elevation of gentry into the peerage and baronetcy, the descent of the younger sons of peers and baronets into the gentry, and the rise of commoners into the gentry. While marriage to an heiress, the acquisition of an estate and the operation of primogeniture clearly played a part in awarding aristocratic status and rank, of outstanding importance was the Crown's willingness to create titles of baronetcy, knighthood and peerage and to sanction, through the heralds' office, coats of arms.

Over half the titles belonging to the hereditary peerage in 1956 had been created since 1900. Of the peerage in 1558 forty-six per cent of the titles were enjoyed by peers of the first and second generation. By 1628 the proportion of first and second generation holders of peerage titles was as high as fifty-seven per cent. In the century after the Glorious Revolution, the proportion of new to old peerage families fell dramatically, as with the baronetcies, but was then revived by the generosity of late eighteenth- and late nineteenth-century governments. However, while new families usually figured prominently in the composition of the peerage, commoners had virtually no chance of admission until the closing decades of the nineteenth century. Over the centuries fluidity of membership within the peerage was not a movement across class boundaries but an upward and downward passage of aristocratic families. Until the last century entry to the baronetcy was similarly confined to aristocrats. The opportunity of commoners to acquire the aristocratic rank of peer, baronet or knight, without needing to acquire gentry status as a preliminary qualification, emerged only in the late nineteenth and twentieth centuries.

The membership of the gentry was prone to even greater fluidity than the peerage. Families could lose their gentry status either by rising into the peerage or by selling their estates, and they could gain it either as the younger sons of peers and baronets or as commoners purchasing estates and receiving coats of arms. The turnover of gentry membership was perhaps at its most extreme in the late sixteenth and early seventeenth centuries. For example, three-quarters of the gentry families in early seventeenth-century Northamptonshire had entered the gentry after 1500. The gentries of Suffolk and Dorset were similarly changeable. Less volatile but far from static were the gentries of Cheshire and Lancashire.

Influential in the process was London wealth and its conversion into land. But the northern parts were also subjected to a high degree of fluidity. Of the 641 gentry families resident in Yorkshire in 1603, 180 had become extinct in the male line by 1642 and 218 new gentry families had surfaced. In this period a replacement rate of one quarter per half century has been calculated for the gentry. Entry depended upon the generation of wealth and the chance to turn it into estates. In other words, entry relied upon the land market. The case has been made for a severe contraction of this market from the late seventeenth century. Damping the market down was probably a petering out of its original stimulus, the sale of church and crown lands, as well as the emergence of legal devices to prevent the fragmentation of estates, the development of mortgage facilities and the falling interest on loans (from ten per cent in 1625 to five per cent in the late seventeenth century) both of which made it less necessary to sell lands in order to clear debts. Yet what effect did this contraction of the market have on the commoner's ability to gain gentry status? The period of rapid flux probably ended in the seventeenth century. Stemming the turnover of gentry membership was not only the relative lack of purchasable land but also the declining tendency of peers and baronets to equip younger sons with a portion of the estate. However, the wealth created by the growth of trade and industry and concentrated in the hands of the employers through low wages compensated for the high price of land, enabling commoners to become gentry no matter what the price of entry. While it does not seem that the gentry increased its numbers from the mid-seventeenth century, there is no sign of contraction. The upward mobility of commoners continued to replace the failed gentry lines. Without a doubt, the more significant turning point in the history of the gentry occurred in the late nineteenth and early twentieth centuries when falling land values choked off recruitment from the commonalty and falling rents as well as the lack of heirs brought many gentry families down.

The termination of commoner recruitment into the gentry preceded by half a century the virtual termination of recruitment to the hereditary peerage and baronetcy. As landowners the latter two groups were similarly affected by falling rents and land values, but ensuring their survival was the fact that their aristocratic identity essentially lay in distinctive titles, not in landownership or life-style. In their case recruitment depended upon government policy. With no informal means of entry, membership was essentially determined by the capacity to beget male heirs and by the government's willingness to grant titles. The baronetcy was sustained by newcomers until the mid-1960s. Before the impact of two Labour administrations ended the practice, the baronetcy was awarded with greater frequency than any other hereditary title in the twentieth century. However, none was awarded between 1945 and 1951 and the Labour government of 1965–70 followed suit. In compensation, the Tory administration created 106 between 1952 and 1965, but then the Heath administration followed in Labour's footsteps. Since 1965 no new creations of baronetcy have occurred. Now a caste, the baronetcy is quite different in character from what it had ever been since its inception in 1611. If the rate of extinction shown earlier this century is maintained and governments persist with the present policy of tolerating existing titles while desisting from the creation of new ones, the baronetcy should last for at least 350 years.

The peerage was also profoundly affected by a change in government policy in the mid-twentieth century. Profusely created by Liberal, Tory and Labour governments – 395 of the 870 titles existing in 1955 had been created since Queen Victoria's death – it suffered after 1965 from a reversion to early medieval practice as new hereditary peerages came to be reserved for the royal family. The main exception is the earldom offered to retiring prime ministers. However, long before the change in policy, the process of creation had slowed down. Apart from what was dispensed to royalty, the last ducal title went to the Grosvenors in 1874. The last marquisate was created in 1936. The rate of creation for earldoms fell dramatically after the second world war. Reducing to a minimum the creation of hereditary peers was a change in the means available to political parties for bolstering their influence in the house of lords. This came in 1958 with the creation of the life barony which soon replaced the hereditary peerage as the major honour conferred upon the citizenry.

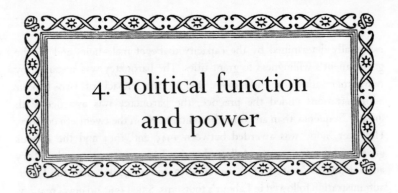

4. Political function and power

(a) Instrument of government

(For reference and further reading, see bibliography, section IV)

In the late seventeenth and early eighteenth centuries the English aristocracy added a governing function to its traditional role as a ruling class. Determining rather than simply applying government policy, it now exercised on a regular basis an authority which it had formerly possessed only in the unusual circumstances of a royal minority, interregnum or the rule of a personally ineffectual prince. Responsible for the change was a successful aristocratic backlash against an attempt to replace constitutional with absolute monarchy. Instead another revolution occurred which established parliament as a vital part of everyday government, and made ministers of the Crown answerable to parliament as well as to the monarch.

Through its domination of parliament, the aristocracy took charge of the state, notably following the constitutional restrictions imposed upon the Crown's authority by the Bill of Rights of 1689, a consequence of James II's deposition, and the practical constraints placed upon the Crown's powers by the succession to the throne, within the space of thirty years, of two foreigners, William III and George I, and two women, Mary and Anne, and by William III's dependence upon English support for his war against Louis XIV. Traditionally, government policy had centred upon the king. The aristocracy's natural function was to advise him and to implement it. By the mid-eighteenth century, the direction of the state was in the hands of an executive of leading aristocrats which took the Crown into account largely to make use of its considerable patronage.

The traditional ruling functions of the English aristocracy were to serve the Crown as councillors, courtiers, members of parliament, local government officials and seigneurs. Having exercised this range of function since at least the fourteenth century, the English aristocracy was, for much of its history, a service elite although one that functioned in the absence of an extensive state bureaucracy rather than in the presence of one, as in absolutist France or Prussia. Furthermore, it was a service elite not because its members were professionally qualified to hold their appointed tasks, or feudally obliged to serve, or exclusively privileged to hold office, but because it was the officially recognised ruling class, because the Crown had no alternative instrument of government, and because, persuaded by a sense of public duty and a need to gain access to royal patronage, it was prepared to work for the Crown.

Its traditional political functions stemmed from certain peculiarities in the development of the English state: first the paradox of its early centralisation and late bureaucratisation, and secondly, the long-term importance of parliament. Unlike France or Prussia, in England the development of a locally extensive and salaried bureaucratic machine did not introduce political centralisation. Centralisation was evident by the thirteenth century whereas bureaucratisation in local government only came in the nineteenth century. Over the intervening centuries the centralised judiciary had to depend not upon trained judges but commissions of gentlemen who served without pay and qualified for service not by training or proven merit but because of the local prestige which their social standing conferred upon them. Moreover, whereas most other nobilities came under the thumb of royal government in the early modern period and were professionalised, operating as civil servants or army officers, the English aristocracy rejected the Crown's bureaucratic innovations, notably the regional councils erected by the Tudors in the north and the Welsh Marches, and so preserved its traditional non-professional administrative functions.

Its parliamentary function was determined by parliament's early acquisition of tax-granting, jurisdictional and law-making powers, their retention and the fact that, until the late nineteenth century, the aristocracy was the predominant element in the house of commons as well as the house of lords. The powers of parliament, and the government's limited, non-parliamentary sources of revenue, gave the aristocracy the

ability to challenge and to influence government policy centuries before a
system of ministerial responsibility awarded it the power to formulate
policy. Frequently on the Continent the traditional diets did not make law
and their fiscal powers, although originally wide, were limited, from at
least the fifteenth century, by the development of revenue systems which
were either non-parliamentary or rested on taxes which, although initiated
by parliamentary consent, did not require it for their continuation.[1] Yet
until the late seventeenth century, the English parliament was not needed
in regular session since direct taxation was regarded as a source of
extraordinary revenue rather than a basic means of financing government
and the making of new laws was accepted as an intermittent, not a regular,
government activity. Only with the Glorious Revolution did parliament
become an essential part of everyday government as well as an essential
part of the constitution. Nevertheless, the extensiveness and durability of
the English aristocracy's traditional parliamentary powers, and their
enlargement in the seventeenth and eighteenth centuries at a time when
royal absolutism on the Continent was either terminating or severely
curtailing representative assemblies, rendered its parliamentary function
comparatively unusual.

In one important respect, the English aristocracy's functional
development closely followed the continental pattern. In the course of the
late seventeenth century England acquired a national army. Its effect was
to end the aristocracy's traditional function of providing the government
with troops. With the demise of the feudal host in the thirteenth century,
the government had raised armies for war abroad by ordering leading
aristocrats to serve with their followings. A second resort was to employ
mercenaries. Furthermore, in the late middle ages, the militia came to be
used for waging war in Scotland, although its normal function was to
defend the realm, and in 1544 Henry VIII established the precedent, upon
which the Elizabethan government acted, of employing it on the Continent.
But the extended use of the militia and the employment of mercenaries
only added further supplies of troops. It did not render the Crown
independent of private retinues: as in France, the provision of troops for
the armies royal remained an important function of the aristocracy well
into the seventeenth century; but because of the emergence of the
standing, professional army, it had ceased by 1700. This reduced the
aristocracy's military function to organising the militia and commanding

the army. The development of a substantial navy in the late seventeenth century had a similar effect. The aristocracy's privateering role of providing their own ships to supplement the activities of the royal navy ended, and they continued to serve only as commanding naval officers.

The higher positions in the army remained an aristocratic preserve until at least the Crimean war, while the officer corps continued to offer gentlemen a respectable career in the twentieth century. The substitution of the persona of an educated gentleman for that of the armed knight in the fifteenth and sixteenth centuries only altered the aristocracy's appearance, not its occupation. Its commitment to the military and the military's commitment to the aristocracy remained strong for the remainder of its history. In 1860, for example, fifty-four per cent of Sandhurst entrants was aristocratic, the proportion remaining at twenty per cent in 1910 and as high as nine per cent in 1930. Furthermore, in 1956, regular military service was still the major occupation of the peerage: at that time, thirty-nine per cent of living peers had served as army regulars against twenty-six per cent with directorships and eleven per cent with the qualification to pursue a career in the law. Upholding the connection between army and aristocracy was the persistent anti-professional ethos of the officer corps and the enduring preference for men of aristocratic birth in the recruitment and promotion of officers. The latter ensured, for example, that in the late nineteenth century, between forty and fifty per cent of generals were of aristocratic birth.

Furnishing troops for the army royal rested wholly upon the aristocracy's private authority since it was fulfilled independently of the tenure of public office. The administrative and judicial functions which it held as lords of the manor and of baronies, honours, hundreds and liberties had a similar private base. However, in many cases they possessed a public character and origin. For example, manors operated as either courts baron or courts leet. While the former merely administered a private function, the landlord's rights over his tenants, the latter operated a public function even though it was privately owned. It derived from the manorial lord's annexation of the views of frankpledge and of the assize of bread and ale, responsibilities which were originally exercised by the royal sheriff in the communal courts of hundred and shire. Furthermore, absent in England were the privatised royal offices of duke, count, viscount and castellany, yet present were franchises whose public authority came of regalian rights alienated by delegation to tenants-in-chief, by grants of immunity from the royal system of government, or by the transference of a hundred court from public to private ownership. Although the sheriff remained a public official, some of his judicial authority fell into private hands, allowing subjects for a time to hold powers of criminal jurisdiction by inheritable right.

Private courts could exercise the broad range of criminal and civil jurisdiction, including pleas of the Crown, their powers only stopping short of the right to try and acquit treason. Such was the case in the marcher lordships of Wales and their northern equivalents, the liberties of Tyndale and Redesdale. In these areas, administrative powers came of the right to exclude the king's writ and fiscal powers came of immunity to royal taxes. These liberties preceded the Conquest, survived the attempts of medieval kings to curb their powers, and preserved their judicial, fiscal and administrative independence until the 1530s. Prior to the final blow, however, many fell to the Crown by a process of piecemeal resumption. In fact, what was abolished by Henry VIII had mostly ceased to be an aristocratic possession.

Then there were the lesser franchises of barony and honour. They originated in the royal authority which was delegated at the Conquest to tenants-in-chief, or they were created earlier by the royal grant of 'sake and soke, toll and team and infangthef' (see glossary). Unlike the liberties, both types of franchise were excluded from hearing pleas of the Crown. With the latter's enlargement in the twelfth and thirteenth centuries, the jurisdictions of the baronies and honours were reduced so that eventually they lost all rights of major criminal jurisdiction. In addition an appeals procedure was developed by the legislation of 1259 and 1267 which allowed the royal judges to monopolise claims to false judgement and, in this way, subjected the remaining criminal jurisdiction of the baronies and honours to royal justice. Their civil jurisdiction was restricted when the statute of Gloucester in 1278 confined it to disputes concerning goods or property not exceeding the value of 40/-. Like the liberties, these lesser franchises were subjected to a process of piecemeal resumption. By 1500 many had become a royal possession.

The privately owned hundreds found their powers similarly curtailed, especially after 1215 when sheriffs were banned from hearing pleas of the Crown, and with the enactment of the statute of Gloucester. The hundreds had fallen into private hands before the Conquest. The courts leet had shallower roots, developing after the Conquest as manorial lords assumed the powers of the sheriff, especially his view of frankpledge. They then lost judicial authority in the thirteenth century as the criminal jurisdiction of the sheriff was transferred to itinerant justices, commissions of gaol delivery and eventually to commissions of the peace and as the statute of Gloucester restricted their civil jurisdiction.

However, these spectacular reductions did not confine private jurisdiction merely to the issue and enforcement of manorial regulations. On the Continent seigneurs preserved greater powers of justice for a much longer period of time, especially the rights of imprisonment and gallows; and royal absolutism as it developed in the seventeenth and eighteenth centuries tended to confer upon the seigneur additional political functions such as tax collection and the organisation of conscription.[2] Nevertheless, although comparatively limited and undergoing no revival, seigneurial authority in England remained an integral part of local government until at least the reforms of the mid-nineteenth century. In the eighteenth century, for example, hundred courts conferred upon their owners a jurisdiction in petty debt and the right to appoint certain local government officials, notably the constable. Manorial courts with powers of court leet retained in the early nineteenth century a jurisdiction that encompassed nuisance, debt, trespass, breach of promise and consumer offences arising from the assize of bread and ale. Besides having a petty criminal and civil jurisdiction, courts leet made bye-laws and often appointed the officials of local government, notably the constables and tithingmen, the ale conners, the pound keepers, the bread weighers, the town criers and the weights and measures inspectorate. These tasks were a genuine part of traditional local government. Although privately owned, their function was a public one.

To deal with the essentially private landlord–tenant matters, the court baron had the power to decide disputes between tenants, to administer the succession and conveyance of customary tenures, to determine manorial regulations and to appoint the manorial officials, the reeve, bailiff, beadle and hayward. This authority endured until the abolition of customary tenures in the 1920s although the conversion of tenures to leaseholds had, over the centuries, limited its effect. The powers of the court leet receded at a slightly earlier date, its powers reduced by the failure of statutes, from the early seventeenth century, to use it for enforcing the common law – the last statute to do so was enacted in 1623 (21 James I, c. 21) – and the tendency from the late eighteenth century for public bodies such as parish vestries to take over the tasks of appointing local officials and making bye-laws, and for the jurisdiction of courts leet to be transferred to special statutory courts such as courts of conscience and courts of requests, or to commissions of the peace. However, only the reform of local government in the mid-nineteenth century terminated the government role of the court leet.

Because of the survival of seigneurial courts with public authority, English aristocrats could serve the state not only by holding public office but also by exercising private rights. Eventually, the aristocracy became no more than a social elite, its members exercising a public function because they had competed successfully for office as professional administrators, soldiers and politicians. However, throughout its history, many of its respected members failed to hold public office simply because the numbers of aristocrats exceeded the available posts. For example, of the 120 gentry resident in Sussex in 1524 only fifty-six served in an official capacity; only twenty-one aristocrats out of eighty-three did so in Buckinghamshire; only fifty-one out of one hundred did so in Suffolk; and only seven out of thirty-five did so in Rutland. Compensating aristocrats for the lack of public office was either employment in the service of magnates or the exercise of their own seigneurial authority. Although having failed to obtain royal office, aristocrats could hold public authority, nonetheless, as the paid officials of magnates and as lords of the manor.

As ministers, MPs, JPs, deputy lieutenants, lord lieutenants, the English aristocracy remained a dominant part of government throughout most of the nineteenth century. Certainly by 1850 it was still firmly entrenched in the political system, dominating parliament by occupying the majority of Commons seats as well as through the house of lords; holding the senior positions in the civil service and army; occupying most seats in the cabinet; controlling local government through the lord lieutenant and his right to select its higher personnel; and because of the enormous administrative and judicial authority exercised by the justices of the peace who were mostly of the gentry. Challenging this political dominance was: (1) the County Councils Act of 1888 which transferred to elected councillors the administrative functions of the JPs; (2) the implementation of the

Northcote–Trevelyan reforms concerning recruitment to the civil service
(formulated in 1854 and successfully applied between 1870 and 1918); (3)
the second and third Reform Acts (1867 and 1884) which, in conjunction
with the Secret Ballot Act of 1872 produced a house of commons which,
for the first time since the fourteenth century, was not a predominantly
aristocratic body; (4) the Parliament Act of 1911 which denied the Lords
their traditional right to sanction legislation; and (5) the removal from lord
lieutenants after 1910 of the authority to appoint deputy lieutenants and
JPs.

Only the nobilities of eastern Europe showed an equivalent capacity to
survive as a ruling class in the late nineteenth century. Elsewhere the
professional politician, the professional administrator and the professional
soldier took over. This eventually happened in England, but with
remarkable belatedness. English aristocrats were highly capable of
adaptation, figuring as elected county councillors, as MPs elected by
manhood suffrage, as elected members of the boards of guardians which
administered the New Poor Law and as members of the school boards that
operated the 1870 Education Act. But the complications and answerability
of the democratic process persuaded many aristocrats to retire from public
life. Initially they were replaced by commoners, usually professionalmen,
with an outlook closely akin to the aristocracy's and a social affinity to
aristocracy imparted by family ties and a public school education.

For much of its history, the English aristocracy performed a dual service
function. Besides serving the Crown as officials and officers, it operated as
the service elite of other aristocrats, acting as household servants, keepers
of castles, estate officials and the administrators of courts of private
jurisdiction. Aristocrats had also served aristocrats because they were
under feudal obligation. This was still the case under the early Tudors in
the honours and baronies of the north where the Dacres, the Cliffords and
the Percies could call upon the feudal services of gentlemen tenants. Some
aristocrats, prior to the seventeenth century, were legally contracted to
serve other aristocrats by indenture of retainder, a repercussion of the
statute *Quia Emptores* of 1290 which outlawed subinfeudation. Since the act
prevented a subject from legally placing another under feudal obligation by
making him his tenant, a substitute contract was needed to enable lords to
secure dependant gentry. The solution was an indenture which bound a
retainer to serve his lord in peace and war for life and obliged the lord to

protect the retainer and perhaps to recompense him with an annuity or with less defined favours. The first known indenture of retainder is dated 1278. By the late fourteenth century it had acquired a standard form. The retainer differed from the household or estate official in not residing in the lord's house and in being summoned only upon special occasions to serve the lord's cause. He differed from the feudal tenant in having no necessary landed connexion with his lord. The retaining system was given legal definition by the statute of 1390 which captured it exclusively for the aristocracy, enacting that only aristocrats were entitled to be retained and only peers could retain.

Retaining somewhat resembled the contractual obligations which, in the same period, developed between the Crown and certain leading noblemen. Both emerged as a substitute for the old feudal relationship between king and tenant-in-chief and tenant-in-chief and vavasour. However, whereas the contracts between the king and individual lords were temporary and confined to military matters, the contract between lord and retainer often proposed or implied a general and permanent service. Retainers served their lords in both a civil and a military capacity and contracted for life. Since the retainers were aristocrats with extensive estates, a tenantry to array and usually a public function as royal officials, seigneurs and members of parliament, the system awarded lords a means of influence within the framework of royal government as well as the opportunity to raise a substantial military force manned by their own tenantry and that of their retainers.

By the early seventeenth century retaining and feudal service had faded away. Moreover, the gentry who still served nobles in full-time employment and, as residents and attendants, formed their entourage, tended now to be the younger sons of lesser gentry. Nevertheless, a century earlier all three ties had remained strong. Moreover, the attachment of gentry to the service of the higher nobles was restored in the eighteenth century following the disappearance of monarchy as an independent political force and the lord lieutenants' capture of the right to make appointments to the higher offices in local government (see ch. 8). Needless to say, the capacity of aristocrats to serve aristocrats did not distinguish the English aristocracy. Traditionally, the lesser nobilities of Europe had functioned as the service elite either of the Crown or of the magnates.

(b) **In opposition**

(For reference and further reading, see bibliography, section VIII (b)).

The English aristocracy's durability as a non-professional service elite and the early decline of its private rights of criminal jurisdiction were only two distinctive features of its political function. Yet another was its long-term ability to oppose the government and to withstand its attempts to enlarge the powers of the state at the expense of the subjects' traditional liberties. The peculiarities in the English state's historical development, notably the traditional strength of its parliament and the feeble, backward nature of its bureaucracy, owed much to the aristocracy's capacity to deny the political innovations of the Crown.

Its anti-tyranny function was performed most spectacularly in the seventeenth century, a time when the nobilities of France and Brandenburg-Prussia found new life in submitting to royal absolutism. On two occasions aristocratic parties rose effectively against the Crown and realised a political revolution, although they aimed merely to prevent the Crown from transforming the polity through force of arms, conspiracy and parliamentary pressure. In the seventeenth century, the English aristocracy took action against the Crown. This was not without precedent. In fact, the Tudor age was an exceptional lull in an onslaught upon the Crown which lasted from at least the thirteenth to the eighteenth centuries. In no continental monarchy were there so many usurpations of the throne or constitutions pressed upon kings. Only the nobilities of Poland and Hungary had a better record of minimising the powers of the Crown; and in western Europe only the nobilities of the Crown of Aragon had an equivalent record of effective resistance to the government. And, with the exception of the Hungarian, these nobilities were eventually subjugated by the Crown.

Accounting for the high incidence and effectiveness of aristocratic revolt in England was the Crown's long-term indebtedness which, by restricting its resources of patronage, limited its means of enlisting aristocratic support, and which drove it to resort to questionable and provocative devices for raising extra revenue. Furthermore, the centralised nature of the state easily allowed English aristocrats to fight for national rights rather than provincial liberties, and enabled it to act through a national representative assembly rather than provincial estates. The

English aristocracy, moreover, was normally under little pressure to accept a strengthening of the state. Lacking was the justification of a warring frontier capable of imperilling the nation. What is more, English governments could not use privilege to persuade aristocrats to support royal absolutism since the more important privileges were parliamentary and therefore alien to a Crown bent on enlarging its powers, and the seigneurial rights which became the basis of aristocratic support for strong monarchy in eastern Europe, had by this time faded beyond the point of revival. Neither was there the fear of class hostility to compel aristocrats to accept an increase in government authority.

Lacking in England, then, were the considerations which on the Continent persuaded nobilities to accept royal absolutism. It could therefore cling to its traditional role as opponent rather than servitor of strong royal government. Moreover, by the seventeenth century the English aristocracy was sustained by a tradition of resistance which gave to its revolts self-confidence and special goals, notably the deposition of the monarch and the restriction of his constitutional powers.

The tradition of aristocratic revolt ended with the successes of the seventeenth century. Yet the aristocracy retained a capacity for opposition: the ministries of the eighteenth century were the target of extensive aristocratic criticism on the issues of heavy taxation, war, political corruption, oligarchic rule, even parliamentary reform. Opposition continued in the nineteenth century on the key issues of extending the parliamentary franchise, abolishing the corn laws, Irish home rule and Catholic emancipation. Yet apart from the fiasco of the Jacobite uprising of 1715, aristocratic resistance failed to take the form of armed revolt (see ch. 8 (b)).

(c) **Power**

From its dual function as an instrument of, and an opposition to, government, the English aristocracy drew enormous power as well as authority. This probably reached its peak in the eighteenth century, an interlude between, on the one hand, the repudiation of the regional forms of government erected by Yorkists and Tudors and of the interference in local government practised by the Stuarts and, on the other hand, the nineteenth-century revival of the attempt to control the localities by centralisation and bureaucratisation. In the intervening period England was, in practice, a patchwork of self-governing territories whose autonomy was safeguarded by the virtual absence of bureaucracy and the magnate's control of central government. In the middle ages, magnates had enjoyed a similar power but only as a result of civil war or because the government was weakened by the personal inadequacies of the reigning monarch: in other words, because of a temporary fault in the system rather than because of its intrinsic nature. Generally, the power of the aristocracy consisted of excluding central government from the localities or of serving as its agent. In the course of time the exclusion of royal government – for example, by means of franchisal rights – came to be replaced by an aristocratic take-over of the authority and machinery of royal government. In this process the magnate element was domesticated and demilitarised and firmly attached to the service of central government. This was a well-recognised achievement of the Tudor monarchy. But then in the course of the seventeenth century the control of government was wrested from the Crown, producing a magnate rule in the eighteenth century which contrasted sharply with the Continent where strong royal rule mostly prevailed. No matter what the nature of a magnate's power, he needed, in common with the Crown, to exert control over other aristocrats. Magnate rule, both in the middle ages and in the eighteenth century, was successful because the magnate proved more adept than the Crown in enlisting the aristocracy's allegiance. (For the power of magnates, see ch. 8 (a)).

The aristocracy's role as a political elite clearly depended upon popular deference. This deference was not simply an expression of dependency since the deference remained after the dependency had gone. The leadership role conferred upon aristocrats by popular, as well as governmental, respect helped the aristocracy to impose itself politically and socially without the constant use of force. But can the changes in the aristocracy's political power be explained as a consequence of its changing relationship with the people? Prior to the nineteenth century, its ability to command popular allegiance seemed to have no correlation with its effectiveness vis-à-vis the state. Its search for power did not compel it to be generously paternalistic. Material needs always kept its paternalism in check. Nor did its search for power cause it to preserve lines of dependency with the people. While it was firmly upheld as a ruling class by a system of landownership which rendered the bulk of the population dependent upon it as tenants, the aristocracy was not averse to reducing the number of dependent families by encouraging the engrossment of farms. Benefiting materially from the development of agrarian capitalism, the aristocracy did little to oppose its social consequences or to re-establish dependency by substituting, through its own participation in farming, a dependency reliant upon wages for one reliant upon rent. Agrarian capitalism freed the bulk of the rural population from direct aristocratic control. However, in failing to stop it, the aristocracy did not appear to suffer. This was because the aristocracy's political power was essentially determined not by its behaviour towards the people but by its relationship with the state.

Notes to Chapter 4

1. See Bush, *Noble Privilege*, ch. IV (2).
2. *Ibid.*, ch. VI (1 (f) and (i)).

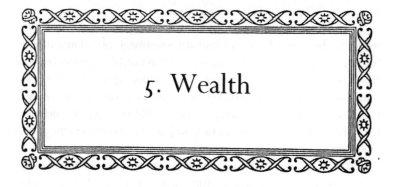

5. Wealth

(a) The degree of wealth

In the late eighteenth century the English aristocracy was distinguished by the extent of its wealth. The wealth of the peerage and baronetcy was spectacular by both the noble and non-noble standards of the time. Moreover, the gentry was far from indigent, even though its members were on average much less affluent than peers and baronets. Lacking in England was the multitude of poor nobles that characterised most European nobilities. Whilst excluding the poor by a process of social demotion, the English aristocracy usually managed to absorb the very rich. Until the closing years of the nineteenth century most millionaires were landowners of aristocratic status: between 1809 and 1858 this was true of 181 out of a total of 189; and from 1858–79, of 117 out of 146. The aristocracy's wealth was predominantly in capital assets, although a plentiful supply of ready cash was necessary to uphold their conspicuous life-style. (For reference and further reading, see bibliography, section V).

(b) Landed income

The aristocracy's basic source of wealth was landownership. The basic means of acquiring it was rent and the exploitation of the estate's natural products, especially timber and minerals. Its wealthiness in the eighteenth century depended upon not only estate size and the profits drawn from mining and urban development but also the nature of the landlord–tenant relationship. Having escaped from the peasant rut, English farming by the eighteenth century was capitalistic and highly productive. Moreover, unencumbered by seigneurial rights and able to exact economic rents and to impose short-term leases, the landlord was strongly placed to reap large, financial rewards. Sustained by agrarian and industrial capitalism, by 1800 the English aristocracy was undoubtedly wealthier than ever before. The source and nature of its wealth, however, was not intrinsically different: in the traditional manner, it shunned farming, and since poverty denobled the gentry, the English aristocracy had always been something of a plutocracy.

For centuries, the English aristocracy drew its landed income mainly from dues and rent. High agricultural prices and low labour costs had persuaded lords to farm their demesnes in the thirteenth century for the market as well as for home consumption, but the extent of its farming even in this period is easily exaggerated. Throughout this time, the aristocracy remained a rentier rather than a producing class: rents and the profits of justice provided the bulk of its landed resources, direct farming making only a supplementary contribution to its income. Furthermore, by the close of the fourteenth century, the problems of finding cheap labour and falling food prices, both the result of extreme depopulation, had persuaded the aristocracy to lease their demesnes almost totally to tenant farmers and peasants. Later periods of inflated food prices caused landlords to graze sheep and cattle and even to grow corn, notably in the late sixteenth and late eighteenth centuries, but not at the expense of their landlordship. Aristocrats in the sixteenth century only supplemented their income with direct farming. In the eighteenth century they certainly interested themselves in agriculture, using the home farm for agricultural experiment, organising agricultural shows and founding agricultural societies; but the main producers remained the tenantry. High and low, the aristocracy had continually aimed to profit from farming by extracting dues and rents from a tenantry. If aristocrats farmed their lands, it was because their estates were too small to support a tenantry. A vital change in approach only came in the late nineteenth and early twentieth centuries when persistently falling rents and land values and a system of taxation which punished unearned income and rewarded earned income with tax rebates persuaded many aristocrats to farm either to maintain a standard of living or even to remain landed. A spectacular example of conversion was that of Lord Wantage in the Berkshire Downs. By 1895 he was farming 15,000 acres of his 20,000-acre estate. His move into farming began in 1863 and quickened from 1879. Compelling him to behave ignobly was his unwillingness to have tenants paying an uneconomic rent. Rarely was the reaction this extreme among the peerage; but for many gentry direct operation became the only alternative to completely liquidating the estate.

An earlier change in estate management profoundly affected the aristocracy's relationship with the farming community. Pressed by high inflation in the sixteenth century, aristocrats were forced to adopt other ways of extracting revenue from their estates. Instead of switching from landlord to farmer, they concentrated on maximising the income from the tenantry either by abolishing or by exploiting seigneurial rights. Thus, some landlords preserved the customary tenures and sought to raise seigneurial dues, notably the entry fines. Others incorporated the tenures into the demesne. By doing so they turned them into leaseholds and replaced the fixed rent by a revisable one, a conversion which made the exaction of seigneurial dues unnecessary. In the long run the second solution proved preferable. By the eighteenth century the typical tenancy was the leasehold. Deprived of the protection of inheritable tenures and fixed rents, the farming community became much more vulnerable to the landlord. Accompanying the destruction of the customary tenures was the engrossment of holdings. In the course of the sixteenth and seventeenth centuries the number of farms fell dramatically as large farmers swallowed up the smaller ones. Thus, although the source of the aristocracy's landed wealth remained rent, its character was transformed. It became, predominantly, an exaction made of agrarian capitalism rather than of peasant farming, the total elevated by the abolition of the customarily fixed rent and by the higher productivity of capitalist farming.

The traditional mainstay of the aristocracy's landed wealth was farming and forestry. However, in the course of time other sources of landed income, notably urban development and mining, reduced, without completely severing, the dependence upon agriculture. Aristocrats were developing parts of London from at least the sixteenth century: to equip themselves with suitable residences but also to profit from the high rents which could be charged for accommodation and shops. However, the major opportunities came between the 1780s and the 1880s with the urban growth promoted by industrialisation. In the same period the leisure industry of spas and seaside resorts opened up further opportunities for aristocratic gain although neither was highly profitable and, in the absence of willing builders and developers, the latter required a large outlay of aristocratic capital and involvement. In contrast, the development of London from the seventeenth century onwards and of industrialising provincial towns called for little aristocratic investment and little participation. Aristocrats were sometimes responsible for the laying of sewers and roads but rarely for the construction of houses.

For the aristocracy the connecting factor with urbanisation was its rights of landownership. Some sold the freehold; others turned rights into profit through a variety of leasing arrangements. The former was the practice in Nottingham, Leeds and Leicester. For ready cash landlords sold their rights to developers and builders. But at least half the land made available for urban building in this period was leased either in perpetuity and for a fixed annual rent, as in Manchester and Bristol, or on a variety of terms: 999 year leases in Manchester and Sheffield; three lives in Liverpool, the lease closely resembling the traditional copyhold with a beneficial rent and an entry fine payable when the tenure was renegotiated; or for forty to 120 years, a practice associated with London, Birmingham, Bath and Sheffield. The buildings as well as the land reverted to the ground landlord upon the expiry of the lease.

The aristocracy's incentives to promote urban development were irresistible, in spite of its unseemly social repercussions. As an investment, farming in its prime bore no comparison with the fruits of urban development. When a private bill for releasing the Colmore estate from the terms of a strict settlement was under discussion in 1746, a witness in evidence to a house of lords committee reckoned that if the land was converted from farming to building use the value per acre would increase from 30/– to £15. This quickly proved to be correct as the bill was passed and the estate became home for part of the Birmingham population. By leasing their estates to builders and developers aristocrats made large fortunes with the minimum of capital outlay and personal bother.

Industrialisation also enlarged the landed wealth of aristocrats by promoting a demand for minerals, the ownership of which resided with the landlord. Slate, clay and lime were needed for building houses and factories; coal and iron were essential to industrial production. While aristocrats frequently mined the coal and iron on their estates in the early seventeenth century, they rarely did so by the early nineteenth century. Aristocrats, in fact, were inclined to lease out their rights and to receive an income from a fixed annual rent plus a royalty on the value of the minerals extracted. The aristocrat's relationship with mining tended to reflect the one with farming and urban development. The fact that by the eighteenth century the aristocracy had been granted full ownership of the minerals beneath its land probably had no special effect upon their exploitation but was of great material benefit to the aristocracy, allowing it to profit from mining without needing to be directly involved, and in freeing it, before the twentieth century, from the obligation of paying a proportion of its mining revenues to the state.[1]

The value of these non-agricultural forms of landed income rose sharply with the failure of farming in the late nineteenth century. Yet, inevitably, they benefited only the handful of aristocrats whose estates were blessed with mineral resources or were fortunately located close to growing townships. For the majority of landowners neither mining nor urbanisation compensated for a failing agriculture. The only remedy open to them was to move their wealth into non-landed investments.

Land was valuable to the aristocracy not only as income but also as a means of credit. Over the centuries land was a major security for loans, originally hazardous because of the lack of legal protection against foreclosure, but by 1700 a safe alternative to the sale of assets for raising capital. In the early sixteenth and seventeenth centuries the credit was mostly provided by wealthy London tradesmen and merchants. By the late nineteenth century the aristocracy had gained access to the wealth generated by industrialisation as the savings of shopkeepers and manufacturers throughout the realm were invested in mortgages.

Over the centuries, landed wealth weathered a succession of crises: notably the fall in landed incomes resulting from the depopulating plagues of the late fourteenth and fifteenth centuries; the devaluation of landed incomes in the sixteenth century by high inflation and the fixed rent of the customary tenure; the depression of rents by low farm prices in the late seventeenth and early eighteenth centuries; and the severe fall in rents and land values from the 1880s when the influx of cheap foreign corn, meat and wool caused the failure of tenant farming.

With the exception of the last crisis, the aristocracy's reaction was broadly the same. It abandoned neither its landownership nor its landlordism. In the fourteenth century its remedy was to remit rights of serfdom, to lease the demesne and to enlarge seigneurial exactions. By these means, it managed to uphold its income. Although the population fell by at least thirty per cent in the late fourteenth century, landed incomes in the 1370s seemed only about ten per cent lower than in the 1340s. Careful estate management prevented the scarcity of tenants from causing a dramatic reduction in revenue. What suffered was the old relationship between landlord and tenant. The decline in demesne farming, the high death rate, the problem of replacing the dead tenants of villein tenures, as well as the profit to be made from the manumission of serfs, caused the rapid disposal of serfdom. When the peasant rebels of Kent and Essex met the king at Mile End in 1381 and demanded of him the abolition of serfdom, it was in decay. Although serfdom persisted in parts, by the sixteenth century the aristocracy had become master to a class of free tenants from whom it still extracted a mixture of rents and seigneurial dues but not the weight and range of exaction that was normally required of serfs. This process of emancipation so weakened the landlord's power over the tenant that another change was required to restore his ascendancy and to improve his means of tenant exploitation, especially with the unprecedented price rise of the sixteenth century when prices rose at least fourfold. Sacrificing neither its landownership nor even its landlordism, the aristocracy responded to this challenge eventually by converting the tenantry into a class of commercial farmers subjected to short leases and rack-rents. This restored the landlord's control. In the restructured rural society the tenant farmers were much more deferential than the former peasantry to their landlords, partly because they were no longer protected against landlord exploitation by fixed rents and hereditary tenures but also because of the fearful presence of a rural proletariat of farm labourers, now an overwhelming majority in the countryside, and produced, like the tenant farmer, by the engrossment of farms.

Thereafter the landed wealth of the English aristocracy was heavily dependent upon the profitability of tenant farming. The aristocracy survived the difficult years of the early eighteenth century, its landlordism intact. The survival of an agrarian crisis was easier now because in many parts rents had lost their customary restraints and agriculture had escaped the limitations of peasant farming. In contrast the failure of tenant farming in the late nineteenth and early twentieth centuries compelled a large-scale departure from landlordism into farming and also a massive transference of aristocratic capital from land to banking and industry. A family deeply committed to agriculture were the Cokes of Holkham. Until the mid-nineteenth century, nearly all their income came from agricultural rents. Then they began investing their estate income in railways: twelve per cent of it in the 1870s to forty-three per cent in the 1880s. Agriculture remained the main source of income but by 1890 one quarter of it came from dividends in railways, brewing and banking. This was the conservative expression of a clear trend. The wealthy aristocrats diversified their income, sometimes selling parts of the estate in order to raise capital for investment on the stock exchange. Many of the gentry sold their estates. Two-thirds of the Norfolk gentry sold up as the value of land was halved and rents fell by forty-five per cent between 1873 and 1894. Responding to the situation Burke's *Landed Gentry* admitted the landless to its 1914 edition.

(c) Non-landed income

Until the twentieth century the English aristocracy's non-landed revenue rarely did more than to supplement its landed income. In the fourteenth century the extended wars against France and Scotland allowed lords to make money fron contracting with the Crown for the provision of troops, from looting and from ransoming captured nobles. But this income was no more than a windfall, its profit often cancelled by the expenses of going to war. In the early seventeenth century large numbers of aristocrats became heavily involved as investors in joint-stock trading companies. But few raised capital for the purpose by selling their estates. Most invested the surplus capital accruing to offices or estates. And few became managerially involved: management and direction were left to the merchants. Moreover, apart from those investing in the East India Company, few made money from such investments and the financial backing provided seemed motivated by patriotic or missionary considerations rather than commercial interest. From the late seventeenth century the financial returns from landownership came to be rivalled by those of long-term mortgages, government stock and investment in commerce and banking. While this may have diverted the capital of commoners which previously had been drawn to land, it had little effect upon the aristocracy's capital investments even though at the time agricultural rents were held down by a general depression in food prices and landed incomes suffered the burden of land tax. Income from civil and military office had long been an important source of aristocratic income but only for a minority of aristocrats, since the majority of royal offices were without salary or fee and a majority of aristocrats failed to hold royal office. The massive increase in government revenue, following the introduction of a regular direct tax in 1692 and resulting from a growth of trade whose wealth could be efficiently tapped by the national debt and by indirect taxation, provided leading officials with greater profits from office than ever before. Nonetheless, the income from office remained for the most part no more than a useful supplement to an income drawn mainly from landownership. Take the case of Thomas Pelham-Holles, the duke of Newcastle, with land in eleven counties, five homes to maintain and a continual career in politics from the 1720s to the early 1760s. In 1740 his official income was about £5,000, a huge sum but easily dwarfed by his gross landed income of £27,000. Moreover, the official income was probably nullified by the expenses incurred in the tenure of office. Other families of the time with large incomes from office, for example, the Cavendishes, the Watson-Wentworths and the Carterets, were likewise mostly dependent upon their landed wealth.

For profit making industrialisation added massive opportunities to those already created by the expansion of trade. But before the twentieth century the English aristocracy remained disinclined to invest heavily in industry and commerce. Aristocrats mined, constructed docks and ports and sank capital in the improvement of the transport system. But these new openings for investment failed to unseat land as the aristocracy's main capital asset and basic source of income. In 1833 the Sutherland family's holding of government stock realised an income larger than the net revenue of its family estates. Another major source of income was its investments in canals and railways. But this example was only typical in that much of its non-landed income was used to buy land, especially large tracts of barren moorland in the Scottish Highlands. With exceptions, throughout the nineteenth century the English aristocracy remained aloof from the industrial process unless its profits could be tapped by landlordship or stocks and shares. Between 1850 and 1900 agriculture's share of the gross national product slumped from twenty per cent to six per cent. But even in these circumstances the aristocracy was slow to adapt. Even with the development of a stock market for manufactured goods, the aristocracy retained a strong penchant for investing in government bonds, breweries, railways and banking. Its actual involvement in manufacturing was even more laggard: in 1956 only twenty-six per cent of all peers held directorships, in spite of the entrée smoothed by their wealth and status. The titled directors, moreover, were mostly twentieth-century creations.

Professional salaries were probably negligible as traditional sources of aristocratic income, but existed in connection with posts in the service of great nobles, high offices of state and military service. Legal training was common among the gentry from the sixteenth century but, except for landless, younger sons, its purpose was to produce future JPs rather than professional lawyers. A radical change only came with the collapse of farming in the late nineteenth century when the law, the army, the civil service, politics and professional writing in the case of Rider Haggard, became a basic source of income for gentry who had failed to make ends meet as landlords or farmers.

(d) **Expenditure**

The early development of commercial farming and of industrialisation in England, the size of their estates and the ease with which English landlords could exploit capitalist farmers, mine operators and property developers made aristocrats exceptionally rich. Yet their abiding landlordism and their unwillingness to participate in agricultural, trading or manufacturing activities was utterly conventional. Equally typical was their mode of expenditure. Improving the estate and the family residences remained over the centuries the main form of capital expenditure. Investment in any form of production, apart from forestry and mining, was minimal. Current expenditure was lavishly devoted to conspicuous display and consumption. Little of it went in charity or in acts of paternalism. Since the bulk of the English aristocracy needed to subscribe to an aristocratic life-style in order to compensate for its paucity of privilege, and, what is more, possessed the necessary wealth, it was probably more prone than many continental nobilities to waste its resources in the expected manner. Much of its life-style depended upon the possession of wealth. However, prior to the twentieth century it was the life-style which determined the nature of its wealth, not the need for wealth which determined its life-style.

Notes to Chapter 5

1. For the less advantageous systems of extraction in operation on the Continent, see Bush, *Noble Privilege*, ch. VII (2).

6. Ethos

(a) Changes in mentality

The mentality of the English aristocracy underwent at least four major changes. (For reference and further reading, see bibliography, section VI.) The first occurred between 600 and 750 AD and featured the conversion of the Anglo-Saxon nobilities to christianity. The second was encouraged by changes in the nature of warfare and the opposition of christian humanism and early protestantism to the eroticism and savagery of knight errantry. During the fifteenth and sixteenth centuries, the civilian ideals of humanism replaced the military ideals of chivalry in the aristocracy's recognised code of conduct. The gentleman as governor rather than the gentleman as knight became the aristocratic goal. The Ciceronian emphasis on civic responsibility was combined with Plato's appreciation of the learned governor to propose a new way to virtue. Knight errantry gave way to public service preceded by a preparatory academic education. As a result, the aristocracy ceased to be content with the training in courtly manners and the rules of chivalry which has been traditionally imparted by aristocratic households. Instead they placed their sons in grammar schools, universities and inns of courts to receive instruction in the law or in the humanities.

The aristocracy, then, became civilian rather than military. Chivalric ideals, even a preference for military occupations, persisted, but aristocrats now preferred to present themselves as educated gentlemen rather than as warriors. Elegance and learning became substitute virtues for ruggedness and military skill. The aristocrat's house became a residence of pleasing aspect rather than a stronghold. This change in life-style underwent no reversal. By the early eighteenth century the homes of aristocrats harboured libraries, classical artifacts and the curiosities of natural science. Moreover, the gothic revival of the nineteenth century, with its castles, tournaments and great halls bristling with trophies and arms, and the contemporaneous cult of fox hunting marked no genuine return to a chivalric past: aesthetic appearance, not security, style, not military effectiveness, were the prime considerations.

A third significant change involved the aristocracy's acceptance of capitalism. By 1700 its estate management had permitted the emergence of a tenantry consisting of capitalist farmers rather than subsistence peasants; and by 1850 it had also accommodated industrial capitalism, having allowed its estates to be ravaged, if necessary, by pitheads, slag heaps, quarries and smoky townships.

The final major change in mentality subjected the aristocracy to a process of bourgeoisification: in morality in the early nineteenth century and in occupation in the early twentieth century. Moved by the French revolution and the evangelicalism of the Clapham sect, the English aristocracy became less unself-conscious in its pursuit of leisure and more prone to advocate that its members practised the virtues of sobriety, frugality, piety and hard work which it had traditionally associated with the worthy commoner rather than the true aristocrat. Furthermore, in a bid to survive, aristocrats in the early twentieth century became professional politicians, civil servants and soldiers, their land no longer a tenanted estate but a back garden or, at most, a park, their houses no longer seats of authority but mere retreats from work.

Yet all these changes upheld, as well as destroyed, traditional aristocratic values. The adoption of christianity, for example, did not transform the aristocracy's warrior culture. It simply gave nobles a further cause to fight for. The renaissance insistence upon academic education as the prime requisite for a ruler had revolutionary implications since it proposed that education might confer as much as, or even more than, birth. But it lacked revolutionary effect. Doctored by the aristocratic apologists of the time, this humanist ideal was made to present the learned aristocrat as intrinsically a better ruler than the learned commoner. In fact, the ideal was merely grafted onto the well-founded belief in an aristocratic ruling class. Education became a means of social distinction rather than of mental improvement. The aristocracy's code of conduct was altered, but its essential values and ideals were left untouched. Likewise, its acceptence of agrarian and industrial capitalism did not affect its rentier nature. The bourgeois ethic contradicted the aristocracy's basic beliefs in the virtue of amateurism and the sufficiency of birthright by valuing a service which was performed in the expectation of adequate remuneration and which implied an expertise dependent upon an extensive training. However, by the nineteenth century the values of the bourgeoisie, especially those of professional men, with whom aristocrats had a much closer affinity than with businessmen, were strongly imbued with aristocratic ideals. Professional men showed a similar aversion to trade and expressed identical aspirations of social leadership and public responsibility. They shared the belief that social evaluation should be determined by family background as well as by deeds, expressed the same social superciliousness, and equally revered continuity and tradition. And, like the aristocracy, they felt that they deserved to be distinguished from the people by means of a special code of conduct. Since the bourgeois ways which aristocrats adopted possessed a strong aristocratic bent, English aristocrats could undergo *embourgeoisement* and yet remain true to many of their traditional values.

(b) Anti-bourgeois attitudes

Over the centuries an aristocratic ethos persisted to which Saxon thegn, medieval knight, Tudor courtier, Georgian squire and Victorian gentleman subscribed. Basically responsible for its durability was the abiding political and economic importance of land but also the aristocrat's continual need to distinguish himself from other social groups, particularly the wealthy commoner. On the other hand, the latter's inclination to adopt aristocratic ways made it difficult for the aristocracy to maintain this distinction.

Over the centuries, the aristocracy's most highly prized occupation was that of landowner and its basic aspiration was to enlarge the family estate. Aristocrats did not regard landownership simply as a means of income. To emphasise the point, the equivalent of several farms was usually maintained as non-productive parkland and, prior to the nineteenth century, low rents were charged to preserve a following. Nor was landownership regarded as an opportunity to farm. Ideally, the aristocratic landowner was a landlord, the resources of his estate worked by a tenantry and attained by him in the form of dues and rent. In view of the profits to be made from commercial farming in, for example, the late sixteenth and late eighteenth centuries, the ability of aristocrats to leave production to their tenantry, unless poverty or the smallness of their estates forced them to do otherwise, is staggering evidence of the obduracy of this ideal. So too is the aristocracy's willingness to leave to the businessman the profit to be made from industrialised manufacturing. The lavishness of their life-style certainly gave aristocrats an urgent need to make money, but they stubbornly sought to make ends meet without having to participate in commercial activities.

However, the English aristocracy was only averse to its own direct involvement in farming, commerce and manufacturing. Over several centuries, it was remarkably appreciative of capitalist developments. From at least the fifteenth century, it encouraged the growth of commercial farming, allowing the engrossment of farms and consenting to, and sometimes financing, enclosures (see ch. 10). Moreover, in the eighteenth and nineteenth centuries, it promoted industrialisation, releasing mineral resources, selling or leasing land for urban development, and helping to fund the improvement of roads and the construction of canals, railways, ports and dockyards. Even if the English aristocracy dissociated itself from production, its members could be persuaded by the prospect of profit to encourage large-scale, capitalist enterprises. Not as entrepreneurs but simply by leasing out their proprietorial rights, the English aristocracy realised huge profits from commercial farming, urban development and mining (see ch. 11). It therefore bent with the forces of social and economic change while maintaining its traditional contempt for trade. Rewarded with easy and sizeable profits, other European nobilities proved equally adaptable, appreciating and promoting commercial developments whilst upholding the customs and sometimes laws of derogation which reserved them for commoners. In eastern Europe several nobilities went a step further, heavily involving themselves in commercial farming and the marketing of farm produce.

Whilst the English aristocracy was incapable of acting ignobly as an order, individual aristocrats became entrepreneurs. Moreover, the contempt for trade did not prevent aristocrats from purchasing apprenticeships for their younger sons. Trade was only regarded as beneath the dignity of the eldest son or the landed sons. For those sons whose lack of privilege and lands tipped them into the commonalty, trade was regarded as a perfectly respectable occupation.

Separated from the business world of farmers and industrialists by its unwillingness to produce, the English aristocracy also distinguished itself in the long term from the professional bourgeoisie. This it did by firmly believing that its occupation should be determined by birthright. Furthermore, reacting against the professional ethic, the English aristocracy practised a cult of amateurism which rested upon a belief in unpaid and untrained aptitude. As an aristocratic ideal, this belief became even more pronounced in the course of the nineteenth century in reaction to the rise of the professions and the imposition of their values upon the bourgeoisie. Another aristocratic reaction against the professional ethic was the fundamental belief in a general service function. Whereas professional men had specific functions, aristocrats conceived themselves as having, in contrast, a more general role to play, not as experts but as leaders and representatives. On the Continent, nobilities could show a greater flexibility. Especially in association with royal absolutism, they became professionalised through state service. In England the aristocracy's professionalisation was latterday, coming only with its termination as a political elite. However, its contempt for the professions extended only to aristocratic participation. And like trade, the professions were regarded as a fitting occupation for gentlemen demoted by the rule of primogeniture.

Because thrift and moderation were traditionally associated with the bourgeoisie, the aristocracy was inclined to practice waste and ostentation. Moreover, whereas the bourgeoisie was never more than a social elite, the aristocracy presented itself as a ruling class. In contradistinction to bourgeois wealth which was expected to have a productive use, aristocratic wealth was ideally devoted to consumption, property accumulation, hospitality and charity. To distinguish itself from the socially mobile bourgeoisie, the aristocracy stressed that rootedness and ancient lineage were superior as measures of success to the acquisition of wealth or social promotion. In contrast to the bourgeois emphasis upon work, the aristocracy shamelessly presented itself as a leisured class. In contrast to bourgeois frugality, the aristocracy valued generosity. In contrast to the material values of the bourgeoisie, the aristocracy, at times, believed fervently in honour, even in the willingness to die for this nebulous virtue. The selflessness of the aristocracy, an ideal which implied acts of hospitality, paternalism and charity as well as a deeply ingrained sense of public responsibility and concern for the common good, was juxtaposed against the wealthy commoner's avaricious individualism. Moreover, in contrast to the bourgeoisie, the aristocracy regarded itself as essentially rural, believing that rural life was less debasing than the town. This sentiment was intensified by the urban growth which came of industrialisation and by Romanticism's appreciation of a communion with nature.

Yet the English aristocracy frequently fell short of these ideals. Its paternalism was a selfish lust for power. Its charity consumed a minute proportion of its income and time, commendable only when measured against the resources of the recipient. When measured against the resources of the donor, aristocratic charity was meanness itself. Furthermore, its hospitality tended to be lavished upon other aristocrats. It had strong urban connections. Alongside the need for a country seat was the desire for a town house. Not only London but also the provincial capitals, county towns, the spa towns and the foxhunting towns of Melton Mowbray and Rugby contained aristocratic residencies. In fact, the English aristocracy only avoided full-time residence in towns and only shunned certain types of township, notably ports and manufacturing centres. Absent in England was a purely urban or a purely rural aristocracy: the possession of property, and the habit of short-term residence, in both town and country made it amphibious.

Continually upstaging the aristocracy was the imitativeness of the bourgeoisie. Over the centuries, aristocratic apologists condemned the bourgeoisie for acquiring the trapping of aristocracy, but with little effect (see ch. 8 (d)). The influence of aristocratic values upon the commonalty was evident in the latter's investment of wealth in land and also in a prevailing contempt for trade among both the business and professional bourgeoisie, a contempt which was more extreme and rigorous than that of the aristocracy, extending not only to commercial involvement but also to commercial activity itself.

Satisfying the bourgeois need for aristocratisation were the public schools and the debased grammar schools of the nineteenth century. The older foundations, such as Eton and Winchester, mainly preferred to admit the sons of aristocrats but opened their doors, towards the end of the century, to very wealthy commoners; the new foundations admitted commoners from the start. Such schools subscribed to, and sought to implant, a code of values which was predominantly aristocratic.

The aristocratisation of the bourgeoisie combined with the eventual *embourgeoisement* of the aristocracy to redraw the dividing lines of society. In place of the divide which traditionally separated the bourgeoisie and aristocracy, it established one that distinguished the gentility, a compound of aristocracy and bourgeoisie, from the working people.

PART TWO

DEVELOPMENT

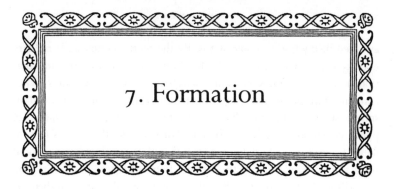

7. Formation

(For reference and further reading, see bibliography, section VII.)

(a) Pre-Conquest developments

The roots of aristocracy in England reached beyond the Norman invasion, the Danish invasions, the Saxon invasions, possibly even the Roman invasion. Since the nobility was originally those members of the ruling family without the title of kingship, the concept of nobility as an hereditary and juridical order was as old as monarchy itself. None of these invasions extinguished nobility. By introducing new types of noble and further privileges, they rather upheld and developed it. To the royal nobility, Roman rule added a senatorial and patrician aristocracy. Its privileges were no more than honorific, but they clearly defined its hereditary noble status. Although initially accessible to commoners through an imperial grant of senatorial or patrician status, it became, like the royal nobility, a nobility of the blood with the termination of Roman rule, and gradually faded away as families failed to produce male heirs and either became extinct or were merged by marriage with other dynasties.

The Saxon settlement of England imparted a whole range of noble privileges, most of them corporate. These privileges centred upon the wergeld, a system of compensation for murder in which the victim's family was entitled to receive a sum of money from the convicted party. Certainly by the end of the seventh century, the law of wergeld firmly distinguished between the amounts a noble and a commoner family could claim. In Frankish law and the laws of Scandinavia and Iceland the wergeld only made distinctions between office-holders and other freemen. In Anglo-Saxon England it not only gave special recognition to officials but also awarded distinction to noble status. By the tenth century an hereditary nobility was declared by several other forms of differentiated compensation, notably for house-breaking (burgbryce) and for acts of violence committed in the company, or in the house, of a man which offended his sphere of protection (mundbryce), and by the fines (wites) imposed in public courts for breaches of the law. For example, the noble's fine for failing to serve in the fyrd differed from that of the ceorl (freeman without noble status). In addition, as the oath of a noble had greater authority than a ceorl's in the local public tribunals, its intrinsic value distinguished the one from the other.

These legal distinctions could be lost as well as gained. Nobles forfeited them along with their noble status if found guilty of cowardice and perjury, while ceorls attained them through the ownership of a minimum of five hides of land (a hide was at most 120 acres) for at least three generations, or in reward for royal service, or even by trading overseas on three and more occasions. This nobility, then, was not simply of the blood. However, its emphasis was upon birthright. The offspring of nobles, the families of ex-kings and the collateral heirs of reigning monarchs were probably the major sources of recruitment to its ranks.

The basis of social stratification in Anglo-Saxon England was nobility and free status. Both nobles and freemen were distinguished from the rest of society and from each other by the hereditary privileges conferred upon them by the legal system. Besides the privileges of noble status, there were privileges of noble rank. Wergeld differentiated not only noble from ceorl but also landless from landed nobles and nobles within from nobles without the royal service. Heriots, that is, the arms owed a lord by his follower, were similarly graduated. Gradations of wergeld and heriot created a hierarchy within the nobility, but one which, in resting upon office-holding and landownership, was quite different from the rank which was later determined by peerage titles.

The corporate privileges of nobility allowed aristocratic status to exist apart from landownership in Anglo-Saxon England. Yet landholding and landownership were a central part of the Anglo-Saxon noble's character. They were his major source of power, income and rank. Aristocratic estates came in two forms: bookland and folkland. As the rights of bookland were determined by royal charter, they differed according to the terms of each charter, but generally bookland granted perpetual ownership and also a wide range of immunity that included exemption from military obligations, the payment of public taxes and the forms of public justice. Since the corollary of immunity was the private right to exercise the powers equivalent to those which the immunity covered, bookland granted considerable rights of lordship, especially the levy of taxes and the dispensation of justice. Moreover, ownership of at least five hides of bookland for three generations secured enoblement and when bookland was held by a nobleman it authorised a higher wergeld than nobles enjoyed without bookland. In contrast, folkland was a terminal and conditional form of landholding, not an expression of ownership. It granted no immunity and nobles with folkland fulfilled military and civil obligations of service.

Powers of lordship were a prominent feature of the Anglo-Saxon nobilities. Not all of them derived from landownership. Seigneurial authority originated not only in the rulership rights associated with bookland but also in the rights of masters over slaves. Also separated from landownership was the lordship implicit in the conditional tenure of arms. The Anglo-Saxon nobles were identified by specific arms as well as by privileges and estates: by the tenth century the weapons of the nobles were distinct from those of the ceorls. They consisted of the sword, helmet and byrnie. Lords awarded these weapons to their aristocratic retainers on the condition of service. Upon a retainer's death his family was obligated to return them to the lord in the form of a heriot which could be a money payment. In this respect, the heriot expressed a form of lordship which involved neither land nor slavery.

Thus, prior to the Conquest, an aristocracy emerged in England which was a *de jure* order rather than a *de facto* class. Yet its social identity did not lie simply in its privileges. It was imparted by other shared characteristics, notably landownership, lordship, a political function combining the military and the civil, and the fact that it was not a caste. It had ceased to be an order of royal relatives or a fading senatorial/patrician elite to which admission was only possible by birth.

The surviving evidence is thinly scattered over several centuries. Quite clearly, the nobility evident in the laws of the late seventh century or in *Beowulf* was not identical with what the Normans encountered in 1066. Furthermore, because of the co-existence of several Anglo-Saxon monarchies before the tenth century, several nobilities are found, each distinguished from the other by differences in the legal system to which they were subject. Nonetheless, certain essential features were held in common and constantly present over several centuries, so much so that the changes of nomenclature, notably from gesith to thegn, appear to have only superficial effect.

(b) The Conquest

The Norman conquest and its aftermath preserved and modified this nobility. One outstanding peculiarity was maintained. On the Continent offices of state such as duke, count, viscount and marquis became titles of higher nobility and sources of private lordship as a result of their impropriation by subjects. In contrast, under the Anglo-Saxons the equivalent royal offices of eolderman and reeve remained in the king's gift. Moreover, when the Norman kings introduced the hereditary title of earl, they did not confer upon it the authority formerly possessed by the Anglo-Saxon eolderman or the Danish earl. As it developed in post-Conquest England the earldom was not a territorial unit of power. *Per se* it had no official function. Until the emergence of the house of lords it was merely an honour. The other peerage titles, founded in the course of the fourteenth and fifteenth centuries, followed suit. Lacking in local authority, they were quite different from the higher titles of the French nobility which, created by a process of feudalisation, were territorial not personal and possessed a bannal authority deriving from their origins as royal offices.

Some of the changes introduced by the Conquest failed to affect the aristocracy's long-term development. Within a century and a half, hereditary rights of landownership had subverted the conditional tenure which the Norman rulers applied to all land in England. Furthermore, the formal stratification imposed by the Conquest upon the aristocracy was shortlived. By the fourteenth century the basic distinction between tenant-in-chief (baron) and sub-tenant (vavasour) had given way to the non-feudal distinction between peer and gentry. Of greater import was the Conquest's elimination of the thegn, except in the far north, its introduction of the dubbed knight and the peerage title of earl, its confinement of most noble privileges to the king's tenants-in-chief, and the great estates which it founded.

Before the Conquest noble status was given meaning by the existence of a range of corporate privileges. Soon afterwards, most of these privileges had withered away. In their stead are found the privileges of knighthood and of the tenurial baronage. The distinctive feature of the English aristocracy – its vestigial corporate rights and the reservation of most of its noble privileges for special types of aristocrat – was not evident prior to the Conquest but was fully formed by 1100. With the peerage eventually annexing the privileges of the tenants-in-chief, the English aristocracy acquired its familiar form.

Having retained a quarter of the land for the Crown, William distributed the remainder to 1,400 lay and ecclesiastical tenants-in-chief, something like one half of the total land passing to laymen. Distribution was far from equal in that ten tenants-in-chief were in receipt of one quarter of the land. Except on the borders of Scotland and Wales, these estates, although individually massive, were not in contiguous blocs. However, while fragmented, each great estate founded at the Conquest tended to be concentrated in a particular region. Furthermore, within a century some of the land passed to lesser lords as, following the practice of the Crown, the tenants-in-chief granted land to tenants in return for military service. Yet this process of subinfeudation did not destroy the great estates even though it was quickly followed by the acquisition of proprietorial rights which transformed tenancy into virtual ownership: most tenants-in-chief subinfeudated less than one third of their total estate. By imposing a top layer of foreign lords, the Norman settlement certainly produced dramatic changes in the membership of the aristocracy. Nonetheless, lower down the aristocratic scale the changes were probably not so spectacular since thegns survived as landlords by submitting to the Norman system of conditional tenure. In doing so, they temporarily lost rights of landownership and permanently lost the title of thegn but preserved their aristocratic status, their estates and their seigneurial rights.

(c) Early peculiarities

The obvious differences between the early development of the English aristocracy and of the other nobilities in western Europe pose several questions (1) Why should a recognisable nobility crystallise at such an early date in England? (2) Why should offices of state in England fail to become hereditary? (3) Why should the corporate privileges of nobility flourish prior to the Conquest but not after it?

Its early emergence reflects upon the sophisticated organisation of the Anglo-Saxon monarchies, evident especially in their degree of centralisation, the vigour of their public institutions and the failure of tribalism to become a political bond. In these circumstances elites could emerge, formed of royal officials and the king's kin, and laws could be made which recognised and formalised a social structure that was not a loose conglomeration of families cohering only because of their allegiance to the same figurehead king but a hierarchical and uniform organisation firmly subjected to the Crown. The effectiveness of the political system and the power of royal government also helps to explain why the offices of state should remain Crown property. Because weak monarchies tended to be gobbled up by neighbouring monarchies in Anglo-Saxon England, their political deficiency did not cause them to fragment into a multitude of principalities; it simply subjected them to the rule of a more effective monarchy. In fact, the centralisation and governmental strength achieved after the Conquest was only the culmination of a long process of political consolidation – promoted by the unifying effect of barbarian attack as well as by the annexation of one monarchy by another – which had ensured that nobles should function as the service elites of kings instead of becoming princes ruling in their own right.

The political strength of central government, particularly after the Norman conquest, helps to explain why the English aristocracy should have such a limited range of corporate rights. Having also been subjected to a form of feudalism by a Norman conquest, the Sicilian nobility had equally restricted corporate privileges. Notably lacking in England was the right of fiscal exemption. On the Continent this privilege was sometimes confined to the fiefholders but it was frequently imparted by noble status. Largely responsible for its development was the establishment of national systems of taxation since it was often granted both as a means of persuading nobles to allow their dependants to be subjected to royal taxation and in recognition of the special military function expected of knights.[1] In England the strength of the Norman and Angevin monarchy made concessions of this sort unnecessary. Fiscal exemption existed in England only for a short period of time and never as a corporate privilege. In fact, the only tax immunity to survive the Conquest was the tenant-inchiefs' exemption from paying the danegeld on their demesnes. Moreover, on the Continent judicial as well as fiscal exemptions were granted to persuade nobles to accept the extension of royal justice into their territories.[2] In England the ascendancy of public justice, maintained by the communal courts of shire and hundred as well as by the judicial powers directly exercised by the Crown both before and after the Conquest, restricted the concession of judicial indemnity, confining it to the peerage and the tenants-in-chief.

Working against the establishment of corporate privileges of nobility in England was the ability of commoner freemen to stop the aristocracy from monopolising the traditional rights of the freemen. Most noble privileges were the annexed rights of other social groups, notably rulers, commoner knights and commoner freemen. Whereas the basic source of rank privileges was rulership, the basic source of corporate rights was freeman status. The nobility normally acquired exclusive possession of the freeman rights when they were confined to the knights and the nobility and then to the nobility alone as it absorbed the knights into its order.[3] In England this process was thwarted by the failure of the knights to take over the freeman privileges and by the failure of the nobles to monopolise knighthood. The survival of freeman rights as a commoner privilege also owed much to the condition of the political system. The decay of public authority in tenth- and eleventh-century France and the Low Countries extensively subjected the commoner freemen to private jurisdiction, leaving the freeman's right of public tribunal the exclusive possession of the nobles. This did not occur in England. Furthermore, in England landownership did not become a noble, as opposed to a freeman, privilege since the Conquest confined landownership to the Crown, making all landed subjects its tenants. Finally, the commoner freeman's right to bear arms was not impaired by the emergence, as the main instrument of warfare, of a warrior aristocracy in Anglo-Saxon times and the mounted knight with the Conquest. In parts of France the commoner's right to carry arms disappeared as his obligation to serve the ruler was converted into a tax and the rights originally deriving from the military service requirements of the freemen passed to the knights: those freemen, that is, whose military function was left to stand.[4] In England the commoner freeman proved more tenacious, both of his rights and his obligations. Moreover, in England knighthood retained greater independence of the aristocracy. In the course of the twelfth and

thirteenth centuries, it tended on the Continent to be included within the
noble order. Commoner knights disappeared from the scene and
commoners were excluded from the attainment of knighthood. By the end
of the thirteenth century continental monarchs had secured the sole right
to confer knighthoods in exchange for the confinement of knighthood to
those already in possession of noble status.[5] In England knighthood did not
take over the privileges of the freemen; nor was knighthood taken over
completely by the aristocracy. It remained relatively underprivileged and
also a means of ennoblement. Following the Conquest, the strength of the
monarchy enabled the Crown to monopolise the right to dub knights
without having to make concessions to the nobility.

(d)   Feudalism and aristocracy

Crucial to the early development of the English aristocracy was the demise
of the feudal system. Its complete removal occurred as late as 1660.
However, within two centuries of the Conquest, it had ceased to dominate
the relationship between state and society. Instead it became merely a
fiscal device for tapping aristocratic wealth. By 1300 the feudal connection
had ceased to be an important source of following and service. A money
payment had been substituted for military service and royal armies were
raised by contract. Rather than requiring their barons to furnish troops in
accordance with their feudal obligation, monarchs now contracted with
leading subjects to provide a specified number of troops in return for a
reimbursement. Also by 1300, subinfeudation, the means by which
feudalism had penetrated deep down in society, was outlawed. By the
same date the extension of royal justice had deprived the baronial and
honorial courts of most of their criminal jurisdiction.

The withering of feudalism affected the English aristocracy in several
basic respects. It permitted subjects to enjoy extensive rights of
landownership, especially of inheritance and alienation. Such proprietorial
rights were not an explicit part of the landholding system established at the
Conquest. In this system the allod (see glossary) was unknown. The king
was the only landowner. All estates were tenancies except for those
directly held by the Crown. The establishment of landownership rights
rendered the aristocracy's public functions unconditional although still a
vital necessity since the decline of feudalism was not accompanied by the

installation of a bureaucracy capable of fully operating the system of government.

In spite of the king's final ownership of the land, a right based on conquest, and in spite of the conditional tenure, an essential feature of feudalism, by 1100 the Crown was prepared to allow its tenants-in-chief hereditary landownership. It did so by confining its rights of intervention to forfeiture of the estate in cases of treason, to the temporary annexation of the estate when it passed to a minor and to approving the heir when a baronial family failed in the direct line. In other feudal parts of western Europe, a similar form of landownership was acquired by aristocrats in the course of the eleventh and twelfth centuries. In permitting it in England, the Norman kings were probably admitting a practice already established in Normandy. In 1100, however, the hereditary landownership of the sub-tenants was not so secure, their mesne lords having retained the right to confiscate the estate upon the tenant's death. Nevertheless, a century later there was little to distinguish the landholding rights of baron and vavasour. In the course of the twelfth century these lesser lords acquired equivalent rights of inheritance to those of the king's barons, particularly after 1135 when protracted civil war gave them the opportunity to trade allegiance for the acknowledgement of hereditary landownership. Thus, by the end of the twelfth century a ruling order of greater and lesser landlords had established itself whose land tenure had become a right of descent rather than an obligation of service and was therefore a contradiction of feudalism's basic principle.

The decay of feudalism also removed the distinction between tenant-in-chief and sub-tenant as a major feature of the aristocracy's structure. In its place the aristocracy gained a stratification which was not connected with land tenure. The barony by patent and the other peerage titles replaced the barony by tenure as the mark of higher nobility. Tenancy, moreover, was restricted to the relationship between peasant and lord: it ceased to govern the relationship between lord and overlord in the manner established by the Conquest and the subinfeudation of the late eleventh and early twelfth centuries.

From the Conquest, the operation of English feudalism depended upon a profusion of professional knights willing to place themselves at the disposal of the barons, enabling them to fulfil their tenurial obligations. In this respect, the feudal system relied upon a class of professional men, serving as knights and estate officers, and failed when the changing nature of warfare in the eleventh and twelfth centuries and the growing cost of the knight's basic military equipment severely reduced the number of knights capable of effective service. In place of the professional soldier living on a wage, the knight became a man of substance with considerable landed resources to sustain his knightly function: the professional knight, in fact, became the aristocratic knight. In this process subinfeudation had a part to play in converting household knights into landed knights. But the contribution was transitory. The extension of feudalism was of less importance than its decay. The feudal system also declined because kings found it less complicated to enlist the service of knights by contract than by feudal obligation. From the start, the Norman kings had fought with stipendiary troops. By 1300 the Crown's reliance upon them was complete. Commuted to a sum of money the feudal obligation became a means of raising the revenue required to hire military service.

The aristocratisation of the knight was a political as well as an economic and military development. In the twelfth century royal government expanded at the expense of baronial government. By the late fourteenth century an administrative machinery had been founded, composed of commissions of the peace, gaol delivery and oyer and terminer and officers such as the escheator, the coroner and the assize judges. A notable feature of the machinery was its heavy reliance upon non-bureaucrats. Paid officials operated at Westminster and in the royal household, and the judges of assize functioned as professional men with an expertise refined by extensive training and in receipt of an income commensurate with their service. However, most of the work of local government fell upon officials who were no more than substantial landowners. In fact, they were the same men who came to fulfil the military functions of knighthood. The commutation of feudal obligation, the contraction of baronial justice, and the conjunction of a high degree of political centralisation with a low level of bureaucratisation produced a lesser aristocracy exercising a general rather than a specific political function.

As a military system, feudalism had conferred upon the aristocracy a martial bearing. Essentially, the aristocrat was a knight. With the decay of the system, the aristocracy lost its inevitable military affiliation. To some extent this was a consequence of the excess of royal offices over knights and the need to give special recognition to other groups of landlords required to serve in local government. Recognition came with the conversion of the coat of arms from an indicator of military occupation to an indicator of class and the equation of the right to a coat of arms with aristocratic status. The development of the aristocracy as an armigerous class in the fourteenth and fifteen centuries was accompanied by the inclusion within its ranks of esquires and plain gentlemen as well as knights. In this way a lesser nobility developed that was alien to feudalism in that it was defined by privileges rather than obligations and by civil rather than military functions.

The emergence of the gentry was a concomitant of a waning feudalism. So was the formation of the peerage which largely took over the basic privileges of the tenurial baronage. Between the mid-twelfth and early fourteenth centuries the only peerage title in existence, the earldom, was granted so infrequently that in 1327 there were no more than seven families with the title. Its privileges were no more than honorific. The rise of the peerage, a phenomenon of the fourteenth and fifteenth centuries, saw a rapid growth in its membership and its privileges. The increase in numbers came of the creation of new earldoms and the introduction of new titles: dukedoms in 1337, marquisates in 1385, baronies by patent in 1387 and viscountcies in 1440. By 1420 there were forty peerages, mainly the creations of Edward III and Richard II; by 1450 there were sixty peerages, mainly the work of Henry VI. From being a socially peripheral group on the verge of extinction, the peerage, in little more than a century, became a substantial, highly privileged and central component of aristocracy. Besides the inflation of honours, the rise of the peerage involved the acquisition of special privileges. These were predominantly connected with parliament. Since the house of lords had originated as the king's great council to which the tenants-in-chief were summoned in order to advise the king, those summoned to attend were initially the tenurial baronage and leading ministers of state. However, by the end of the fourteenth century it was normal for peers to receive writs of summons and rare for non-peers, even tenants-in-chief, to be summoned unless as ministers. In this way, the peers were able to usurp a basic privilege of the tenants-in-chief and to avoid sharing it with other aristocratic groups.

By 1400 the English aristocracy was distinguished from many nobilities which had similarly grown upon a feudal base in lacking privileges imparted by the ownership of a fief. Although the fief in England had originally conferred the fiscal privilege of exemption from the danegeld and the political privilege of advising the mesne lord, by this time the fief awarded no more than seigneurial rights. This distinction owed much to the rise of the peerage but also something to the decline and fall of feudalism.

(e) The territorial magnate

Unaffected by the demise of the feudal system was the territorial magnate, an aristocrat distinguished not by privilege, although he tended to be a peer, but by the extent of his landed possessions, wealth and private power. The great estate was a legacy of the Conquest. By the thirteenth century the material resources of certain magnates were so considerable that they were bound to prove a political problem for the Crown. Simon de Montfort in the late thirteenth century, Thomas Earl of Lancaster in the early fourteenth century, the progeny of Edward III, especially John of Gaunt in the late fourteenth century, and its descendants in the mid-fifteenth century, were immensely powerful: because of the extensiveness of their landed possessions and because of the support they could enlist from other aristocrats by forming alliances with them and by taking them into their service. The aristocrats who contracted to serve John of Gaunt in the early years of Richard II's reign included one earl, three barons, eighty-three knights and 112 esquires. In 1311 Thomas of Lancaster had a private retinue of fifty-five knights. Gaunt inherited the estates of the greatest magnate of the early fourteenth century, Thomas of Lancaster, who had inherited the forfeited estates of perhaps the greatest magnate of the thirteenth century, Simon de Montfort.

The situation was conducive to the magnate. By the close of the fourteenth century the greatest inheritances, notably those of Lancaster, Mortimer and Arundel, were probably larger than any since the Conquest. Responsible for their formation was the conjunction of inheritances brought about by female inheritance and marriage. The huge patrimony of Thomas of Lancaster, for example, which included the earldoms of Leicester, Derby, Lancaster, Lincoln and Salisbury, owed something to his marriage to the heiress of Henry de Lacy. In addition, the Crown had a central part to play. Most of the great magnate dynasties were the creations of the Crown, the result of rewards dispensed to royal kin

(Thomas of Lancaster was a nephew of Edward I, while John of Gaunt was the fourth son of Edward III) or royal favourites. Once established by the Crown's liberality, they were allowed to survive by the Crown's forgiveness, their titles and lands retained in spite of committing the crime of treason, or allowed to grow through the Crown's willingness to consent to marriages which amalgamated great inheritances.

In spite of frequently causing political disorder, magnates were not regarded as excrescences on the body politic. The government accepted them as an integral part of the political system. In the late thirteenth century governments were raising armies for campaigns abroad by contracts with pay rather than by feudal obligation. But this hardly affected the magnates' political function. Apart from serving as military leaders in the armies royal, they continued to supply the king with troops. All that changed was that the obligation of a private contract which had no connection with land tenure replaced the obligation of the fief. In the fourteenth and fifteenth centuries kings raised armies principally by contracting with their magnates to provide troops. In civil matters magnates served the Crown by holding high offices of state, through their membership of the upper chamber in parliament and by exercising extensive rights of private jurisdiction. The limitations placed upon honorial and baronial jurisdictions in the twelfth and thirteenth centuries did not apply to the liberties, areas of independent jurisdiction where the king's writ did not run and the pleas of the Crown, apart from treason, were exercised by the owner. The Crown remained capable of creating franchises until the accession of the Tudors. On the other hand, it was also capable of resuming them. By 1350 the greatest of the lay franchises, the palatinate of Chester, was no longer magnate property. It had been annexed by the Crown and reserved for the king's eldest son. Edward I examined the validity of the existing franchises, resuming several for reasons of illegitimacy. Edward IV did likewise. Yet Edward III created a franchise of enormous proportions in 1351, the palatinate of Lancaster, granting it to his favourite, Henry of Grosmont, Duke of Lancaster, who was the descendant of Thomas of Lancaster and the father-in-law of John of Gaunt. This franchise had a short life as the possession of a magnate, but only because it was inherited by Henry Bolingbroke who managed to usurp the Crown. Edward IV, moreover, not only resumed franchises but also created them. The franchise of Norfolk was granted to the Mowbray family, and a palatinate of the West March was planned for his brother, Richard of Gloucester, but foiled by Edward's death in 1483 and Richard's succession to the throne. No medieval king completely opposed the existence of the franchises. In fact, they regarded them as a necessary part of the polity. For this reason, the power of the medieval magnates lay in their capacity either to control or to exclude the machinery of royal government. The one was accomplished by holding royal offices and by enlisting the allegiance of royal officials; the other, by securing the right to prevent the royal writ from being served in their territories.

The power exercised by the Crown and the magnates was very much alike. In both cases, it depended upon binding the aristocracy to their cause. In spite of the decay of feudalism, magnates continued throughout the middle ages to be served by aristocrats who were under obligation to them as mesne tenants. Yet after subinfeudation was outlawed in 1290, feudalism ceased to be a legitimate means of recruiting fresh support. Instead, magnates enlisted support by taking gentry into full-time employment, or by paying them pensions, or, from the late thirteenth century, by subjecting them to an indenture of retainder, a legal agreement in which a retainer bound himself to serve a lord in peace and war for life, and in return the lord was bound to offer protection and occasionally an annuity. Dependent essentially upon enlisting gentry support, the magnate's power relied upon the attractiveness of his lordship. Having taken control of royal patronage, and equipped with the patronage which they dispensed in their own right, magnates at times in the late middle ages could compete effectively with the Crown for this support. The close relationship between gentry and magnates was successfully challenged only by the expansion of effective royal government into outlying regions under the Tudors and by the Crown's acquisition of resources of patronage which were so considerable that the magnates could not hope to compete with them. In response, the gentry inclined to the Crown. Swiftly adapting, the magnates found a new source of power as courtiers manipulating the royal patronage and as lord lieutenants presiding over local government.

(f) The significance of the fourteenth century

By 1300 the English aristocracy had already acquired many of its basic characteristics. With the disappearance of wergeld, the corporate privileges were left in a state of attenuation. With the decline of feudalism, the conditional tenure gave way to hereditary landownership and the aristocracy ceased to be operated by feudal obligations. With the success of the barons in opposing John and Henry III, the English aristocracy had already established itself as the formidable opponent of royal absolutism. Yet it was still only partially formed. In structure, political function, landownership, great differences existed between the landed ruling elite of the thirteenth and the seventeenth centuries.

By 1400 these differences had mostly disappeared. Structurally, the former distinction between baron and vavasour had given way to the familiar distinction between a peerage with extensive privileges and a minimally privileged gentry: the result of the Crown's willingness to dispense peerage titles to subjects not of the royal family, the peerage's capacity to annex the privileges of the tenurial baronage largely by converting the upper chamber of parliament into a house of peers and the emergence of the gentry, a social group identified by its right to a coat of arms, its landownership and the ruling function expected of it. Instrumental in this latter development was the decision of the royal heralds to recognise the escutcheons of other than knightly and peerage families and the government's abandonment of the attempt to reserve for dubbed knights the leading offices of local government and the county seats in parliament (see above, p. 32).

Politically, the familiar functions of aristocracy crystallised in the course of the fourteenth century, especially with the emergence of the JP and the formation of parliament as a bicameral assembly. To fill the gap created by the political centralisation that came of the extension of royal justice in the twelfth and thirteenth centuries and the government's failure to establish a professional bureaucracy capable of operating it, the commission of the peace emerged. In 1360 it became a permanent police and administrative institution; in 1362 quarter sessions came into being. In the next two centuries the scope of its work was extended to deal with most aspects of local government. In this way the basic civil function of the English aristocracy was founded and the nature of its political function defined: neither feudal in the sense of resting upon tenurial obligations nor professional in the sense of being paid and determined by expertise, nor controlled by the privilege of reserved office. In the course of the century the ideal that local offices should be held by dubbed knights was abandoned and other criteria for appointment were adopted such as land held in fee or land of a certain value.

Over the centuries aristocrats functioned as MPs as well as JPs, with a seat either in the upper or the lower chamber. In the course of the fourteenth century not only did the upper chamber become a house of lords, with a membership confined to the peerage, but the lower chamber established itself as an essential part of parliament. Of the first seventy parliaments which sat from 1258, almost sixty were not attended by elected representatives of the commons. Such parliaments were essentially meetings of the king's great council attended by judges, ministers and selected tenants-in-chief. A change came in the reign of Edward II. Between 1311 and 1327 knights of the shire and burgesses attended every parliament but for two. Then from 1327 the Commons were inevitably present at a parliamentary session. In the same century the function of the aristocracy was determined by the development not only of parliament's bicameral structure but also its basic legislative, jurisdictional and tax-granting powers. By 1327 the law could only be changed with parliamentary consent and taxes were negotiated not by local agreement but only in parliament. In 1377 parliament was recognised as a final court of appeal against judgements made in the courts of common law. Since the Commons quickly washed its hands of this function the Lords acquired it as its sole preserve.

In the formation of the English aristocracy, the political changes of the fourteenth century, both in local and central government, were of outstanding long-term significance. Before the nineteenth century later changes made no attempt to undo them. But also highly significant were the social changes of the fourteenth century. These included not only the emergence of a peerage and a gentry but also alterations in the relationship between landlord and tenant which stemmed from the Black Death of 1349.

From at least the Conquest the aristocrat was very much a seigneur. The extension of royal justice in the twelfth and thirteenth centuries had questioned his private judicial authority but it had also confirmed his lordship by making a clearer distinction between free and unfree tenants, especially through awarding the former greater access to the royal courts. Furthermore the commutation of labour services to rent in the early twelfth century had been followed by an enlargement of seigneurial dues and services and the tendency to define the tenantry as a serf class. For example, heriot and merchet only emerged in the late twelfth century. From the Conquest to the fourteenth century the enlargement of seigneurial right was the prevailing tendency. A turning point came in the fourteenth century. The intensification of seigneurial rights had stemmed from the demesne farming of the thirteenth century, especially the demand for labour services. Other factors were the inflationary pressures falling upon landlords who, in spite of their farming activities, remained heavily dependent upon rents and dues, and a rapid growth in population which favoured the landlord by creating an excess of tenants. By 1300 the tenantry was largely unfree and easily exploited because of its subjection to a wide range of dues, notably heriot, entry fines, merchet, lerywite, banalities, chevage and tallage (see glossary) as well as onerous, week-work labour services. In contrast, by 1400 landlords found themselves with a glut of vacant tenancies, the result of a process of extreme and persistent depopulation beginning with the Black Death of 1349 and continuing until the early sixteenth century.

In these disadvantageous circumstances, the landlord had three remedies. One was to extend his own farming activities. This was discouraged by the aristocratic belief that landownership should involve landlordship, the high cost of labour and the low profitability of farming. The second remedy, to exploit the tenantry by means of the seigneurial system, was practised with some success throughout the late middle ages. The problem was that it generated an extreme bitterness between tenant and landlord which declared itself in the peasant revolt of 1381 and a multitude of riots. Moreover, prior to the demographic recovery of the early sixteenth century, harsh landlordship created vacant holdings as well as hostile tenants as tenants were attracted to landlords offering favourable terms. The need to find an amenable tenancy promoted a third policy. In the late fourteenth century lords sought to counter the fall in landed incomes by selling manumission from serfdom and by converting customary tenures into leaseholds. Both measures worked against the seigneurial system: the former reduced the range and weight of its demands upon the tenant, the latter terminated his seigneurial obligations. In the fourteenth and fifteenth centuries, reducing seigneurial exactions was the lord's response to a tenantry made precious by its scarcity. In the sixteenth century the lord's actions against the seigneurial system were a response to high inflation and the proprietorial rights of the free tenantry which, by preventing him from raising the rent, devalued his land revenues. By the seventeenth century the aristocracy was tending to rule its tenantry not by seigneurial exaction but through the short-term, rack-rent lease. Encouraging the conversion from customary tenure to leasehold was not only peasant revolt but also the emergence of commercial farmers. In the late middle ages they helped to solve the problem of a tenant shortage by amalgamating farms, while in the sixteenth century they appeared a better proposition than a populous peasant tenantry because they were capable of paying rents equal to, or in excess of, the income extractable from a peasantry by seigneurial means. Although it was not fully evident before the seventeenth century, the landlord's inclination to escape from the seigneurial system and a peasant tenantry was established in the late fourteenth century.

Notes to Chapter 7

1. See Bush, *Noble Privilege*, ch. II (4).
2. *Ibid.*, ch. III (1).
3. *Ibid.*, ch. I (2 (b)).
4. *Ibid.*, ch. V (3).
5. *Ibid.*, ch. V (4).

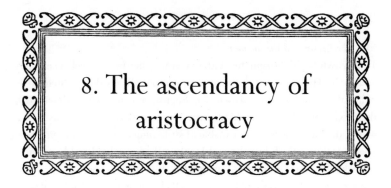

8. The ascendancy of aristocracy

(a) The appreciation of the Crown

(For reference and further reading, see bibliography, section VIII (a).)

Since royal absolutism in England was stopped by aristocratic revolt, the English aristocracy escaped the close association with monarchy which on the Continent caused Crown and nobility to be opposed in conjunction as complementary parts of the old regime. Instead of suffering, the aristocracy in England gained from the reduction of the Crown's authority. Nevertheless, it would be wrong to regard the two as mutually opposed and independent. Until the early eighteenth century when government policy and patronage was, in practice, taken out of its hands and transferred to an executive of ministers, the Crown was a vital force in shaping the aristocracy: destroying feudalism by granting rights of hereditary landownership and by banning subinfeudation, failing to equip the centralised system of royal government with an adequate bureaucracy, preventing the development of extensive corporate privileges while cultivating a peerage, having to bend compliantly on occasions in response to aristocratic demands and retaining a deeply ingrained belief in the need for an hereditary, privileged ruling class and therefore willing to dispense honours and privileges as hereditary rights and ever-ready to rely upon aristocrats in running the state. This appreciation applied to aristocrats great and small. The magnate flourished over the centuries not because of the Crown's political weaknesses but because of its incapacity to conceive an aristocracy in which the magnate did not form an essential part.

(i) *The Crown and the magnate*

The Crown treated magnates with extreme generosity as well as extreme meanness. The nature of the treatment was not wholly determined by the political strength of the Crown. No English monarch every objected to their existence. Moreover, kings firmly in control of the state, as well as feeble, dangled rulers, were capable of sustaining and even enlarging their power and wealth. Edward I and Henry VII proceeded harshly against a remarkably large number of magnates, but also generously provided replacements. The house of Lancaster which dominated the political scene for much of the fourteenth century was the creation of Edward I; and the dynasty of Jasper Tudor – nipped in the bud by extinction – was the creation of Henry VII who also promoted the house of Stanley, conferring upon it an earldom and awarding it, through the grant of estates, an ascendant position in Lancashire. Henry VIII rigorously dealt with large numbers of magnate families but also established a string of them equipped with resources to match those of the fallen.

The Crown favoured the territorial magnate principally by forgiving defecting dynasties, by permitting the conjunction of dynasties through marriage, by founding new dynasties, and by granting magnates either independence of the system of royal government or, alternatively, an official control of it. The restoration of disgraced magnates was a normal occurrence.

Rarely were magnate dynasties terminated by royal order. In the fourteenth century, for example, the baronial opposition of Edward II's reign was forgiven by Edward III, whilst in the thirteenth century, the baronial opposition to Henry III was mostly forgiven by Edward I. Furthermore, of the nine peers attainted in Henry VII's reign, six had their attainders reversed. Of the peers attainted in the reign of Henry VIII, most were eventually restored, mainly in the reigns of his children, Edward and Mary. The inclination of the early Tudors, however, was not to make a complete restoration of the titles and estates. Only one of the five attainders imposed and reversed in Henry VII's reign was a full restoration. In the reign of his son, the attainder of the house of Stafford in 1521 was so decisive that the family never recovered the bulk of its estates or its ducal title; and the reversal of the attainders of the house of Fitzgerald and of the Courtenays did not restore the whole inheritance. Nonetheless, all three families managed to survive royal reprisal as territorial magnates equipped with extensive estates and peerage titles. The Crown's policy of forgiveness allowed certain magnate families to defect repeatedly and to survive as large landowners and high-ranking nobles in spite of suffering the penalties of treason. Thus the Percy earls of Northumberland were brought down twice in the fifteenth century (in 1408 and 1461) and twice in the sixteenth century (in 1537 and 1569), on each occasion suffering the forfeiture of their estates, yet survived as a magnate dynasty.

Magnates could improve their position by marriage: materially, by marrying the heiresses of other magnates and socially, by marrying princesses of the blood royal. In both cases, the right of marriage could lie with the Crown: for reasons of feudal overlordship which empowered the king to determine the marriage of a tenant-in-chief's heiress or for reasons of kinship (for example, by right of paternity). In the fourteenth and fifteenth centuries the princes of the blood and other close royal relatives had the pick of the magnate heiresses. This told a familiar story: the Crown's inclination to reward its own kith and kin even at the expense of creating magnates endowed with massive private resources. The Tudors were without male kin to reward and, fortuitously, the opportunities were lacking, in the absence of sole heiresses of magnate estates, for one great family to acquire by marriage the possessions of another, lock, stock and barrel. However, essentially the Tudors followed tradition. Magnates were allowed to enlarge their estates by marrying the heiresses of other magnates and several magnate/princess marriages occurred, mostly with the royal permission, in spite of the political danger evident in increasing the number of subject dynasties with a claim to the throne. Thus, not only Henry VII but also three of his subjects married daughters of Edward IV in the opening years of his reign. Tudor monarchs were certainly incensed when the royal permission was not sought: as in 1514 when Charles Brandon married Mary Tudor, or in 1536 when Thomas Howard married Lady Douglas, or in the 1560s when Edward Seymour and Catherine Grey arranged to marry. In Henry VIII's reign, moreover, a law was even passed making it treason for a subject to marry or cohabit with a princess unless authorised by the royal permission given under the great seal. Nonetheless, the Tudor dynasty was not intrinsically against such alliances and allowed several to take place.

The Crown also upheld the magnates by adding to their number. In fact, a magnate family's estates and titles usually originated in a royal gift. Compared with his late fourteenth- and fifteenth-century predecessors, Henry VII created very few new peerages. Credited with only nine, some of which were restorations of forfeited honours, his behaviour seemed a reversion to the peerage policy of the thirteenth century when new creations were rare and the peerage was prone to contraction because the peerages created failed to compensate for those suffering extinction or absorbed through marriage by other peerage families. Henry VIII was also remarkably mean in the early years of his reign: by 1529 only seven peers had been made. A spate of creations between 1529 and 1558 added thirty titles to the peerage, but parsimony returned with Elizabeth. During the length of her reign only ten peerages were created.

Between 1330 and 1480 and under the early Stuarts the size of the peerage was spectacularly enlarged whereas under the Tudors the creations only compensated for the failure of lines. Yet this evidence does not prove that the Tudor monarchy was anti-magnate or lacked sympathy for the magnate. Elizabeth's unwillingness to create new peerages seemed to spring from a desire to uphold the nobility as an order of ancient, or of socially elevated, lineage. Only two of the ten peerages created were bestowed on families lacking either ancestral connections with the peerage or kinship with the Crown. Furthermore, the paucity of creations between 1485 and 1529 may have been a natural counteraction to the generosity of the Yorkists whose openhandedness had made the peerage large enough. Furthermore, compensating for the Tudors' sparing creation of peers was their generous dispensation of estates to old peerage families and to leading gentry. While magnates were felled, others were raised in their stead. Accounting for the Crown's generosity was not only its lack of antipathy to the magnate but also the resources at its disposal. These resources came partly from the dissolution of the monasteries and chantries in the 1530s and 1540s and partly from the Crown's absorption of magnate inheritances in the late fifteenth century. The latter was principally due to the frequency of usurpation. The annexation of magnate inheritances by forfeiture offered only a limited gain since forfeited estates were usually restored. Of greater effect in placing magnate inheritances permanently in the Crown's possession was the simple fact that in the fifteenth century a succession of great magnates seized the Crown and, by deposing the reigning monarch, incorporated their private inheritances with the Crown lands. Instead of retaining them, the Crown quickly fritted away these massive resources, largely to raise revenue for dynastic wars against France and Scotland.

The major recipients of this landed wealth was the aristocracy. Possession was gained by purchase or by royal gift. The land market now provided the means for establishing a magnate dynasty. In the medieval period the only means of constructing a sufficiently large estate had been marriage and royal patronage. Nonetheless, in the traditional manner, many of the new magnate families of the sixteenth century relied upon royal favour for their elevation. Inevitably, some of the royal gifts of land went to kinsmen of the Crown. Following Jane Seymour's marriage to Henry VIII and the fortuitous birth of Edward VI, her brother Edward received a huge estate in Wiltshire and Somerset as well as a viscountcy and an earldom. Overnight the Seymour family was converted from old gentry to new magnate, with private resources for asserting itself in the overmighty manner. The Parrs were likewise raised into the magnate class by a royal gift of titles and lands after Katherine Parr's marriage to Henry VIII. Having married Katherine Parr's sister, William Herbert also benefited materially from the Parr–Tudor match. Earlier, the Boleyns became a magnate family as a result of Henry VIII's association with Mary and Anne Boleyn. When he died in 1536 at the age of sixteen Henry Fitzroy, Henry VIII's illegitimate son, was already a large landowner and a duke, thanks to his father's munificence. All this happened in accordance with a long tradition. Over the centuries a leading source of magnates was the generosity inevitably extended by kings to members of their own family. Yet Henry VIII's liberality also fell upon those outside the royal family. In the course of the reign the Russells acquired titles and estates that justified the appellation of magnate. To solve the problem of government created in the West Country by the fall of the Courtenays in the late 1530s, the Crown deliberately established the Russells as their replacement, awarding John Russell not only a barony but also estates, formerly of Glastonbury Abbey, worth £1,000 p.a.

The gains made by certain families in the reign of Edward VI at the expense of the Crown's resources can be attributed to the Crown's vulnerability. But the men who were best positioned to gain from the royal minority had already acquired the capacity of magnates as a result of Henry

VIII's generosity and tolerance. The huge estates which Protector Somerset forfeited to the Crown in 1552 were, for example, mostly accumulated in the closing years of Henry VIII's reign.

Medieval kings had favoured the magnates by permitting them a range of private powers, notably to judge, to possess armies and to build castles. Franchises were set up to provide border defences, to solve by delegation the problem of governing outlying regions and to reward loyal servants and close favourites of the king. In contrast with the tolerant policy of medieval kings, the Tudors failed to create new franchises, absorbed many of the old ones and then in 1536 deprived them of their basic right to exclude the king's writ. By incorporating the franchises within the political system, the Tudors departed from tradition. Furthermore, their attitude towards private armies was relatively unsympathetic. Less licence was granted under the Tudors to subjects for developing their own military resources than ever before. Yet the Tudor regime was not against the private possession of armies, castles and armouries. It could not afford to be since it depended upon these magnate resources to curb popular disorder, to provide a quickly organised home defence and to furnish the means of waging war abroad. In 1536 the magnates Norfolk, Suffolk and Shrewsbury were the instruments of action for dealing with the northern revolts; while the popular disturbances in East Anglia and the West Country in 1549 seemed to get out of hand because the local magnates, the Howards in East Anglia and the Courtenays in Devon and Cornwall, had fallen into disgrace and therefore could not be directed against them. The followings of magnates, moreover, remained a basic means of raising troops to defend the northern border and to wage war abroad, in spite of the reforms of the militia. The abiding primitiveness of the military system maintained a vital role for the private army in the Tudor state. The restrictions placed upon retaining, notably by the statute of 1504 and by proclamation, do not prove a royal antipathy to private armies. Furthermore, magnates failed to build castles under the Tudors because of changes in habit rather than because of Tudor disapproval; and the Tudors placed no restriction upon the private possession of armouries, so much so that a statute of 1557 obliged the peerage to keep them well-stocked. Distinguishing the Tudor regime, then, was its abstemiousness in creating new titles and in granting private governmental and military rights, but not a disbelief in the political and social need for territorial magnates. The Tudors upheld the aristocracy not only as a two-tiered order of peers and gentry but also as a class of great and lesser landowners and prepared the way for a revived magnate control of local government by developing the office of land lieutenant. (See pp. 116 and 134–5.)

In the course of the sixteenth century the composition and power of the magnates was transformed. To what extent was the transformation the direct outcome of Tudor policy? The glut of magnates of the blood royal in 1450, a legacy of Edward III's fertility and a cause of the civil wars of the fifteenth century, had disappeared a century later. This owed something to the Wars of the Roses in which several blue-blooded magnates fell without male issue and three leading subjects of the blood royal ceased to be magnates because they became kings. But to what extent was the reduction of the royal race due to deliberate action on the part of the Crown? The Tudors dealt severely with troublesome relatives; and they also took some care to ensure that their female offspring married foreigners and therefore did not impart the blood royal to subjects. Yet they did not systematically remove the offspring of fallen blue-blooded magnates, the only final way to eradicate claims to the throne; nor did they succeed in preventing subjects from marrying princesses. Henry VII could not prevent Lord Welles, Lord Courtenay and Thomas Howard from marrying the daughters of Edward IV. Henry VIII could not prevent the marriage of Charles Brandon, duke of Suffolk, to his sister, Mary. Nor did he prevent the two daughters of this match from marrying the marquis of Dorset and the earl of Cumberland whose daughters, in turn, were permitted to marry subjects. Occasionally the Crown made objection, but not with much effect. In fact, the reduction of the royal race owed much more to the operation of chance than to the policy and actions of the Crown.

Although Henry VII was unlucky to be faced with so many unmarried Yorkist princesses when he ascended the throne, it was fortunate for him that only one, apart from his own wife, produced surviving offspring and that amounted to no more than a single boy. He became the marquis of Exeter and fathered only one child, a son who died without issue. The Brandon–Tudor match produced only daughters and their marriages produced only daughters. The De la Pole family, a Yorkist line, became extinct not because of Tudor action against it but because the seven De la Pole brothers produced one daughter who became a devout nun. The fact that Henry VII was an only son and that, upon ascending the throne, Henry VIII and Edward VI were brotherless, also worked against the production of magnates. Moreover, the infertility of the last generation of De la Poles and two of Edward IV's daughters was exceeded by the children of Henry VIII, all of whom died childless. Genetic failure was not always so absolute. Margaret Clifford, the granddaughter of Mary Tudor, produced Ferdinando Stanley, earl of Derby. However, after holding his title for no more than a year, he died without male issue.

By the late sixteenth century the only surviving magnate with a fair claim to the throne was the earl of Huntingdon who chose to remain a loyal servant of the Crown. The high infertility of the royal race and its tendency to produce daughters rather than sons ensured that the prominent challengers to Mary and Elizabeth should come from women, notably Jane Grey and Mary of Scots. Unable as women to claim the throne through their own military leadership in the manner of the fifteenth-century claimants, both were at a political disadvantage.

As a result of this coincidence of genetical failure, the magnates ceased to be dominated by dynasties of the blood royal. But the decimation of the royal race does not wholly explain why in the sixteenth century the over-mighty subject should disappear and the Crown should regain its political ascendancy.

The strength of the late medieval magnate lay in the allegiance owed him by lesser aristocrats, serving as feudal tenants, indentured retainers, annuitants and full-time employees. By the late sixteenth century the magnates were noticeably less well-followed than in the past. In general terms, this was because of the Crown's success in persuading the aristocracy to accept a political system centring upon the royal court. Partly responsible for its success was a curtailment of the patronage dispensed by the courts of magnates. The legal restrictions placed upon retaining, the abolition of the franchises as independent units of local government, the extension of effective royal government into outlying regions through the establishment of regional councils, limited the patronage that magnates could dispense in their own right. But also responsible was a lavish dispensation of patronage by the Crown which made the royal court the primary focus of aristocratic allegiance. Initially the Crown proceeded by adopting the devices of the magnates: attaching gentry to its service by giving them offices in the royal household and by admitting them to its own retaining system. But crucial to the conversion of the aristocracy from magnate to royal rule was the enormous accretion of royal patronage which followed the dissolution of the monasteries and chantries. The enlargement of the Crown's patronage combined with the extension of effective royal government to make the royal court more attractive than magnate courts, and the inability of magnate patronage to rival royal patronage persuaded the aristocracy to accept the Crown as the primary fount of reward, favour, employment, protection and justice. In addition, the increased prospect of royal reprisal helped to persuade aristocrats, both high and low, to accept royal rule. As a result, magnates became less willing to ally with each other against the Crown and the gentry became less ready to fight for a magnate cause which ran counter to the monarch.

Royal action, or the prospect of it, cannot be ignored as a dissolver of the old relationship between the magnates and other aristocrats. But some importance must also be attached to changes in aristocratic habit. Habits changed under the influence of the price revolution and the Italian renaissance, notably its advocacy of bookish learning as a preparation for rulership and of fencing with the rapier as the essential means of acquitting an aristocrat's honour. The Wars of the Roses were a succession of duels fought in the traditional manner as battles between large numbers of seconds to settle an issue of honour either between individual magnates or a magnate and the Crown. By the late sixteenth century, the magnate, now a non-martial courtier, was inclined to settle his affairs by other means than private war. For the acquittal of honour, an army became unnecessary. The retaining system faded away as much because the magnates ceased to have need of it as because of the Crown's prohibitiveness.

Furthermore, pressed by the price rise and the problems created by customarily fixed rents, magnates came to regard their estates primarily as sources of revenue rather than of following, and were therefore prepared to increase land revenue at the expense of forfeiting a tenantry's loyalty. This change in estate management could alienate both the peasant and gentry tenants. Just before his death in 1521 the third duke of Buckingham was frightened to visit his marcher lordships in south Wales because of the hostility of local gentry who had formerly served the Stafford family as loyal supporters and were now bitterly antagonised by increased feudal dues and rents. Similarly, the earl of Cumberland in the mid-1530s could no longer command the support of the gentry families who were his vassals and retainers, largely because they now regarded him as a mean landlord. The pressures of inflation also drew magnates to the royal court, attracted by the profits to be made from the royal favour and from royal office. Moreover, they dissuaded magnates from supporting large private followings which could not be easily afforded and which, in the changed political climate, were no longer a necessity.

The domestication of the magnate was partly a process of repression and partly a process of accommodation. Magnates complied with the Crown because of what it had to offer. Abundant royal patronage enlisted the support both of magnates and gentry. For the magnates there was also the chance of securing political power by submitting to, rather than by seeking to oppose or exclude, royal government. The Tudor monarchy found the independent power of the magnate anathema; but it found magnate power exercised in the royal name and interest fully acceptable. Thus, the development of the Tudor state was not completely at the magnate's expense. It simply required him to change his political function. The changes in local government, for example, were not against the magnate interest. There was a place for magnates on the councils of the north and the Welsh marches; and the development of lords lieutenancy as permanent appointments to all counties rather than temporary appointments to troublesome regions placed local government firmly in the hands of the local magnates. Charged as lord lieutenant with the administration of the militia and the oversight of county government, the magnate no longer needed the retaining system as his means of locally influencing the operation of royal government. This was the first step in a process which by the early eighteenth century had enabled the magnates to take full charge of local government in the counties where their estates were situated. In this respect the magnate rule of the eighteenth century was a continuation rather than a complete reversal of Tudor policy.

The sixteenth-century change in the relationship between Crown and magnate also owed much to a change in the gentry's attitude towards the magnates. The growing dependence of the magnates upon the Crown was accompanied by the gentry's increasing independence of the magnates. The relative attractiveness of royal and magnate patronage played a part and so did the political effectiveness of the Crown, but also responsible were changes in cultural habit. Moved by the Italian renaissance, the English aristocracy quickly changed its life-style and aspired to appear as the educated gentleman rather than the warrior knight. The new emphasis upon a bookish learning caused gentry to send their sons to school, university and inns of court rather than to other noble households for their education, reducing the numbers of gentry attached to magnates as household servants and courtiers and blocking off an important avenue whereby gentry had been recruited into magnate service. Working against this development were the powers allowed the lord lieutenants in the seventeenth century to nominate the leading officials of local government and to dispense leases on Crown lands. This capture of royal patronage by the lord lieutenant eventually allowed the magnates to regain control of the local gentry.

(ii)   *The Crown and the gentry*
A corollary of the interpretation which presents the Tudor monarchy as anti-magnate is the view that it was especially favourable towards the gentry. This interpretation attributes to Tudor rule not only the fall of the medieval magnate but also the rise of the gentry. Questioning its validity is, on the one hand, the Tudors' establishment of new magnate dynasties and the use made of magnates in their system of government and, on the other, their failure to make an exception of the gentry when proceeding against the aristocratic order as well as their inclination to continue, rather than to transform, the gentry's traditional political functions and privileges.

Defecting gentry were treated with a rigour at least equal to the treatment of defecting magnates. The chances of restitution for a fallen gentry family were probably less promising than those of a fallen magnate family. Moreover, the exceptional severity of the early Tudor proceedings against the franchises and retaining was paralleled by the decisive exploitation of the king's feudal prerogative. For centuries monarchs had sought to prevent their tenants-in-chief from evading feudal dues. Yet they had tolerated the Use, a legal device to evade such payments. When the government denied the Use this power in 1536 it proceeded with unprecedented harshness against the private interests of the aristocracy. The measure was only a temporary success. By 1540 the statute of wills was enacted permitting a tenant-in-chief to escape feudal dues on two thirds of his estate on the condition that the full dues were paid on the remainder, a compromise indicating the early Tudor dependence upon a contented aristocracy. At the same time, the episode reveals the Tudor willingness to take action against the aristocratic interest, no matter whether that interest was of the gentry or the peerage. Furthermore the conciliar developments of the early Tudors served to check the local power of the gentry as well as of the magnates. The eventual revolts against their regional councils came from the aristocracy as an order rather than from a segment of it.

The Tudors used the gentry in the traditional manner. No attempt was made to equalise the grossly disproportionate privileges of the peerage and the gentry. The gentry, moreover, remained the main source of recruitment to offices of state but, in the traditional manner, achieved the higher offices only through ennoblement. This was especially true of high military commands. In the late 1530s the wardenships of the northern marches were occupied by gentry but on a temporary basis and only because of the absence of suitable magnates. Military leadership was confined to magnate families with a history of military achievement. Edward Seymour broke into this exclusive sphere in the early 1540s only because he had been raised into the peerage and because the failure of the Brandons and Howards gave him the opportunity to receive high military office. Some high administrative offices became newly available to the gentry at the centre of Tudor government but not at magnate expense. Rather they were taken from the clergy and expressed the secularisation, not the gentrification, of government. In the traditional way, the gentry remained the key figures in local government, forming the basic membership of the commissions of the peace. Additional tasks were bestowed upon them in the course of the century but only in their capacity of JPs.

During the sixteenth century the gentry were subjected more than ever before to the Crown which came not only to provide its major source of employment and patronage but also to determine its membership. For the first time, the convention that gentry families should sport a genuine escutcheon was enforced by visitations of royal heralds. The latter's task was to confirm and to admit coats of arms. Membership of the gentry thus became an armigerous act and for this reason entry to the gentry became as dependent upon the Crown as entry to the peerage. The growth in the size of the gentry, a remarkable feature of the late sixteenth and early seventeenth centuries, owed much to the willingness of the Crown to admit, through the royal heralds, new armorial bearings. Nevertheless, landownership remained the key of entry; and the enlargement of the gentry rested upon the capacity of commoners to purchase suitable estates. Creating gentlemen in the sixteenth century was the wealth made in commerce, farming and law coupled with the vigour of a land market originally stimulated by the land unloaded by the church and the Crown, an unloading that placed at least one quarter of the total landed area of the country on the private market between 1534 and 1660 and which was essentially the responsibility of an indebted Crown. As a result, the gentry between 1500 and 1700 tripled whereas the population only doubled, its share of the land increased from roughly thirty per cent to fifty per cent; and its presence became more widespread. Whereas in the early sixteenth century the majority of village communities lacked a resident squire, by the late seventeenth century only one third was in this position. However, since the growth in gentry landownership was accompanied by a spectacular growth in gentry numbers, the gentry *per capita* did not become wealthier or holders of larger estates. Moreover, because the growth in gentry landownership fed upon the estates formerly belonging to the church and the Crown, it was not at the expense of the higher nobility whose landholding in the same period doubled (from five per cent to ten per cent). Apart from increasing the gentry's presence, the growth in its size only intensified the competition for local office and enlarged the proportion of gentry, always a considerable one, that was unable to secure public office and therefore exercised a ruling function only as lords of the manor.

(b)   **Aristocratic revolt**

(For reference and further reading, see bibliography, VIII (b).)

Although important in the sixteenth century, the relationship established between the Tudor monarchy and the aristocracy was of little long-term consequence. By the early eighteenth century, the territorial magnates were again in the political ascendant with central government ruled by a cabinet of them and local government directed by the magnate lord lieutenant. Moreover, although pacified and attached to the royal interest by Tudor rule, the aristocracy broke loose in the seventeenth century and attacked the royal authority with such persistence and vigour that two kings were deposed and a political system emerged which by 1720 was so different from the traditional polity that the Tudors would not have recognised it. Aristocrats seeking merely to arrest the political innovations advocated by the Crown realised a political revolution. The opposition to the Crown in the seventeenth century was not exclusively aristocratic; nor was it the work of an aristocracy acting in unison; but neither was it marginally aristocratic and essentially popular. In the armed revolts of the 1640s and the 1680s, members of the aristocracy figured as prominently as in the parliamentary opposition to the Stuarts.

The aristocratic opposition of the seventeenth century was the culmination of a long tradition partially concealed by the relative acquiescence of the Tudor aristocracy. Under the Tudors, aristocrats (on occasions) openly and forcibly opposed the government, notably in the opening years of the regime, in the northern revolts of 1536 and 1569 and in Wyatt's rebellion of 1554. Moreover, a parliament dominated by the aristocracy made frequent criticisms of government policy. But compared with the periods before and after, the opposition was remarkably feeble and infrequent. In spite of the problems created by religious schism, the rule of a minor and two queens and an unsettled succession, only one Tudor monarch was deposed and that was Jane Grey, unseated by the monarch whose succession her own usurpation had forestalled. In the two centuries prior to the Tudor accession five kings were deposed by their aristocratic opponents and in the period 1460 to 1485 the Crown had forcibly changed hands six times. Under the Tudors no control was placed upon the monarch's choice of ministers, yet in the late middle ages aristocratic resistance secured their dismissal and appointment. No constitution was pressed upon the Tudor monarchy, whereas over the centuries a succession of them were forced upon the Crown: the Petition of Right of 1628 and the Bill of Rights of 1689 had their forerunners not only in Magna Carta (1216) but also in the Charter of the Forest (1217), the Provisions of Oxford (1258) and the ordinances of 1311. Expressed through parliament as well as by insurrection, this tradition of revolt affected the aristocracy's mentality, instilling the role of a responsible opposition to royal tyranny. Acts of resistance were sustained by the knowledge of earlier acts: the opposition to Henry III followed the example set by the baronial revolt against King John; in leading the opposition to Edward II, Thomas earl of Lancaster saw himself performing the part of Simon de Montfort, the leading opponent of Henry III, and the ordinances impressed in 1311 upon Edward II were partly inspired by the ordinances imposed upon Henry III in 1258 which were, in their turn, inspired by Magna Carta. The two major aristocratic rebellions of the seventeenth century likewise made reference to Magna Carta, their supporters believing that they were acting in a long tradition of protest to defend immemorial custom against the absolutism of the Norman kings and their successors.

(i) *Medieval revolts*
The medieval revolts shared two preconditions. They occurred in a situation of military defeat and were incited by the offensiveness of the king's personality. Frequently the protest was a constitutional one, an allegation that the government was overriding the rights of subjects. Often the charge was that evil councillors had caused the king to ignore his bounden duties. As a corollary, these evil councillors were accused of excluding leading members of the aristocracy from the affairs of state and from the king's favour. The evil councillors were usually either upstart favourites or bureaucrats of foreign, clerical or commoner origin. The aim of the opposition was to determine the government's leading personnel, to force the king to consult his leading nobles more frequently and to insist that all taxes levied by the government and all laws enforced in the common law should receive the consent of the realm. The general outcome was the creation of a constitutional polity which denied the monarch the arbitrary right to legislate and tax. However, the restrictions which aristocrats imposed upon the Crown did not seem to derive from a plan to transform the constitution. In proceeding against the government, aristocrats felt that they were safeguarding a political tradition. For the most part, the opposition was so effective because indebtedness forced the king to bow to parliamentary demands and because the private financial and military resources of great magnates made them at times politically irresistible.

Basic preconditions for aristocratic revolt were the long wars with Scotland, Henry I's annexation of Normandy in 1106 and the accession to the English throne in 1154 of the Angevin dynasty which at that time owned two-fifths of the kingdom of France. A long struggle ensured between the English and French for the continental possessions of the English Crown, a struggle which waxed and waned from the late twelfth century until the 1450s when the English Crown lost all its French territories but for Calais.

For the English, the wars against France and Scotland were marked by a succession of dramatic and expensive military failures, failures which usually coincided with outbreaks of aristocratic hostility towards the royal court. Thus John's loss of Normandy, Anjou and Brittany formed the background to the baronial revolt which produced the great charter. Henry III failed as a soldier in Wales and Scotland as well as in France. The revolts of 1234 and of 1258 occurred in the circumstances of military defeat. Edward II was another notable military failure. During his reign the aristocratic opposition was principally aroused by military setbacks in Scotland. In contrast, Edward III was supremely successful in upholding the Angevin interest in France and in withstanding the Scots. In spite of the financial cost, the gains made from protracted wars in Scotland and France maintained harmony between him and his subjects. The tide turned, however, after 1369. The military defeats of the 1370s were so decisive that by 1380 the English Crown retained only Calais, Cherbourg, Bordeaux and Bayonne; and the Scottish border counties, taken by the English in the 1330s, had been lost. Incited by military defeat, a vigorous parliamentary opposition managed in 1371 and 1376 to rid the government of obnoxious ministers and to replace them by its own appointments. A similar, if not so extreme or successful, reaction occurred in the reign of Edward I. In the late 1290s an aristocratic opposition developed because there were no longer any military successes to justify the government's heavy financial exactions. Also prone to military defeat and lacking any compensation for the weight of taxation or the oppressiveness of the king's perverse and extravagant nature, the government of Richard II was dogged by aristocratic resistance, both armed and parliamentary. Furthermore, the Wars of the Roses began with the humiliating defeats of the 1450s which undid the triumphs of Henry V and deprived the English Crown of virtually all its French possessions.

The long wars against Scotland and France contributed to the success of the aristocratic opposition. In making the Crown insolvent and heavily dependent upon taxation, they forced it to comply with parliamentary demands for the redress of grievances. It was the indebtedness of the

Crown, mainly the fault of war, that accounts for the successes of the aristocratic opposition in the reigns of Henry III, Edward I, Edward II, in the 1370s and in the reign of Richard II.

McFarlane stated that when conflict between Crown and aristocracy occurred it was

> almost always the fault of the king: which is as much to say that it depended how often the hereditary succession brought those unfit to rule to the throne. Edward II, Richard II and Henry VI were the penalty that monarchy paid for its dependence upon the chances of heredity.

He overlooked the fact that every monarch in the thirteenth and fourteenth centuries got into difficulty with his leading subjects but, nevertheless, his point stands. Although the struggles between monarchs and nobles were not simply caused by heredity, some monarchs, on account of their inadequate personalities, had much greater difficulty than others in managing their aristocracy. John, Henry III, Edward II and Richard II were all notably incapable of moderation. John's manic efficiency was irritating in the extreme as was the sharpness of his tongue. Henry III's claim to arbitrary powers by divine right, the extravagance of Edward II and Richard II, as well as their arbitrariness and their domination by favourites, proved highly offensive. All were highly adept at making determined enemies of high-ranking subjects simply through being true to themselves.

The constitutional grievances of this aristocratic opposition rested on the charge of breach of contract and the king's obligation to respect his subjects' feudal and customary rights. His obligation derived from the feudalism established by the Conquest and from his coronation oath, a surviving feature of the monarchy's original elective nature. Because of his suzerainty and because of his coronation oath, the monarch was under obligation to the realm. The one contract reinforced the other. The baronial opposition to John took its stand both on feudal right and the historic principle that the validity of the royal prerogative rested upon the consent of his free subjects and was permitted on the condition that, in keeping with the promises of his coronation oath, the king would respect their rights. Magna Carta was a feudal document emphasising the lord's obligation to his vassals and a reasserted coronation oath binding the king to respect the customary rights of the freeman. Both types of contract were deemed at times to justify opposition to the king, even his deposition.

Provoking conflict was the king's failure either to summon his tenants-in-chief and to consult with them on matters of government policy or to secure the consent of the representatives of the realm, originally the barons and by the fourteenth century the members of parliament, before making laws and exacting dues which feudal custom failed to authorise. What especially ignited conflict was the illegitimate manner in which revenues were raised and the extravagant way in which they were spent; the king's ignorance of his leading subjects in the making of policy; the confiscation of property without good cause and the government's use of the royal household rather than the exchequer for the administration of its finances. In complaining of the king, the aristocracy took its stand upon ancient rights, but, in the course of time, particularly with the development of parliament and because of the concessions made by the Crown in return for revenue, these basic rights were undoubtedly extended so that, in spite of its claim to stand on tradition, the aristocratic opposition of the fourteenth century was fighting for some rights of recent creation.

The aristocratic opposition of the thirteenth and fourteenth centuries essentially resisted the arbitrary conduct of the king. But it was more than simply a defence of rights. Objection was made not only to royal absolutism but also to the behaviour of the royal court. Much of the opposition was moved by personal interest and was the expression of an envious country aristocracy opposed to the royal court because it felt excluded from its favours. The type of complaint frequently focused upon the evil minister, especially one who was not of the aristocracy. As royal favourites, evil ministers were opposed for capturing the king and for encouraging him to behave irresponsibly; as bureaucrats, evil ministers were charged with imposing heavy financial exactions. But the basic ground of complaint was exclusion from royal favour and respect. The grievances, then, might be presented in public and constitutional terms but, to some extent, they were private and personal, the result of a rift between a magnate and the king. Much of the conflict sprang from personal quarrels which were depersonalised and presented as principled in order to enlist the maximum support. A central feature of the aristocratic opposition to Henry III was the personal feud between him and Simon de Montfort. Generating and sustaining the aristocratic resistance to Edward II were the personal differences between him and

Thomas of Lancaster; the opposition to Richard II owed much to the duke of Gloucester and the earls of Arundel and Warwick and their hatred of him.

Characterising the aristocratic revolts of the middle ages were their frequency and success, although the latter is easily exaggerated. The Crown's powers of counteraction were often greater than its need to make concessions. For example, the Oxford Provisions were operative only between 1258 and 1261. By 1265 Henry III had defeated the baronial opposition. Securing the repeal of the ordinances, he successfully reclaimed the sole right to appoint the leading state officers. With the fall of Thomas of Lancaster in 1322, the ordinances of 1311, which had been a dead letter since 1313, were revoked. Edward I was made to confirm the great charter in 1299, 1300 and 1301 but then proceeded to violate its terms, notably by imposing an arbitrary tax on wool and by suspending Winchelsey as archbishop of Canterbury. The requirement of the Good Parliament of 1376 to control the appointment of royal ministers had been undone within a year. In the 1390s Richard II broke free from the restrictions imposed upon him in the 1380s. The very recurrence of complaint suggests the short-term effect of aristocratic resistance.

Nevertheless, its influence on the rise of parliament in the thirteenth and fourteenth centuries was of permanent effect. Furthermore, it caused a procedure to become ingrained in the aristocratic mind which made revolt and resistance easier to imagine and achieve. Its short-term effects were spectacular: not only kings but also their ministers and favourites were deposed; and in 1258, 1311 and 1386 committees were established to run the government. Although the life of these committees was short, their establishment, along with the deposition of kings and ministers, set examples from which the future could learn.

Aristocrats continued to oppose kings in the fifteenth century through the military might of magnates and in parliament, but their opposition underwent some change in aim. In the closing years of the fourteenth century it became dominated by dynastic ambition. The Crown did not fall to Bolingbroke simply as a result of Richard II's overthrow but because his family had for some time coveted the throne. The plethora of families of the blood royal in the fifteenth century and the example of usurpation set by the house of Lancaster in 1399 ensured that the struggle between Crown and aristocracy should be strongly dynastic. Outside parliament, the struggle featured magnates of the blood royal seeking to obtain the

Crown for themselves, supported by fellow magnates of enormous wealth and private authority such as the Beauchamps and the Percies. The dynasticism of the armed conflict worked against the restriction of the Crown's powers. Whereas in the past a basic aim of aristocratic revolt was to curtail the Crown's authority, now, with the rebels designing to possess the Crown, there was no good reason to impose constitutional limitations upon its powers. Constitutional restriction, however, remained a goal of the parliamentary opposition which sought to add to its right of fiscal consent the right to appropriate the fiscal revenue.

(ii)   *Modern revolts*

The glut of blood royal eventually ran out and the strong rule of the early Tudors put a stop to the high incidence of deposition and usurpation. But there was no immediate reversion to the type of revolt which sought to impose a constitution upon the king. The northern rebels of October 1536 opposed base-born councillors, notably Riche and Cromwell, and those of 1569 objected to Lord Burghley's apparent control of the Queen. Both were revolts against the court, objecting to its favouritism of southerners. But Tudor revolts did not criticise the government for pursuing an extravagant and unprofitable foreign policy, or charge monarchs with being the playthings of favourites, breaking their coronation oaths, and committing arbitrary acts. Moreover, the revolts against the government's religious policy introduced a new element. Also distinguishing the aristocratic revolts of the sixteenth century was their limited effect. Compared with the risings of the previous three centuries, they were easily suppressed and had no noticeable impact upon the Crown's policy or constitutional position.

The aristocratic opposition expressed in Tudor parliaments was also comparatively weak. In the course of the century parliament certainly refound its vociferousness; but, compared with the parliaments of the fourteenth and seventeenth centuries, Tudor parliaments, even in Elizabeth's reign, were subservient to the Crown and incapable of swaying government policy. In sharp contrast, under the early Stuarts the aristocratic opposition recovered its former strength. Both in parliament and by force of arms it acted decisively against the government. Aroused by the medieval condition of a heavily indebted Crown that could not afford to dispense with parliament no matter how critical it was, and

placed in a modern situation of religious conflict, parliament became
unmanageable. Moreover, with a wayward Crown offending the
aristocracy through the way it disposed its patronage, its absolutist
ambitions and its religious inclinations, the aristocracy proved capable of
mounting two rebellions, each of them at least as successful as the major
medieval revolts. In spite of the religious discord present and the
leadership provided by members of the gentry in the English Civil War,
there is no good reason to regard these rebellions as different in kind from
the great revolts of the past. They were no more revolts of a
commercially-minded aristocracy against a feudally-minded monarchy
than previous revolts; and, in keeping with a long tradition, they did not
seem intent on overthrowing the traditional polity. On the other hand,
they cannot be explained, in the medieval manner, as revolts of magnates
against a fickle prince whose extravagance, military incompetence or
domination by favourites had made him intolerable.

The traditional preconditions of military defeat and government
insolvency were present in the Civil War but absent from the Glorious
Revolution. The indebtedness of Charles I's government, however, was
due not simply to war but the inadequacy of the revenues earmarked to
pay the normal expenses of government. It compelled him to summon
parliament and also to search for new sources of revenue. Summoning
parliament, in the 1680s as well as in the 1640s, gave expression to a
hostility aroused not so much by the government's misuse of public money
as by its religious policy, especially the high anglicanism of Charles I and
the catholicism of James II. Throughout the century an unresolved
conflict between parliament and the government acted as the basic cause
of armed revolt. Parliament remained obstreperous not only because of the
religious issue but also because of the government's attempts either to
function without parliament or to overrule it. Ancient rights seemed to be
at stake. Charles I and James II were opposed, like John, Henry III and
Richard II, for being political innovators bent on freeing the Crown of its
customary restraints.

At the root of the conflict, then, was a constitutional issue. Like the
medieval revolts, the seventeenth-century conflicts were not between a
progressive aristocracy wishing to transform the political system and a
conservative Crown seeking to preserve tradition, but between a
reactionary aristocracy defending ancient rights and an innovatory Crown

seeking to alter the polity. Yet while the two seventeenth-century rebellions were aroused by a monarchy intent on re-ordering the political system, neither was simply a constitutional conflict. The aristocratic opposition derived its strength and determination from personal antipathy. High anglicanism was offensive to puritans in the 1640s and catholicism to anglicans in the 1680s; but sustaining the aristocratic opposition on both occasions was a deep sense of insult springing from the manner in which the Crown dispensed its patronage and treated its officials. Opposition came not only from men who sensed that their liberties were being reduced but also from men who felt that, in compensation, they had not received their due. The conflict between court and country, a standard feature of medieval revolts, seemed to prepare the ground for the armed revolts against the Stuarts. Both monarchs proved consummate in alienating aristocrats, so much so that their attempts at political reorganisation stood little chance. The absence of an alternative apparatus left the Crown dependent upon the co-operation of aristocracy. As the aristocracy had no means of perceiving any advantage for itself in the planned reorganisation, this was not forthcoming. Unlike the Tudors, the Stuarts were incapable of enmeshing the major elements of the aristocracy in the web of the court. This failing was partly due to a lack of political sense but in the case of the early Stuarts also to an insufficiency of government patronage. Lacking the windfalls of war and the acquisition of new resources, the early Stuarts were relatively starved of patronage. Compounding their difficulties was the growth in the size of the aristocracy which naturally enlarged the demand for royal patronage. In addition, the early Stuarts misused their patronage by employing it to raise revenue. The massive sale of honours, along with the sale of monopolies, alienated as well as enlisted support. The government's interference with public office, either to reduce the fee or to alter the personnel, offered further personal grounds for objection. On the other hand, absent from both rebellions was the dynastic factor. Two monarchs were deposed but not, in the traditional manner, by subjects aspiring to the Crown. The one dynastic revolt, Monmouth's uprising of 1685, was a miserable failure.

In the medieval manner, the aristocratic revolts of the seventeenth century exceeded their original intentions. The attempt to conserve did just the opposite. By elevating the importance of parliament, impeding the process of political centralisation and limiting the royal prerogative, rebellion transformed the polity. Perhaps the conservationist aims of the rebels are easily exaggerated. Essentially it was their rights, not the traditional system, that they were determined to preserve. Moreover, the Bill of Rights (1689) did innovate, outlawing the king's suspending powers, severely restricting his dispensing powers and divesting the Crown of the right to declare martial law. Like Magna Carta, it extended as well as preserved subjects' rights and, in encompassing the king with legal restraints, it altered the constitution. Yet it also resembled Magna Carta in failing to propose a new polity. The political thinking of both documents rested upon the need to protect ancient rights from the Crown. By defining more precisely what a king could do, the outcome was to place new limits upon his lawful actions.

As in the past, the needs of war account for many of the successes of aristocratic opposition. Firmly establishing the revolutionary settlement of 1689 was the way the Bill of Rights was elaborated, substantiated and applied in the following war years. It was the war against France that established a form of parliamentary government. William III's dependence upon British support in his struggle against Louis XIV made him as submissive to his subjects as war had rendered Henry III and Edward III. Occurring at a time when the government was not involved in a foreign war, the revolts of the 1640s had no equivalent effect. They generated a wealth of political ideas but Charles I's execution did not solve the problems of government and a further attempt at solution was to crown his son Charles II. Like his father and in spite of the civil war, Charles II thought that the basic remedy for the problems of state was to increase the power and authority of the Crown. His successor, James II, thought likewise. The consequent revolt, the Glorious Revolution, prevented the remedy from ever being tried again. This was not only because the long war with France left William III heavily dependent upon his British subjects but also because the displaced James II became dependent for his restoration upon France. The war against France was a struggle between two systems of government: between the absolutism of Louis XIV and James II and the 'English' system of constitutional monarchy in which, legislatively and fiscally, government was answerable to a representative assembly and local government was in aristocratic rather than bureaucratic hands. The defeat of Louis XIV in the war of the Spanish succession validated the English system. Sustained by this proof of its feasibility, the system of government, brought about by the revolts of the 1640s and 1680s against royal absolutism, became securely based on a compound of apparent rationality and national sentiment.

Although part of a long tradition, in several respects, the seventeenth-century rebellions were very different from the medieval revolts. Religious discord, notably, gave aristocrats in the seventeenth century an additional reason for objecting to the government. However, instead of providing a completely new dimension, the complaints generated by the government's religious policy tended to intermix with the traditional constitutional and personal reasons for the revolt. Religious schism merely added another medium for the expression of traditional complaints. Furthermore, in contrast with the revolts of the late fourteenth and fifteenth centuries, dynasticism failed to provide the grounds for serious opposition to the Crown. In addition, the seventeenth-century revolts seemed, to a much greater extent than medieval revolts, aroused by the process of political centralisation. The rights at stake in the seventeenth century concerned the aristocracy's freedom from central control in performing the tasks of local government and in determining at the local level the nature of religious worship. The seventeenth-century revolts were very much a protest against the encroachment of Westminster into the shires: the revolt against Charles I was partly an objection to his use of prerogative courts to discipline JPs, and the revolt against James II was partly a reaction to his purging of the lord lieutenancies, the commissions of the peace and borough corporations. True, the opposition to John concerned the interference of central government but the tyranny defined by aristocratic revolt in the middle ages usually involved the freehold of property rather than of office. The fourth notable difference concerned the role of the magnate. In the middle ages the armed and parliamentary opposition of the aristocracy centred upon discontented magnates. They provided the cause, the leadership, the resources. Their private followings and personal grievances were decisive in igniting and affecting rebellion. Sustaining the parliamentary opposition was the clientage of magnates in the Commons and the presence of magnates in the Lords. In contrast, the seventeenth-century rebellions appeared less magnate-orientated. Magnates certainly figured: the earls of Essex, Bedford, Warwick and Manchester, Viscount Saye and Lords Brooke and Wharton were prominent in organising the resistance to Charles I; and the involvement of gentry could still be decided by their allegiance to magnates. Thus, in the civil war the Wiltshire gentry were moved by the feud between the Herberts and the Seymours and the Leicestershire gentry were swayed by the mutual antipathy of the Greys and the Hastings. The earl of Shaftesbury and Lord Russell led the opposition to Charles II while Danby, Devonshire, Shrewsbury and Delamere played a crucial role in replacing James II with William III. Nevertheless, the magnate was no longer the prime mover of revolt; and their private armies were less decisive in determining its course. The royalists of the 1640s and the 1680s were defeated by professional troops, the new model army in the 1640s and the army which William brought with him in 1688. Furthermore, much of the aristocratic opposition occurred independently of the magnate interest. For example, the opposition expressed in the Commons had a mind and dynamism of its own. It was activated not by a sense of loyalty to offended magnates but by a sense of injustice and constitutional propriety. On the other hand, the gentry's dependence upon magnates in the medieval revolts has been undoubtedly exaggerated, whereas the importance of the magnate in the seventeenth-century revolts has been understated. Possibly the role of the magnate in medieval and modern revolts differed only because of the gentry's willingness in the seventeenth century to make their protest directly rather than through the medium of the magnate.

(iii)   *The end of rebellion*

There was a high road to the rebellions of the seventeenth century; but it did not have its beginnings under the Tudors. Temporarily obscured by the harmony established in the sixteenth century between lord and king, it stretched back into the distant past and was clearly evident in the medieval aristocracy's capacity to withstand royal government. Then, following the rebellions of the seventeenth century, it abruptly stopped. Why? By 1750 the burning religious and constitutional issues which had driven aristocrats to rebellion in earlier times no longer divided the political establishment. Furthermore, with the establishment of parliament as a regular part of government, its continued domination by the aristocracy, the develop-ment of a respectable opposition party to complement the party in government, aristocratic resistance became tamer and mostly institution-alised. From the aristocracy's point of view, the system of government by the mid-eighteenth century had become pliant and flexible. This was largely a consequence of the defeat of royal absolutism. There was no longer any question of an independent royal government proceeding against the basic interests of the aristocracy. There was no longer any question of an inevitable conflict between the Crown standing on its prerogative and an aristocracy standing on its privileges. That was all part of the past. Government remained strongly influenced by the Crown but, in practice, essentially controlled by an aristocratic parliament. Nor was there any question of a conflict between a royal government insistent upon state control and bureaucratic centralisation and an aristocracy insistent upon maintaining tradition. The system of government created by the failure of royal absolutism was not the old medieval system revived: the eighteenth-century monarchy lacked the central control which medieval kings had exercised. However, the new system did allow the larger landowners the local independence of medieval magnates by excluding the possibility of bureaucratic supervision or interference. It also provided the magnates with the opportunity to determine policy through their control of parliament and the cabinet. Basically, it substituted magnate for royal domination. In place of the father of the people, divinely appointed and privileged by birth to decide policy, appeared for a time 'the great oaks that shade a commonwealth', their rule dependent upon a managed parliament and the absence of an extensive, independent bureaucracy. In the cabinet they exercised executive authority through actual membership; in parliament they exercised legislative control through the Lords and a manipulated Commons; in the country they exercised administrative control through the office of lord lieutenant. The freedom enjoyed by the magnates in local government and their control at the centre left them with little cause for profound discontent. However, because of the parliamentary dominance of the house of commons, magnates were unable to exercise their political power by natural right. The privileges of peerage were not sufficient for that purpose. In order to exercise effective power, they needed to enlist the support of the gentry. Although they complained bitterly about the weight of the land tax and the prolongation of war and political corruption, the gentry did not acquire anything like the hostility to a government controlled by magnates and their clients that it had earlier felt towards governments controlled by kings and their courtiers. In spite of the frictions created by the party conflict between Whigs and Tories and the former's long and exclusive ascendancy, the magnate oligarchy was less abrasive than kings and courtiers in treating the aristocratic interest and much more adept in showing it respect. During the years of Whig supremacy, the virtual absence of rebellion owed much to the disinclination of Tories to resort to arms; but this unwillingness owed much to the fact that it was a party of aristocrats whose social interest was being served even though their party was in the cold and even though their political affiliation excluded them from reaping the considerable benefits of government patronage.

The harmony between the government and the aristocracy in eighteenth-century England was also determined by the considerable financial resources at the government's disposal. Sustained by the growth of the economy whose wealth it could effectively tap through taxation and the national debt, the government had no need to employ the fiscal expedients which had offended the aristocracy in the past. Furthermore, because the government needed to avoid the stigma of absolutism, unparliamentary taxation, a familiar cause of aristocratic aggression over the centuries, was ruled out. The Crown's cession of its feudal rights removed another revenue-raising device which had traditionally alienated the aristocracy.

Arguably, maintaining the aristocracy in a reasonably content and acquiescent state in eighteenth-century England was its freedom from royal interference and bureaucratic control rather than the rewards dispensed to it by the government which, although great, only reached a small proportion of its membership. For this reason, the stable relationship established between government and aristocracy in the eighteenth century differed basically from that of the sixteenth century since the latter was mainly sustained by royal patronage, a patronage so munificent that the aristocracy could accept, in return for it, a process of increased political centralisation.

Finally, the fear of revolution, generated by recollection of the English civil war and revived by the French revolution, discouraged aristocratic extremism, while the absence of popular revolution in England left the aristocracy without a counter-revolutionary cause to fight for. Moreover, the radical changes of the political system which occurred in the nineteenth century were acceptable to the aristocracy because through parliament it could influence and modify their formulation and implementation.

(c) **Aristocratic dominance**

The success of aristocratic revolt in the early modern period contrasted with the failure of popular revolt. The one completely undid the Crown's attempt to enlarge its own powers, producing instead an aristocratic oligarchy; the other allowed the gains to be lost which the tenantry had made in the period of depopulation. The outcome was highly beneficial to the aristocracy, leaving it, throughout the eighteenth century, in an unprecedented position of political and social ascendancy. Its new-found dominance lay not only in the replacement of a polity centring upon the rule of a king by an aristocratic oligarchy but also in the abolition in 1641 of the privy council's judicial functions which left the house of lords as the only court of final appeal,[1] in the absolute rights of landownership conferred upon it between 1646 and 1660 by the Crown's abandonment of its feudal rights, by the statutory recognition, enacted in 1689, that the landowner's rights extended to the subsoil, and by the elimination of the tenantry's traditional proprietorial rights, notably the fixed rent and the hereditary tenure. Notably absent in England was an extensive system of noble-reserved office, but a diluted equivalent, and another reflection of its political dominance, came with the high property qualifications enacted in 1710 for MPs and in 1732 for JPs (for reference and further reading, see bibliography, section VIII (c)). Also expressing the aristocracy's political ascendancy was the repeal, in the course of the seventeenth century, of the medieval/Tudor corn and tillage legislation (see below, p. 193). It would be simplistic to regard the aristocracy's political dominance as just the product of successful rebellion. Although clearly evident in the century after the Glorious Revolution, the way was prepared well before by the durability of the large proprietor and by certain long-term political developments, especially the emergence under the late Tudors of the lord lieutenant as a leading official in county government, the unquestioned assumption that his office was the rightful possession of the great landowners, and the Stuart willingness to devolve upon the office the nomination of local officials and the dispensation of royal patronage. The devolution of royal authority began when Charles I permitted lord lieutenants to choose their own deputy lieutenants instead of having them selected by the privy council. The process was completed when Charles II allowed the lord lieutenant to name the JPs and other local officials in the king's gift, as well as to decide the recipients of leases on Crown lands. The aristocracy's political dominance also stemmed from its control of parliament and the failure of royal government in the seventeenth century to subdue, or to dispense with, that body. Aristocratic oligarchy was born as much of these developments as of the defeat of royal absolutism. Furthermore, the conditions favouring the great estate, the failure of the Tory party, the acumen of Walpole and the growing cost of elections in the early eighteenth century only account for the precise nature of oligarchic rule, not its essentially aristocratic nature. That had much deeper roots.

Also deep-rooted were the proprietorial rights which the aristocracy wrested from the Crown in the late seventeenth century. The battle for the subsoil was a long one with gains secured by the aristocracy in the late sixteenth, as well as in the late seventeenth, centuries. The abolition of the Crown's feudal rights was similarly the product of a long struggle. In the middle ages their existence was not oppressive since evasion was easy. Only the rigorous exploitation of the Crown's feudal prerogative under the Tudors and Stuarts made abolition necessary. Its achievement was not a complete submission on the Crown's part. As Lord Chancellor Hardwicke described it in 1757, abolition was 'the bargain which the nobility and gentry made with the Crown soon after the Restoration when they purchased out their own burdens by the tenures and wardships by laying an excise upon beer and ale to be consumed by the common people'. Agreement, then, was reached by shifting the fiscal burden from the aristocracy to the people, the profits from the feudal prerogative being replaced by a tax on consumption which, by its regressive nature, fell heavily upon the poor and lightly upon the affluent.

The subjection of the tenantry was another long process. The tenurial developments of the late middle ages had created an unrealistic situation which the landlord had to rectify or perish by accepting. As a result of the removal of serfdom and the prevalence of tenures granting fixed rents and security of tenure, the balance of advantage tilted decisively against the lord and in the tenant's favour. Essentially, a two-tiered system of landlordship was created consisting of tenancy and sub-tenancy. At the sub-tenancy level there was neither security of tenure nor customarily fixed rents, whereas at the tenancy level the restrictions upon the landlord were severe. Because of these restrictions, the aristocrat found himself excluded from the profits which his tenants made as farmers and landlords.

Pressured by inflation in the sixteenth century, the aristocracy was forced to act. Its survival as a landowning class was at stake. Barred from farming by customs of derogation, and deterred from exploiting seigneurial dues by tenant belligerence, its salvation lay in replacing the tenures with the less protective short-term, rack-rent lease. Eventually the predominant tenancy became the lease rather than the tenure. In the course of the sixteenth and seventeenth centuries, the aristocracy swept away their tenantry's traditional proprietorial rights, giving themselves a freedom of action which was only curtailed by the tenant right legislation of the twentieth century. This subjection of the tenantry was not simply the outcome of a head-on conflict between tenant and lord which happened to go in the latter's favour. Part and parcel of the revision of tenancy was the rise of agrarian capitalism. A system of tenancy freed of kinship rights was in the interests not only of landlords but also of commercial farmers bent on engrossment.

For the landlord the new relationship was both a source of profit and of tenant control. It not only allowed him to tap efficiently and simply the profits of commercial farming, but it also removed much of the tension that freehold and copyhold had generated between landlord and tenant. The tenant farmers' subservience was a fact: evident in their loyalty to landlords and their tolerance of the aristocracy's hunting activities in spite of the damage done to farming by game preservation and foxhunting. Yet this subservience cannot be explained wholly in terms of the landlord's power to rack-rent and evict. The proletariat of landless farmhands produced by commercial farming helped to persuade the tenant farmers that they and the landlords had much in common. Contact in the hunting field, indulgences to hunt game in spite of the game laws, and the possibilities of other forms of association softened the relationship. Less persuasive was the prospect of securing aristocratic status. Tenant farmers achieved a state of gentility, but because of the price of country estates, they rarely made the ranks of the gentry.

Aristocratic dominance was achieved at a time when the growth of the economy, generated by commercial farming, the expansion of trade, the wars against Louis XIV and early industrialisation, was creating massive resources of wealth outside, as well as within, the aristocratic order. Dominance involved ensnaring this non-aristocratic wealth as well as deriving financial benefit from it. The aristocracy accomplished the latter by charging economic rents on agricultural and industrial operations, by investing in government stock and by mortgaging their estates. Their success in the former owed much to the competition for status stemming from the generation of surplus wealth. In the time-honoured manner, wealthy commoners purchased estates; but increasingly they also used their wealth to purchase gentility, a quality achieved by adopting the manner of aristocracy, by receiving the right sort of education, by acquiring 'unearned income', and by gaining access to the social world of aristocracy. Formerly contained within the households of aristocrats and only accessible to their families, friends and servants, it now expanded, finding expression in the assemblies of county towns, town races, the hunting field, the London club and eventually the public school. Access was not gained on terms of equality: farmers were, for example, admitted to the hunt but not to the hunt club or the hunt ball. Yet this did not seem to matter. Admitted to a social culture which included the aristocracy, even if excluded from equal intercourse with aristocrats, commoner wealth could accept aristocratic status as something to respect, even if it could not be attained. In this sense aristocratic dominance relied upon a natural deference, sustained simply by social contiguity, as well as upon enforced subservience. It did not depend on genuine social mobility. Wealth could be converted into aristocratic status, but the bulk of it was content with something less elevated. Gentility was enough.

(d) Anti-aristocratic sentiments

(For references and further reading, see bibliography, section VIII (d).)

In the late eighteenth and early nineteenth centuries, the English aristocracy was rigorously and radically criticised. Some of the criticism repudiated the twin pillars of the old order, private landownership and hereditary distinction. Some of it doubted the aristocracy's long-accepted capacity to serve the national interest.

In 1775 Thomas Spence was expelled from the Newcastle Philosophical Society for proposing that private landownership was against nature and an act of theft. For the rest of his life he advocated a system of communal landownership which was to be realised by the people's seizure of private estates. Although overshadowed in the public mind by the ideas of Paine and the parliamentary reform movement, his idea persisted, finding expression in the works of Thomas Evans, Allen Davenport, George Petrie and Bronterre O'Brien and in the collective community schemes of Thomas Preston, Robert Owen and Goodwyn Barmby. It regained currency in the agricultural depression of the 1880s when H. M. Hyndman reprinted Spence's 1775 lecture and made land nationalisation an aim of the Social Democratic Federation and when A. R. Wallace's schemes materialised in the foundation of the Land Nationalisation Society.

The aristocracy's hereditary right to rule was powerfully questioned in Thomas Paine's *Rights of Man* (1791–2). According to Paine, 'an hereditary governor is as inconsistent as an hereditary author'. With this argument he condemned both monarchy and aristocracy. Paine had no difficulty in ridiculing the peerage and the house of lords. If hereditary legislators, he reasoned, why not hereditary mathematicians or hereditary poet laureates. If a house of landowners, why not parliamentary houses of 'brewers, or bakers or any other separate class of men'. Presenting the upper house as an institution for the defence of large landowners, he argued that, since hereditary membership rendered the house unaccountable, the only means of curing its selfishness was to secure its abolition. Having been founded on conquest, Paine argued, the aristocracy 'is still a monster' and, because it is prone to degeneration through intermarriage, it 'becomes in time the opposite of what is noble in man'. According to Paine, aristocracy was not only unnatural but also useless: its members 'neither collect the honey nor form the hive but exist in lazy enjoyment'.

Paine's writings, like those of Spence, had mostly a lower middle- and working-class appeal, in Paine's case, a very considerable one. Their views horrified the bourgeoisie as well as the aristocracy. However, by the early nineteenth century anti-aristocratic works were appearing with a middle class attraction, notably David Ricardo's *Principles of Political Economy* (1817) and James Mill's *Essay on Government* (1820). The former presented the landlord as an inevitable and harmful parasite. The latter proposed that the aristocracy was a naturally defective ruling order partly because its members were bound to act in their own, rather than in society's, interest, and partly because, having inherited their position and possessions rather than acquiring them by effort and labour, they 'would not possess intellectual powers in any very high perfection'.

This latter idea was first expressed in Godwin's *Enquiry concerning Political Justice* (1793), a work rapidly written under the spell of Paine's *Rights of Man* and the French revolution. Upon publication it enjoyed ecstatic success among young intellectuals and then suffered general condemnation in the anti-Jacobin reaction which followed news of the Terror. Eventually, it made its mark through the poems of his son-in-law, utilitarianism and English Jacobinism.

> The loathsome mask has fallen, the man remains
> Sceptreless, free, uncircumscribed, but man
> Equal, unclassed, tribeless, and nationless,
> Exempt from awe, worship, degree, the king
> Over himself: just, gentle, wise . . .

These lines from Shelley's *Prometheus Unbound* were an evocation of the explicitly anti-aristocratic chapters 10 and 11 of book five of *Enquiry Concerning Political Justice*. Godwin identified the essence of aristocracy as privilege, a monopoly of wealth and hereditary distinction, all of which he clinically condemned. Aristocracy was presented as 'in direct opposition to all sound morality'. It denied the communalty the chance to prove itself and debased the aristocracy by giving it no need to prove itself. In its stead Godwin advocated meritocracy: 'mankind will never be, in an eminent degree, virtuous and happy till each man shall possess that portion of distinction and no more, to which he is entitled by his personal merits'. He argued that 'the dissolution of aristocracy is equally the interest of the oppressor and the oppressed' since 'the one will be delivered from the listlessness of tyranny and the other from the brutalising operation of servitude'.

Capping these dismissals of aristocracy were the St Simonian ideas imparted in the 1830s by James Smith. He translated St Simon's *Nouveau Chrétianisme* which proposed that true christianity was communism, a society without degree or private property. Support or interest came again from middle-class intellectuals; but otherwise the communistic were distracted from seeking the total transformation of society by embracing schemes to establish individual communities (see below, p. 153).

At a time when industrialisation was removing much of the population from the sway of the squire, and the French revolution was inspiring anti-aristocratic beliefs, this upsurge of hostility is no surprise. But to appreciate it properly, it needs to be related to the tradition of complaint.

After all, the aristocracy had lived with criticism, scepticism and contempt for centuries. Furthermore, in the traditional manner, only a small proportion of the criticism doubted the need for an aristocracy. What is more, by 1850 it had died down, in spite of its limited gains. Once industrialised, English society proved remarkably tolerant of its old order.

(i)   *The tradition of complaint*

The people's hostility to the aristocracy in pre-industrial England is as notable as the subservience which set in as the French revolution became a distant memory and industrialisation was fully established. Its traditional capacity to question, resist and contemn the ruling order is clearly evident in the agrarian riots and rebellions of the late middle ages and the early modern period, the Leveller and Digger movements of the 1640s and the social commentary issued over the centuries in treatises, sermons and ballads.

Some of this opposition was thought to question the need for an aristocracy. In fact, the standard reaction to popular revolt was to perceive a revolution. The chronicle accounts of the peasant revolt of 1381 stressed that Wat Tyler had proposed the establishment of a society free of lordship. Faced by extensive uprisings, the duke of Somerset in August 1549 reported that 'a number would rule another while and direct things as gentlemen have done, and indeed all have conceived a wonderful hatred against gentlemen and taketh them all as their enemies'. In the previous month a Devon gentleman had informed the court that some of the western rebels 'would have no state of any gentlemen and yet to put all in one bag', and at the very start of this uprising it was alleged that men had marched through the town of Bodmin crying 'kill the gentlemen and we will have the six articles and ceremonies as they were in King Henry VIII's time'. In the same summer an uprising in Yorkshire was supposed to have featured a radical prophecy foretelling the eradication of king and nobility and their replacement by four governors and a parliament of the commons.

More's *Utopia* suggested that society would be improved if the noble estate was removed. Furthermore, a long tradition of sermons had frequently questioned the superiority of the noble order on the grounds that originally – when Adam delved and Eve span – and physically, noble and commoner were indistinguishable. In the fourteenth century, John Ball had reminded his audience of the levelled nature of pristine society and Thomas Bromyard had preached: 'If God had fashioned nobles from gold and the ignoble from mud, then the former would have cause for pride; but . . . all are of one material'. The early protestants made similar observations. Thomas Becon asserted: 'What is the body of man, cometh it of never so noble house but earth, dust and ashes' and asked: 'are not the carcasses of all personages meat fo worms alike?'

Also questioning nobility was the humanist idea, literally taken from the Greek, that true aristocracy was the rule of the virtuous rather than the rule of the ennobled and the noble-born. Thus Thomas Becon declared that 'virtue is the alone and only nobility' and that 'he with virtue is the best gentleman be his parents never so base'. Reasoning that virtue was inculcated by an academic education rather than by noble birth, he cut the aristocracy at its very root.

In the mid-seventeenth century the Levellers, Diggers, Ranters and Fifth Monarchists presented another radical challenge to aristocracy. The Levellers objected to the aristocracy's birthright to rule and the privileges of the house of lords. They challenged the aristocracy's ruling function by advocating a system of election for local officials as well as MPs in which the right to vote rested upon a personal rather than a property qualification. Power was to reside with the free-born, not the noble-born. To guard against aristocracy's misuse of this democratic system, servants and beggars were denied the vote because it was felt that they would not be able to exercise it independently. The Levellers challenged aristocratic privilege by advocating the abolition of the house of lords. They objected to peers having parliamentary membership 'by the prerogative patents of kings, not by consent and election of the people', and saw no reason why the peers should 'be less liable to any law than the gentry are'. The Levellers did not propose the complete abolition of aristocracy. Their hostility focused upon the peerage and the aristocracy's ascriptive ruling function. Nonetheless, they articulated an attack on aristocracy as a divinely appointed ruling class which, since it was contained within a programme of political reform, was quite unprecedented. What they failed to question was private landownership. This issue concerned the Diggers or New Levellers. Gerard Winstanley condemned private property as a breach of the seventh and eighth commandments 'thy shall not steal or kill'. His complaint was also against the lordship conferred by landownership. He reasoned that God had vested lordship exclusively in

man's relationship with beasts, birds and fishes: 'not one word was spoken
. . . that one branch of mankind should rule over another'. A precursor of
Spence, his solution was more pacific and less practical. Commons were to
be taken over, but Winstanley left it to the landlords to see the error of
their ways and to give their lands to the community. No previous
movement in England had proposed the end of private landownership. In
proceeding that far, Winstanley and his fellow Diggers were advocating a
society without a landed aristocracy. Although the Levellers and the New
Levellers differed fundamentally in their beliefs, both agreed that the
Norman conquest had imposed not only an absolute monarchy but also a
tyrannical aristocracy and saw no point in disposing of the one without the
other.

The Levellers and New Levellers were essentially secular; the Ranters
and Fifth Monarchists were essentially religious. Whereas the former
conceived a shorn rather than a completely abolished aristocracy, the latter
proposed a society in which no vestige of the traditional aristocracy would
be found. The Ranter, Abiezer Coppe, presented God as the mighty
leveller who would remove 'honour, nobility, gentility, propriety'. The
Fifth Monarchists were more conservative, accepting the need for social
hierarchy and private landownership, but were radical in their contempt
for the aristocracy which Christopher Feake regarded as 'an enmity against
Christ', in their belief that Christ's nobility, the elect, were superior to
'earthly kings and their nobilities' and in their assurance that the reform of
society required the destruction of its present structure.

Radical words were complemented by radical deeds. Popular revolts
occasionally featured the murder of gentlemen and the destruction of their
property. Acts of contempt developed, notably the refusal to doff the hat
in the presence of social superiors and the use of the familiar 'thou' as an
address to all and sundry. Such acts were neither created nor confined to
the Quakers. Fifteenth-century Lollards were known to practise them. By
the seventeenth century they were well established as expressions of anti-
authoritarian sentiment.

Yet how revolutionary was pre-industrial society? Much of this radical
evidence reflects upon the aristocracy's capacity to perceive the spectre of
revolution when faced by popular revolt rather than the people's capacity
to conceive revolution. A deep hostility towards gentlemen often figured
in popular disturbances but the petitions and deeds of the rebels suggest

that the existence of gentlemen was not usually in question. The objection was rather to their behaviour as royal officials and landlords. Furthermore, More's *Utopia* was playing with an idea. It was not seriously proposing a society without nobility. Rather than improving society, commentators mostly believed that to remove aristocracy would cause its dissolution. The radical preaching tradition, evident before and after the reformation, basically ordered the nobility to remember its humanity and its social and political obligations; it did not propose the nobility's abolition. Moreover, the humanist doctrine that virtue was not necessarily imparted by noble birth was effectively countered with the socially amenable belief that an educated gentleman would prove a better ruler than an educated commoner. And it never persuaded its advocates to dispense with nobility. Richard Morison accepted the doctrine but firmly and typically believed that 'lords must be lords, commons must be commons, every man accepting his degree'. Furthermore, the Levellers, the Diggers, the Ranters and the Fifth Monarchists were a temporary phenomenon. Surfacing suddenly in the late 1640s, all had petered out within a decade, apart from the Fifth Monarchists and they failed to survive beyond the 1680s. However, this does not rule out the existence of a long revolutionary tradition. The idea of a society without nobility was lodged in the mentality of pre-industrial society even though it did not surface very often and was mainly expressed by fearful aristocrats and clergy when faced with popular revolt.

Prior to industrialisation, society had no difficulty in accepting the aristocracy but found it easy to criticise its members either for failing to fulfil their obligations as rulers or for exploiting the tenantry. Treatises and sermons presented the ideal of a benevolent and public spirited aristocracy ruling wisely and dispensing charity, hospitality and paternalism. Criticism came of its failure to live up to the ideal. Aristocrats were condemned for being bad magistrates, usually because they were inclined to place profit before a concern for justice. This was a theme of the *Piers Plowman* literary tradition, founded in the fourteenth century by Langland's poem and still productive of new works in the sixteenth century. Latimer spat out: 'they are bribe-takers'. They were also criticised for spending lavishly upon themselves but not upon the community, for placing self-interest before the common good. Thomas Becon in his *Jewel of Joy* (1548) claimed that 'God's word cries out on those with so great multitudes of worldly possessions and yet make no provision for poor people, for the virtuous bringing up of youth, but spend it on gorgeous building, lusty horses, delicate fare, idle lubbers . . .'. For this sort of conduct, John Hooper, a contemporary, branded the nobility as degenerate in his *Declaration of the Ten Commandments*. Like that of the unjust magistrate, this type of complaint was a traditional one – it had featured prominently in the *Piers Plowman* poems – but for protestants it acquired an extra intensity when they saw monastic lands passing from rich clerical to rich lay worldlings. Apart from harsh landlordship, the complaint which aroused the greatest anger was the neglect of vocation. The society of orders was thought to be threatened not only by the merchant aspiring to nobility or by the peasant wishing to have all things in common but also by the commercial leanings of the aristocracy. In a bill on the decay of tillage which he submitted to Edward VI's first parliament, John Hales claimed that 'divers your grace's subjects called to the degree of nobility . . . have so much neglected their vocations that they be become graziers, sheepmasters and toilers of the earth'. Edward VI made the same point when, in attempting to define the true gentleman, he wrote: 'I mean not these farming gentlemen nor clerking knights'. Becon, in *Jewel of Joy*, denounced 'greedy gentlemen' and remarked how unnaturally high was the price of victuals and cloth 'since they began to be sheepmasters and feeders of cattle'. The neglect of vocation was an old complaint. It had featured in the preaching tradition of the fourteenth and fifteenth centuries, although then the exercise of arms was the neglected vocation and gambling and hunting were the condemned distractions.

Aristocrats were most frequently criticised as landlords. Exploitation of the tenantry was the grievance; the system of serfdom, the raising of rents, the enlargement of entry fines, the denial of common rights, the engrossing of tenancies and overstocking the common were the principal grounds of complaint. In the fourteenth century Wycliffe, a succession of preachers and William Langland in his *Vision of Piers Plowman* had all pilloried the landlord. In the mid-sixteenth century Latimer fulminated: 'You landlords, you rent raisers, I may say you steplords, you unnatural lords, you have for your possession yearly too much'. Twenty years earlier Tyndale, in *The Obedience of a Christian Man*, had more quietly advised: 'Let Christian landlords be content with their rent and old customs, not raising that rent or fines and bringing in new customs'. The anti-landlord complaint was powerfully expressed in 1536 and 1549. The December articles of the Pilgrimage of Grace (1536) called for the execution of the statute against enclosures, the protection of tenant right for specified areas in the west march and the north riding, and the maintenance of entry fines at two years rent. This was essentially a protest against the changes in tenure which were expected to follow the dissolution of the monasteries and the transference of the monastic estates to the laity. A handbill of the rebels asserted: 'claim ye old customs and tenant right, to take your farms by a God's penny, all gressoms and heightenings to be laid low'. The anti-landlord complaint surfaced again in the uprisings of 1549 just as it had been present in 1381. The raising of rents and entry fines, the conversion of customary tenures to leasehold, the infringement of common rights were all a source of objection in the petition that Ket's rebellion presented to the government. In requiring 'that all bondmen be made free', this petition distantly echoed the demand of the 1381 rebels for the removal of serfdom. No petition has survived for the 1381 revolt but criticism of the landlords was prominent in the rejection of serfdom and the demands for the reduction of seigneurial exactions and the fixing of rent at 4d per acre.

A final complaint criticised the aristocracy for acting as agent to an oppressive government. This was a well-worked theme of the Robin Hood ballads. Written and revised over several centuries, they confined their criticism of aristocracy to this particular issue. For serving as tax collectors or as magistrates enforcing unpopular laws, aristocrats were subjected to verbal and physical attack. Notably in 1537 and 1549 popular hostility to the aristocracy was extreme because of the latter's suspected collaboration with the government in enacting and imposing the Henrician and Edwardine reformations. Similarly, in 1381 aristocrats were roughly treated as tax collectors, just as, in the eighteenth century, they were abused as magistrates for failing to fix prices or for enforcing unpopular acts such as the Militia Act of 1757.

(ii)   *Complaint in the revolutionary era*
The anti-aristocratic hostility of the late eighteenth and early nineteenth centuries, then, was nothing new. Yet there were differences. Radical sentiments probably gained a freer expression in this period, especially as from the 1790s popular movements became more independent of aristocratic leadership. Traditionally, popular protest had sought aristocratic support. Its provision had helped to contain the expression of

radical sentiments. Now, in the late eighteenth century, inspired by the French revolution and incited by the alienating effects of industrialisation, popular protest acquired the ability to stand on its own feet. As late as 1836 William Lovett could state that 'a lord, an MP or an esquire was a leading requisite to secure a full attendance and attention from them (the working classes) on all public occasions', and aristocrats certainly continued to be involved in popular movements, usually in the moderating role; but, less directed by aristocrats, the repudiation of aristocracy could become a more explicit aim of popular protest.

Furthermore, the case against aristocracy became more fully elaborated. Largely due to Paine and the influence of Jacobinism, hereditary rule, the central principle of aristocracy, was frequently questioned. Opposition to aristocracy became easier to conceive as the aristocracy was seen as an interest rather than as an order with a special social and political function. With the aristocracy regarded as 'the landed interest', inevitably looking after itself and naturally incapable of caring for the rest of society, men could oppose it for being true to itself and its ideals. The criticism formerly levelled at the bourgeoisie – that it was intrinsically materialistic and selfish – could now be objected against the aristocracy. Paine was as much responsible for this change in attitude as he was for condemning hereditary rulership.

Also sustaining anti-aristocratic sentiment in the revolutionary era was a greater tendency than before to regard the aristocracy as a parasitic class. Articulated in print and widely believed, it owed something to the anti-noble sentiments voiced in revolutionary France, notably Volney's *Ruin of Civilisations* and to the influence of Paine's *Rights of Man*. Society came to be conceptually divided not in the traditional manner between rulers and ruled but between those who produced and the unproductive classes. Patrick Colquhoun's *Treatise on the Wealth, Power and Resources of the British Empire* (1814) gave statistical meaning to this view of society. Although no radical, he furnished radicals with powerful evidence for dismissing the aristocracy as harmfully useless. The aristocratic ideal of non-involvement in commercial activity, then, continued to be a major source of complaint, with the difference that traditionally aristocrats were criticised for not subscribing to it and now they were criticised for taking it to heart.

Nonetheless, in the traditional manner, a good deal of anti-aristocratic sentiment uttered in this period was non-radical. Much of the criticism was against individuals and types of aristocrat rather than against the order as a whole. Focusing upon evil ministers and corrupt officials, the rich, enclosing landlords, an unrepresentative parliament, the bulk of popular protest did not explicitly question the aristocracy's right to exist. Moreover, in keeping with tradition, it was often the spin-off of other concerns such as misgovernment, the callousness of the rich, the oppressiveness of landlords.

As well as becoming more fully articulated, radical and sustained, the opposition to the aristocracy in the late eighteenth century became less spontaneous. Riot action, marches and meetings continued to be employed, but greater use was made of the press and of parliamentary petitions. Furthermore, the opposition now sprang more dynamically from the town than from the countryside. As the major voice of popular anti-aristocratic protest, the peasant had been replaced by the artisan. In a traditional manner, largely responsible for anti-aristocratic sentiments were traditional elements in society, especially those threatened by the emergence of capitalism, but now it was the victims of industrial, rather than agrarian, capitalism. In these circumstances landlordship lost its former prominence in the corpus of anti-aristocratic complaint. Also contributing importantly to the protest was a gentry element, antagonised against the magnates by the oligarchic system of government, and a middle-class element, as fearful of democracy as the alienated gentry, but rendered temporarily critical by the belatedness of parliamentary reform and the durability of the corn laws.

(iii)   *Industrialisation and complaint*
In view of the hostility and insubordination shown towards the aristocracy in earlier times, the role of oligarchic government and the French revolution in arousing criticism, and society's relative ability to tolerate aristocracy in the late nineteenth century, it would be misleading to regard anti-aristocratic sentiment as essentially a repercussion of industrialisation. Moreover, the urban element was probably more to the fore in protesting against aristocracy in the late eighteenth and early nineteenth centuries as much because of what had happened to rural society as because of industrialisation. With the elimination of the traditional rural society of smallholders and the fading away of the seigneurial system as the basic link between landlord and tenant, a major source of anti-aristocratic

sentiment – evident, for example, in the popular disturbances of fourteenth and sixteenth century England and in France in 1789 – was removed. By the late eighteenth century peasant society in England, but for some regional exceptions, had been replaced by a society of large commercial farmers and a landless agricultural work force. Such a society was much less capable than a peasant society of focusing its social hatred upon the aristocratic landlord. Labourers could revile aristocrats for denying them rights of common and, as magistrates, for implementing offensive laws such as the New Poor Law, but hatred tended to spark between farmer and farmhand rather than between the rural population and the aristocracy. Rural militancy was rife but, in contrast to France where peasants rose against their lords, in England workers rose against their employers, the tenant farmers. In England the conflict became one of class, fought between a middle class and a proletariat. The issue was not so much rents or labour services as wages and employment (and, to some extent, foraging rights). In this respect, the development of class conflict in the countryside ensured that the aristocracy, which mostly retained its traditional role as landlord, was not the main target of popular protest. Frightened by the threat from their employees into a close alliance with the landlords, and subjected to rent rather than seigneurial exactions, the farmers tended to remain subservient to the aristocracy. The cases of opposition, aroused usually by religious differences between lord and tenant, the exaction of tithes, insecurity of tenure, rights of common, the enforcement of the game laws, the depredations of fox-hunting, the damage done to crops by game reared for coursing or shooting and the survival of seigneurial exactions, were not sufficient to produce in England a war against the landlord equivalent to the one waged at that time in France and other parts of Europe.

In the industrial towns, the development of factory production had a similar effect, generating social conflict between employers and employees from which the aristocracy was removed by its steadfast refusal to indulge in commercial activity. On the other hand, traditional urban elements, notably artisans and shopkeepers, became susceptible to the anti-aristocratic sentiments generated by the objection to oligarchy and the French revolution because their way of life was threatened by industrial capitalism, and they reacted in a manner similar to the peasantry of earlier centuries who had complained bitterly of landlords for allowing agrarian capitalism its head.

(iv)   *Oligarchy and complaint*

Central to the anti-aristocratic sentiments expressed in the late eighteenth century was the establishment of the venetian oligarchy of great landowners and its blatant favouritism of the aristocratic interest. Since this oligarchy was upheld by an unresponsive parliamentary system, a reform movement flourished from the 1760s, sustained by a hatred of oligarchy rather than a belief in democracy, and supported by elements from the whole range of society. By the 1790s the movement had become genuinely popular and was capable of proposing, in the Leveller manner, a system of representation resting upon a manhood franchise. It did not wish to deny aristocracy but aimed to protect society from aristocratic exploitation and misrule. The slowness with which parliament was reformed – proposed in the 1760s but only modestly applied sixty years later and with manhood suffrage not achieved until 1884 – maintained a torrent of criticism which fell upon the aristocracy because they clearly dominated not only the house of lords but also the Commons. But, because the aim was to reform the parliamentary system, the grievance held against aristocracy was not its very existence but the fact that royal absolutism had been replaced by aristocratic absolutism.

Society's hostility towards the aristocracy was caused not simply by the oligarchy's monopoly of power but also the selfish and irresponsible way in which this power was exercised. The Corn Laws of 1815 completed a statutory development which transformed a system of regulation designed to favour the consumer to one that instead favoured the producer: in place of the traditional ban on the export of corn, in 1689 bounties were paid on exported corn while in 1815 the sale of corn imports was forbidden unless the price on the home market exceeded a certain level. Clearly designed to uphold the price of corn, these regulations were easily seen as evidence that the landowners were using their domination of parliament to favour themselves at the community's expense. They aroused a massive middle-class opposition which, until the repeal of the corn laws in 1846, held strong, anti-aristocratic views. Incensing society were not only new laws (the rigorous game laws enacted in the eighteenth century, the Combination Acts of 1799 and 1800, the Acts against Sedition of 1792 and 1795, the New Poor Law of 1834) but also the removal of certain old laws. Artisans complained bitterly in the opening years of the nineteenth century about the non-enforcement of statutes regulating wages and the

Apprentices Act of 1563. Parliament's perverse response was to abolish this legislation. The oligarchy's support for a policy of *laissez faire* rather than of paternalism confirmed popular suspicions that a sense of responsibility and a concern for the common good no longer accompanied the possession of power.

(v) *Religion and complaint*

Anti-aristocratic sentiment in the late eighteenth century depended heavily upon a tradition of social protest closely connected with religion. The connection preceded the reformation in the form of a millenarianism which branded the nobility as part of the covetous rich and threatened them with doom on the day of judgement. Although deeply respectful of the social structure, Lollardy presented lordship as an obligation as well as a right, the non-fulfilment of which justified the withholding of rents and services. Much of the social radicalism of industrial England stemmed from the reformation and the sectarianism that followed. The protestant desire to regain the purity of the early christians made a major contribution to the history of radicalism, even if it had little effect upon the protestant way of life. The doctrine of the elect erected a counter hierarchy, Christ's nobility as opposed to the king's nobility. In declaring that 'a Nation is more beholding to the meanest kitchen maid in it that hath a spirit of prayer, than to a thousand of her profane, swaggering gentry', the Fifth Monarchist pamphlet *Failing and Perishing* was only putting in extreme form a commonly held sectarian view of society. Calvinism's appreciation of the election of ministers by the congregation, the studied contempt for the social hierarchy evident in the Quaker refusal to doff the hat and their insistence upon 'thouing', the communal practices of Anabaptists and sects such as the Sandemanians, the principle of consent central to the beliefs of the Baptists, the disbelief in original sin (held by Ranters, Socinians, Antinomians, Familists, Grindletonians) or the belief in an earthly perfectibility (held by Fifth Monarchists, Anabaptists, some Mortalists) which no longer allowed aristocratic overlordship to be justified as a necessary device for containing the sinfulness of man, all produced a social outlook which was bound to be critical of the old order. This outlook was impressed upon society not only by what sectarians said and wrote but also by authority's reiterated fears of what heretics intended. Its repertoire of social criticism was kept alive by the development of dissent in the seventeenth and eighteenth centuries, in spite of the dissenter tendency to seek respectability in social conformity and notwithstanding the inclination of dissenting movements with a radical social outlook to merge with movements which, in the manner of orthodox Methodism or Quakerism, presented salvation as a process of reform within the existing social framework. Thomas Paine, notably, was the son of a Quaker, and Thomas Spence and William Godwin were reared in Sandemanian households. Moreover, both the Levellers and the Diggers had close sectarian ties.

(vi) *Political revolution and complaint*
Industrialisation may have made people more susceptible to radical ideas, but the ideology of radicalism was created independently of it: first, because of a revolutionary folk tradition, secondly as a long-term consequence of the reformation, a realisation of the traditional fear that heresy and revolutionary ideas went hand-in-hand; and thirdly, on account of the contribution made by the American and French revolutions. The republicanism of the former, especially as it was presented through the filter of Paine's *Common Sense* and his *Rights of Man*, sowed doubts about the hereditary rule of aristocrats as well as of kings. Furthermore, by 1791 the French revolutionaries had totally repudiated nobility. Their emphasis upon *egalité* as well as *liberté* inspired English popular protest in the 1790s to conceive a society without a formal hierarchy of status; and the removal of the French monarchy in 1792 recharged English republicanism. Jacobinism survived for twenty or more years in England, directing popular protest against the aristocratic order. Yet it formed only one strand of protest and its appeal was countered by the force of patriotism, by a strong reaction against the free-thinking republicanism of revolutionary France and by an abiding faith in constitutional rather than revolutionary reform. The reaction against the French revolution and the waning of its influence allowed popular protest in England to become less socially defined: the rich rather than the aristocracy became the specific target of complaint. The tendency of social complaint to overlook the aristocracy was promoted by the process of industrialisation which made the large-scale capitalist the villain of the piece. In this respect, industrialisation worked contrary to the French revolution and very much in the old order's interest.

What is remarkable about this period of intense and sometimes radical social criticism is its limited effect upon the aristocracy as a privileged ruling class. The extension of the parliamentary franchise eventually made the government more answerable to the nation and put paid to oligarchic rule, but in 1850 the aristocracy still retained its virtual monopoly of private landownership, its privileges and its political dominance. Whatever winds ruffled the surface, there remained, as in the past, a strong undertow of social deference and subservience. Throughout this troubled time, the aristocracy could rely upon respect and loyalty not only from the propertied and the rich who felt similarly threatened by the masses, but also from the working classes and the lower middle class. Popular movements were capable of opposing, as well as promoting, radicalism. In the 1790s the radicals were hunted down by church and king mobs as well as by a repressive, aristocratic government. The people abhorred, as well as revered, Thomas Paine. Popular reform societies multiplied in the 1790s but so did branches of the John Reeves' Association which aimed to preserve 'liberty and property against republicans and levellers'. Furthermore, withstanding the ideology of the French revolution was England's own revolutionary tradition. Much of the radicalism of the time was moved by it. Having been shaped by aristocratic revolt, it emphasised liberty rather than equality. 'Hunt and liberty'; 'Bread and liberty': the radical slogans of the period looked to the English past rather than across the Channel. The predominant issue imparted by this tradition was not the injustice of an hierarchical society determined by birthright but the tyranny of government, in this case the tyranny of an oligarchy which appeared to have usurped the powers of royal absolutism. In England the message of the French revolution was obstructed by the prevalence of a native revolutionary ideology.

A major problem for the English Jacobins was to overcome the force of patriotism. One solution was to present their cause as the restoration of a democracy which, having existed in Anglo-Saxon times, had been snuffed out by the Normal conquest. In this way, implementing the French revolution in England could be presented as a rejection of the French ways imposed in 1066. However, the idea of the Norman yoke, very much part of the English revolutionary tradition, had been predominantly used to safeguard the subject's liberty against an encroaching Crown. For this reason, it was not so easily adapted to question the need for an aristocracy.

When the Levellers and the Diggers had used it, it was to oppose a tyrannical aristocracy rather than to abolish degree. In fact, a denial of aristocracy, like the advocacy of republicanism, could be regarded as a treasonable pact with the country's ancient enemy, especially since both the American and French revolutions coincided with wars between England and France.

Benefiting the English aristocracy was not only the exclusion of a revolutionary ideology by one already in existence, but also the displacement of one by another form of radicalism. As conceived by the Levellers, Paine, the aged John Cartwright and Jeremy Bentham the establishment of democracy involved the destruction of the house of lords. Yet the emphasis placed upon reforming the electoral franchise in the early nineteenth century steered attention away from the upper house, directing it solely upon the Commons. Moreover, in the course of the nineteenth century, the idea of land nationalisation was to be squeezed out by other, less radical schemes for the abolition of primogeniture, the prohibition of strict settlements, a land value tax, the compulsory registration of land titles, leasehold enfranchisement, the preservation of common rights, the creation of co-operative farms and the recreation of societies of small landowners. By the 1840s radicalism was dominated by the Chartist movement which not only failed to question the need for the house of lords but also found the extension of private landownership to wider sections of society preferable to its complete abolition.

Also upholding aristocracy was the particularism of many radical schemes of social reform. Influenced by Robert Owen, social radicalism was dominated by the desire to establish little Edens, colonies of perfection, in which christian brotherhood was practised and men co-operated rather than competed, and communally shared rather than individually accumulated. Thus communities were planned and sometimes founded in which aristocracy had no place, while the aristocracy was allowed to dominate unchallenged society at large. In the 1830s the St Simonians led by James Smith opposed this trend of radicalism, condemning small-scale co-operative communities and advocating the establishment of one, all-embracing society which practised the community of goods and equality; but they failed to stem it. It seemed more English, and certainly more pragmatic, to found the occasional community than to establish a communist state.

(vii)   *Industrial versus political revolution*

Industrialisation created a world alien to the aristocracy yet, in certain respects, it assisted its survival. In producing a massive proletariat, industrialisation persuaded the middle classes to accept the old order as a buffer against tyranny of the propertyless. In middle-class eyes, the aristocracy was needed, in its ancient role as defender of liberty and property, not to safeguard against royal absolutism but the arbitrary rule of the masses which democracy seemed to sanction. Along with the Reform Act of 1832 and the repeal of the corn laws, industrialisation healed the differences between the aristocracy and the middle class which had developed under Jacobin influence and in reaction to oligarchic rule. Industrialisation helped the aristocracy to weather the storms of working-class protests, first by ensuring that large parts of the population lived in societies where aristocrats hardly figured. The aristocracy's traditional urban connections had only been with certain types of town, notably seats of central and provincial government such as London, York, Norwich and Exeter. However, since, prior to industrialisation, the bulk of the urban population had inhabited this type of town, urban as well as rural society had been very much dominated by an aristocratic presence. In contrast, industrialisation caused the massive growth of towns in which aristocrats had never cared to live, towns with no more than a manufacturing or trading function. As a result, in maintaining the people's capacity to tolerate aristocracy, a weight of indifference was added to the weight of traditional deference. Secondly, the reconstruction of urban society by industrial capitalism, rather like agrarian capitalism's reorganisation of rural society, helped the aristocracy to survive by removing it from the arena of social conflict. As mine and dock owners, aristocrats could bear the brunt of proletarian attack, but rarely did they own factories or operate mines. Removing them from the basic social conflict of industrialised society – essentially a struggle between employee and employer – was their rentier character.

As the nineteenth century wore on, society's anti-aristocratic complaints quietened. Admitted to the franchise and their grievances remedied, the middle classes easily reached a *modus vivendi* with the old order, while working-class criticism was directed elsewhere by the development of a class conflict within the third estate. This does not mean that criticism of aristocracy ceased. Notably in the 1880s and until the first world war, hostility raged in town and countryside. The corporations of industrial towns were critical of the local landlords, especially as the termination of ninety-nine year leases allowed the rent to be raised, and over seigneurial rights of market and the aristocracy's ownership of urban facilities such as docks and water works. Arguably, this was in a long tradition. It resembled, for example, the tiffs between the Russells and the city of Exeter in the sixteenth century. Furthermore, conflict in the countryside occurred in the circumstances of an agricultural depression, especially following the Napoleonic war and in the closing decades of the century. Tension flared into open hostility on the issue of rents, impropriated tithes and, in the late nineteenth century, leasehold enfranchisement and wire and barbed wire fences.

Radical hostility also gained a new lease of life from the 1880s. The Social Democratic Federation backed both the abolition of the Lords and land nationalisation, as did the Independent Labour Party. Inspired by Alfred Russel Wallace, a Land Nationalisation Society was founded in 1888 which in 1906 claimed the support of 130 MPs. The ideas of Ricardo were given a new life and popularity with the publication of Henry George's *Progress and Poverty* (1879), and advocacy, notably by Liberals, for the imposition of a land value tax. Although an opponent of private landownership, George was prepared to tolerate it on condition that land rents (calculated on an economic valuation) were appropriated by the state through a system of taxation. The land value tax movement castigated the aristocracy as receivers of unearned income and proposed punitive taxation. However, with little radical effect. Of greater impact upon the aristocracy was not root and branch radicalism but a hostility which merely insisted upon a reformed aristocracy.

(viii)   *Government criticism of aristocracy*
As well as favouring the aristocratic order, governments had often proceeded against its interests especially when they were seen to be handicapping the Crown. Thus attempts were made to curtail the aristocracy's franchisal and seigneurial rights in the middle ages, to maximise the Crown's feudal income under the Tudors and early Stuarts and, in the early modern period, to increase the Crown's authority in local government. But government hostility also had a broader, less self-interested motive. The tillage legislation of the sixteenth century, an

attempt to prevent landlords from destroying the traditional rural society by promoting large-scale commercial farms, was concerned with the defences of the realm and the spread of vagabondage.

After a period of acquiescence, government hostility to the aristocratic interest was reborn in the nineteenth century: aroused by the intractability of the house of lords to the extension of the franchise, the Corn Laws issue, the need to develop a professional administration and a feeling that the landed interest should be more heavily taxed. The antipathy towards corruption, a long-term reaction to the oligarchic rule of the eighteenth century, eventually produced the Northcote–Trevelyan report on civil service reform in 1854. The widening of the franchise indicated not so much government hostility to aristocracy as the need to comply with popular demands and to admit the irrationality of the old system, but the abolition of proprietary military office (1871) and the attempt to introduce a civil service based on merit rather than patronage represented the establishment of a professional rather than an aristocratic *esprit de corps* in government circles, especially if they were Liberal, which, in a long tradition, was not against aristocracy but only some of its practices. Liberal hostility to aristocracy was intensified by the pressure of events, notably the need to respond to the peasant agitation of the 1880s in the Hebrides and Ireland, its rift with the Lords over Home Rule and the 1909 budget, and the impact of individuals, especially Gladstone, Joseph Chamberlain and Lloyd George, but it also stemmed from a belief in the need for land reform, set afoot in the early 1880s and powerfully supported by Lloyd George between 1909 and 1914. The concern was stated by Campbell-Bannerman in 1905: 'we wish to make the land less of a pleasure ground for the rich and more of a treasure house for the nation'. The intention was to improve tenant security, to establish a land value tax as well as to reform the rating system by transferring the rebates on undeveloped land to cultivated land and by ensuring that, in accordance with Tax on Land Values doctrine, rates fell upon site ownership, and, in a bid for the rural vote, to restrict both the minimum wage for farm work and the rents exacted of the farmers by the landlords. Land nationalisation did not figure, but within the Liberal Party was a strong animus against the aristocracy because of the way in which it managed its estates. The decay of rural society, as farms were converted to game reserves, and urban decay, as rents were enlarged and rebuilding was sluggish, were both seen as the responsibility of the aristocratic landlord. Land reform, however, was not a convincing vote-catcher in a largely urbanised society and therefore tended to be given a back seat. The dismal fate of Lloyd George's land reform campaign of 1913–14 was the fate of the land nationalisation projects associated with the Labour Party. In this respect, industrialisation not only helped to persuade the people to accept aristocracy but also made governments tolerant of its wealth and privileges (for further evidence of government attitudes, see ch. 9 (d)).

Notes to Chapter 8

1. That is, with the exception of the court of delegates, whose final appeal jurisdiction was restricted to ecclesiastical and admiralty cases, and appeals from overseas courts which continued to be heard by the privy council.

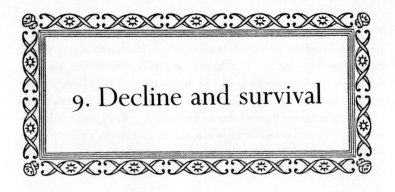

9. Decline and survival

In an industrial and democratic society the decline of aristocracy was a foregone conclusion. Distinguishing the process in England was the postponement of the inevitable. In spite of the preference for elective rather than ascriptive authority, the replacement of the amateur code of values by the professional ethic, the supplanting of private charity by the welfare state, the English aristocracy not only survived but also retained some of its social and political importance: a testament of its capacity to outlive its *raison d'être*. (For reference and further reading, see bibliography, section IX.)

(a) The course of survival

Survival has had two meanings for the English aristocracy. One applies to much of the nineteenth century. It denotes the preservation of a traditional life-style, privileges and political dominance in an increasingly alien world. The other largely concerns the twentieth century and follows the loss of most of its traditional characteristics. Its emphasis is upon self-preservation: the aristocracy's ability to avoid extinction.

In the late nineteenth century, the English aristocracy still retained a firm grip on the political system. As late as 1865 it held seventy-four per cent of the seats in the Commons. As late as 1887 it occupied eighty-eight per cent of the seats on the magistrate's bench. As JPs aristocrats exercised a broad administrative, as well as judicial, authority in local government. Moreover, as late as the 1870s and 1880s it held the majority of cabinet posts and remained firmly entrenched in the upper ranks of the civil service, the army and the church. Although the occasional privilege was abolished or debased, there was nothing to resemble the massive repudiation of privilege which, on the Continent, followed the revolutions of 1789 and 1848: in England seigneurial rights as well as the privileges of peerage and baronetcy outlived the nineteenth century. In 1900 the aristocracy remained the major owner of private land in England and, in the traditional manner, derived the bulk of its resources from rent. Until the twentieth century these resources allowed the average aristocrat to maintain an extravagant life-style without the need to participate in commercial activities. In sharp contrast, the fortunes of most continental nobilities seriously declined in the nineteenth century, even though only the Norwegian nobility had been permanently abolished by 1900; even though the traditional agrarian society endured in much of Europe, and even though government land reforms left the nobility owning much of the land. The actions of revolutionaries and the concessions of counter-revolution swept much away: privileges became vestigial and, as landowners, members of parliament and office-holders, commoners came to rival the nobility. In England, oligarchic rule went in the early nineteenth century, undermined by the 1780s reform of office, which limited the means at the executive's disposal for winning parliamentary support by patronage, and by the electoral reforms of the 1830s which ruled out the management of parliament by bribery. What persisted, however, was a political system dominated by aristocrats and aristocratic values.

By 1950 most European states had disposed of their nobilities. In much of eastern Europe the great estate had also gone, the victim either of land nationalisation or land redistribution. The surviving continental nobilities were no more than social elites, often little more than a segment of the bourgeoisie distinguished only by the honorific attributes of armorial bearings and titles. In contrast, the survival of the house of lords has maintained for the English aristocracy a special political role. Until 1911 the consent of the Lords remained essential for the enactment of all but money bills. For this reason, a crucial part of the legislative process was not answerable to the electorate. Whilst the Parliament Act of 1911 freed most legislation of this undemocratic constraint, it left the Lords with considerable legislative authority. Its consent even remained necessary for a bill aiming to extend the maximum duration of Parliament beyond five years. The Lords also retained an authority to initiate legislation and to amend Commons bills; the latter enforceable through certain delaying powers. Thus, enactment could only occur in the absence of the Lords' consent if a bill was passed by the Commons in three successive sessions (amended to two in 1949). Since the act of 1911 left the Lords with considerable legislative authority, the peerage's privileges retained political as well as honorific value. Elsewhere in Europe, by 1920 the surviving privileges of nobility denoted no more than status or rank.

By 1950 the English aristocracy's political dominance had certainly vanished, but its influence persisted. The aristocracy's membership of the Commons declined steeply in the last three decades of the nineteenth century. However, although it had dwindled to 32 per cent of the membership in 1874, a clear consequence of the 1867 Reform Act and the Secret Ballot Act of 1872, it remained at twelve per cent in 1918 and as high as 4.5 per cent in 1950. The cabinet, moreover, continued to contain large numbers of lords. Until 1895, aristocrats by birth formed the majority of every cabinet; and the aristocratic presence remained strong until 1906. Thereafter, aristocrats tended to occupy only a minority of cabinet posts but, nonetheless, a number grossly disproportionate to their size. Thus, between 1916 and 1935, the cabinet membership consisted of twenty-five aristocrats against eighty-three commoners. Between 1935 and 1955 the ratio was 21:78. And there were certain cabinets, notably the Churchill ministry of 1952, the cabinet formed in November 1956 and the Thatcher cabinet of 1979 which were heavily endowed with peers, baronets and gentry. Aristocrats in the twentieth century also continued to hold prestigious and important offices, especially in the fields of foreign and imperial affairs. For example, the first commoner to hold the office of foreign secretary was Ramsay MacDonald who combined it with the premiership in 1923. Its tenure by Lord Halifax between 1937 and 1940, by the fourteenth earl of Home between 1970 and 1973 and by Lord Carrington between 1979 and 1982 marked the endurance of a long tradition. Furthermore, the first landless prime minister was not appointed until 1908.

Eventually, the English aristocracy became part of a social elite which also incorporated a bourgeoisie of business and professional men. Yet within that elite it retained a superior position. Massive land sales followed the first world war and, as landowners, the aristocracy was hard hit by the long decline of rents and land values, a process started in the 1870s and only stopped after the second world war. Nonetheless, the aristocracy remained closely associated both with the ownership of large estates and the possession of great wealth. Changes in the aristocracy's spending habits and display of wealth followed the first world war: the lavish establishments in town and country disappeared, the great London houses converted into hotels, the large social gatherings evident in the surviving country seats now consisting of visitors organised by the National Trust rather than the house guests of a lord. The aristocracy became less vulgar than formerly in its display of wealth and less prone to use its riches to finance wasteful extravagance. However, relative to the rest of society, the English aristocracy did not become impoverished as a social group. Many of its members, especially peers and baronets, remained a part of the rich. Several families even preserved the traditional aristocratic way of life until the second world war when heavy taxation and the absence of servants delivered the *coup de grâce*.

These generalisations, arguably, more readily apply to the peerage and the baronetcy than to the gentry. Undermined by the commoner assumption of gentry privileges and the depression of land rents and values from the 1870s, the gentry proved less able than the peerage and baronetcy to maintain social distinction. In fact, the history of the gentry in the nineteenth and twentieth centuries – marked by an emphatic decline – seems closely in accordance with the continental pattern. But significant differences existed since the decline of the gentry was not the direct result of government policy, and the people contributed to its decline not by revolutionary action but by assuming gentry privileges, by failing to furnish replacements for falling gentry families and by fragmenting the large estates through converting farm tenancies to freeholds by an act of purchase. After 1900 the capacity to survive was most evident in the peerage and baronetcy. Their position was seriously challenged only in the late twentieth century, notably by the failure of governments in the late 1960s and 1970s to grant hereditary titles. However, prior to 1965, hereditary peerages and baronetcies were granted in profusion, and after 1965 honours continued to be dispensed in the form of personal titles (life peerages and knighthoods); while no serious attempt has been made either to abolish the house of lords or to confiscate existing titles. Hereditary titles were even restored in the 1980s as a form of government patronage.

A process of decline has clearly been at work. It featured the end of oligarchy in the early nineteenth century, the transference of the Lords appellate jurisdiction to a committee of law lords, the fading away of the gentry in the late nineteenth and early twentieth centuries – a process which converted the hereditary aristocracy into a peerage and a baronetcy –, a general bourgeoisification, the demotion of the Lords' legislative powers in 1911 and, from the late 1960s, the ossification of the hereditary peerage and baronetcy through the virtual absence of new creations. Yet countering this decline was a process of survival, reflected in the aristocracy's capacity to retain a political ascendancy in the nineteenth century and the peerage's capacity to retain political influence in the late twentieth century. How did the English aristocracy survive the immediate impact of industrialisation and democracy? And why did it have greater staying powers as a political elite than its continental counterparts?

(b) The wealth factor

In *Lark Rise to Candleford*, an account of rural life in Oxfordshire in the 1880s, Flora Thompson described a gentry family on the way down. The Bracewells, an unmarried son and a lordly mother, occupied the manor house, expected the local inhabitants to defer to them as if they were royalty and dispensed charity although known to be 'poor as crows'. Of the mother, she wrote:

> As the old servants in and about her house died or were pensioned off, they were not replaced. Only a cook and a house parlour maid sat down to meals in the vast servant's hall where a large staff had formerly feasted. Grass grew between the flagstones in the stable yard where generations of grooms and coachmen had hissed over the grooming of hunters and carriage horses, and the old mare which drew her wagonette when she paid calls took a turn at drawing the lawn mower, or even the plough.

As for the squire, he

> took his responsibilities less seriously than his mother did hers; spending most of his days roaming the fields and spinneys with a gun under his arm and a brace of spaniels at his heels, leaving her to manage . . . what was left of the family estate . . . His one indoor accomplishment was playing the banjo and singing negro songs.

Aristocratic families of this sort were not peculiar to late nineteenth-century England. The novels of Gogol, Verga and De Montherlant portray a variety of minor nobles caught in the same poverty trap. Moreover, in earlier times the poor noble was as prominent a feature as the rich noble of most European nobilities, the result of the transmission of substantial corporate privileges to everyone of noble birth and either the partible inheritance of estates, which led to their successive fragmentation, or systems of inheritance which heavily favoured the eldest son. So long as the corporate privileges retained significance, the poor noble was in no danger of denoblement unless the government intervened. In contrast, the poor aristocrat in England stood much less chance of retaining his noble status, especially if he was of the gentry. As the scarcity of corporate rights and their assumption by commoners rendered the maintenance of a noble way of life an essential ingredient of the gentry's identity, impoverishment easily questioned its members' aristocratic credentials. For this reason the English aristocracy was more likely than continental nobilities to be a plutocracy, especially since demotion by poverty was countered by the ability of the wealthy to acquire aristocratic status through the purchase of a suitable estate and the adoption of an apposite life-style. However, between the 1870s and the mid-twentieth century poverty among the gentry occurred on a devastating scale. The Bracewells became fairly typical. Moreover, the traditional compensation of members of the middle classes rising into the gentry ceased to happen. Basically at fault were falling rents and land values. Both stemmed from the competition of foreign farm products. The price of English wool began to fall after 1864 under the impact of Australian sheep farming. The introduction of refrigerated ships from 1891 brought down the price of mutton and beef. Bad harvests in England between 1874 and 1890 acted, in conjunction with an influx of cheap American wheat, to depress English arable farming. Although rents recovered in the first world war as the demand for supplies restored agricultural profits, they continued to decline in the 1920s and 1930s. Falling rents reduced the aristocracy's disposable income while falling land values reduced its credit worthiness.

The damage done by the fall in landed incomes was compounded by an increase in the aristocracy's fiscal liability, notably between the budgets of 1909 and 1919. Not only was the assessment rate of income tax raised and a minerals tax enacted (1909) but a tax on capital, the estate duty, was introduced in 1889 and enlarged between 1894 and 1919 from a maximum rate of eight per cent to one of forty per cent.[1] In addition, in 1909, a special tax on the landed, the supertax, was imposed. Although lacking the privilege of fiscal exemption, the English aristocracy had been favoured over the centuries by a system which relied heavily upon regressive taxes on consumption and direct levies that taxed income rather than wealth. In response to these fiscal reforms, the rich eventually turned tax evasion into a fine art. However, for a time the increased liability badly affected an already reeling aristocracy. Hit by the failure of farming, the aristocracy followed the obvious course and sought to diversify the investment of its capital resources. Traditionally its capital had been sunk in property or government stock. Now, in the closing years of the nineteenth century the aristocracy also invested in commerce and banking and to a much lesser extent in manufacturing, frequently selling land to raise the capital for the purchase of shares. Diversification allowed aristocrats to survive comfortably and wealthily, even as landowners, but rarely in the manner to which their forebears were accustomed. Those who retained estates were driven to abandon the traditional ritual of ostentation and wasteful consumption. The gentry families who were forced to sell their estates lost their badge of aristocratic status. The gentry families with estates which were too small to allow capital to be raised from their partition had the choice of selling the whole of their estate or of farming it. Both courses were damaging to their aristocratic status since it was difficult to distinguish landless gentry and gentlemen farmers from the commonalty. Falling rents, moreover, forced the lesser gentry to become engaged full-time in the making of money. Unless they became professional politicians, administrators or soldiers, survival involved an abdication of traditional functions. Falling rents, then, not only caused a massive demotion of gentry into the commonalty, a loss which was final since the fallen families were not replaced by elevated commoners, but also enforced radical changes upon the life-style of those aristocrats who managed to preserve their noble identity (thanks either to the possession of a peerage, a baronetcy or an estate).

Landownership remained a poor investment until the late twentieth century. Accompanied by the pressures of the estate duty, tenant right legislation and the fears of further punitive government action caused a massive retreat from rentier landownership. Large-scale land sales occurred notably after the first world war when, within the space of three or four years, one quarter of England changed hands. Some aristocrats merely sold off parts of their estates, but their tendency to invest the capital realised from land sales in stocks and shares helped to break their traditional dependence upon land rent. Moreover, the estates which were sold were frequently purchased by tenant farmers and therefore lost to the aristocracy for good. In a desperate attempt to retain a connection with the land and to benefit from tax relief, aristocrats also retreated into direct farming, in spite of its lack of profitability. The extent to which land sales or direct farming occurred at the expense of rentier landownership is measurable in the changing proportion of farm land cultivated by the owner rather than the tenant. In 1888 it stood at 15.4 per cent. By 1908 it had fallen to 12.3 per cent, presumably because landowners had temporarily switched back to tenant farming sensing that the worst of the depression was over, but by 1927 thirty-six per cent of cultivated land was owner-occupied. Tenant farming made no further come-backs. Only sustaining it was the institutional ownership of land, massively extended in the mid-twentieth century with the land acquisitions of the Forestry Commission, the National Trust and finance and insurance companies. Owner occupation accounted for thirty-eight per cent of farm land in 1950 and fifty per cent in 1965.

The degree to which survival necessitated a complete break with landownership is evident in the emergence of the landless aristocrat. Although frequently found on the Continent, they were rarely evident in England before the twentieth century. Bending with the times, Burke's *Landed Gentry* from 1914 admitted landless gentry families on condition that their escutcheons were recognised by the College of Heralds. By 1937, one third of its families were landless. Moreover, by 1956 only one third of the peerage possessed estates. Encouraging landlessness was not only the need to sell, but also the disappearance of a demand for, aristocratic estates. Over the centuries estates put on the market had passed into aristocratic, or imminently aristocratic, hands. For this reason land sales had exerted no profound effect upon the aristocracy as a landed order. Yet from the closing years of the nineteenth century, this ceased to be the case since aristocratic estates tended to be sold piecemeal to the tenantry. By the mid-twentieth century they were being bought by institutions such as the National Trust, insurance companies, unit trusts and pension funds. Furthermore, the newcomers to aristocracy, profusely admitted in the early twentieth century through the grant of peerages, baronetcies and

knighthoods, were not under the traditional compulsion to possess a
tenanted estate. For the most part their landownership was merely the
parkland girding a country house, or a substantial garden attached to a
country cottage, or a farm. The country houses bought by the newly
ennobled were rural retreats rather than foci of authority and dependence.
Furthermore, the houses of aristocrats, new and old, ceased in the early
twentieth century to be communities in the traditional manner. In
describing Oxfordshire society, Flora Thompson remarked: 'in the large
country houses around lived squires and baronets and lords who employed
armies of indoor servants, gardeners and estate workers'. Between the first
and second world wars these armies of employees disappeared as the need
for economy and the cost and scarcity of labour made service on the old
scale totally impractical. If the decline of aristocracy essentially involved
the abandonment of traditional characteristics, the pressures brought
upon it by the long-term failure of farming in the late nineteenth and early
twentieth centuries were of vital importance, bringing the gentry down
and subjecting the remaining aristocracy to an irresistable process of
embourgeoisement.

Nevertheless, the surviving aristocracy remained part of a plutocracy
whose wealth was preserved by the government's concentration upon
alleviating poverty rather than disposing of the rich. Furthermore, the
generous ennobling policy of governments in the early twentieth century
and their inclination to honour the affluent, injected considerable wealth
into the aristocracy. Having the same effect was the eventual appreciation
of the old aristocracy's capital assets. Those that retained their estates
benefited from the recovery of land values after 1945. This recovery
became spectacular in the 1960s and 1970s as speculation fever and the
policy of city institutions to invest in land bumped up its price. Whereas
the average price of rural land had risen by only £3 per acre between 1876
and 1950, in 1970 it had risen by £147 per acre and in 1974 by £547 per acre.
In the same period the bric-a-brac of country houses became a fertile
source of capital. Furthermore, since aristocrats had no difficulty in
gaining access to the public schools, Oxford and Cambridge – on account
of their wealth and social prestige – the way was educationally paved for
attaining high-ranking positions. The Fleming Commission of 1944
revealed that the public schools had educated three quarters of a sample of
top officials in the national and imperial civil services, of bishops, judges,

directors of banks and railway companies, with one half of the public school contingent coming from schools with a strong aristocratic preference. Little change had taken place ten years later, in spite of the Education Act of 1944. Public schooling also produced the preponderance of MPs. In the 1950s and 1960s, a period when no more than three per cent of school children were privately educated, three quarters of Conservative MPs and one half of the Commons' membership were from the public schools. In occupying these offices, aristocrats were essentially acting as professional politicians, professional administrators, professional lawyers and businessmen. Their behaviour was bourgeois rather than aristocratic, and they competed for office not simply with other aristocrats but mostly with commoners. However, thanks to the restricted pool of recruitment, and the access conferred by a prestigious school and university education, it was not difficult, for those who tried, to exercise the public functions which their forebears would have claimed by natural right.

(c)   The failure of revolution

The English aristocracy's survival owed much to the inability of popular anti-aristocratic sentiment to force the government to take radical action. On the Continent revolutionary movements between 1789 and 1848 fixed upon noble privilege as the outstanding social evil. As a result, the nobility rather than the rich came under attack. Both revolutionary and counter-revolutionary governments proceeded against it, the former in order to apply a revolutionary programme, the latter to prevent revolutionaries from securing mass support. Aristocrats could survive this sort of repudiation but not in their traditional form. In this respect, political revolution was a central fact in their decline. In England the only political revolutions to occur were the work of aristocrats, and served to increase the aristocracy's control of the political system.

On the Continent the downfall of nobility owed much to the revolutions of 1789, 1848 and 1917–18, all of which depended upon a standard set of political and social circumstances. In the first place, they were reactions against royal absolutism. Although radicals in late eighteenth-century England presented the government as absolutist, it differed quite fundamentally from the absolutist monarchies of the Continent. This type of polity prepared the way for revolution by creating, and then alienating, a professional political elite. Revolution came of this elite's dissatisfaction with the political system and its ability to blame the nobility for its defects. In England a successful revolt against an attempted royal absolutism prevented the development of a similar professional elite. In reaction to royal absolutism, the government became lodged in a state of primitive bureaucracy, the instrument of government remaining the traditional aristocracy. In England, moreover, professional groups had less reason to feel socially frustrated simply because the development of the economy and the empire created for them a cornucopia of profitable employment. A third precondition of revolution was government bankruptcy. In the era of revolution, however, the revenues generated by economic growth allowed the English government to remain solvent. Revolution tended to occur in agrarian societies dominated by peasant farming and aristocratic landlordship: societies burdened with a top-heavy, bureaucratic, rather than capitalist, structure. The normal background to revolution was widespread peasant militancy. Revolution occurred when the largest social group, usually the peasantry, could be drawn into revolution not necessarily because it subscribed to the current revolutionary ideology but because its hatred focused upon the same social object as the revolutionary leadership. Revolutions were essentially temporary alliances between outraged peasants and aggrieved professional men, the one opposing the nobles as landlords, the other opposing nobles as favoured servitors of the state; the one opposing nobles for imposing heavy rents and for being undertaxed, the other opposing nobles for appearing to deny them promotion in the state services. For both groups the aristocracy appeared to be in the wrong, not so much because of its wealth but because of its seigneurial rights and certain of its noble privileges, especially fiscal exemption, parliamentary membership and reserved office. Privilege, then, was at the root of the discord. In England, privilege gave less cause for offence, the seigneurial system having wilted into a state of harmlessness, the fiscal and reserved office privileges having disappeared centuries ago and the parliamentary privileges rendered tolerable on account of their confinement to a minute proportion of the aristocracy and the house of commons' ascendancy over the house of lords.

Revolution failed to repudiate the English aristocracy because of the nature of the political system and the absence of predominant social groups strongly aggrieved against aristocracy. In preventing revolution, industrialisation and commercial farming, as well as the defeat of royal absolutism, had crucial parts to play. Agrarian and industrial capitalism removed the bulk of the population from the direct proprietary control of the aristocracy. If the aristocracy had been farmers or industrialists, this would not have happened. For the most part, they were neither. While agrarian capitalism replaced a peasant society easily antagonised by landlords with a rural proletariat whose social hostility was directed against the tenant farmers, industrial capitalism produced a proletariat easily antagonised by their employers. In both cases, the essential source of friction was wages and employment, issues which did not involve the aristocracy. In these circumstances the people could adopt towards the aristocracy an attitude of indifference.

Preventing the repudiation of aristocracy was not only a corpus of popular indifference but also a weight of popular sympathy and support. The accommodating relationship between tenant farmer and landlord differed totally from the traditional relationship between lord and peasant. Absent were the extreme irritants of seigneurial dues and services as well as the independence of spirit imparted by the proprietorial rights of freehold and copyhold tenures. Present was the tenant-controlling, short-term, rack-rent lease and its consequence, a subservient loyalty. Concord between tenant and lord was also maintained by the threat of an alien work force. Faced by the masses, the product of industrialisation and commercial farming, the middle classes sided with the old order. The threat of full democracy cemented the relationship.

By the late nineteenth century a remarkably harmonious relationship existed between the bourgeoisie and the aristocracy. An essential lubricant was not so much the prospect of promotion, or aristocratic support for bourgeois interests, as the possibility of association, particularly through the education provided by the private schools which mushroomed spectacularly in the mid-nineteenth century. For the most part these schools presented themselves as country houses and aimed to educate an elite of leaders, if not of rulers, recruiting from both bourgeois and aristocratic backgrounds. Also maintaining bourgeois/aristocratic harmony was the middle-class feeling that the aristocracy was no longer an order apart but that the two were components of the same social group, the gentility, and, in this respect, equally distinguished from the rest of society. This feeling of community was cemented by the bourgeoisie's unopposed usurpation of gentry privileges and the development of an outlook, a mixture of aristocratic and bourgeois attitudes, which both were prepared to adopt.

Imparted by social ambition and the public school system, the middle classes acquired the outlook of aristocrats. The public schools imposed upon middle class and aristocrat alike a compound of ideals with aristocratic roots: a sense of leadership and of public responsibility, the belief that leaders should not be specialists, a strong aversion to trade which was seen as self-seeking, socially humiliating and materialistic, a supercilious attitude towards the rest of society, a firm faith in the efficacy of continuity and tradition and the conviction that social evaluation should be determined not simply by performance but also by family or school background. Just as Tudor theorists had de-radicalised humanism by insisting that an educated aristocrat would prove to be a better ruler than an educated commoner, the public schools avoided advocating a meritocracy manned by an academic elite by insisting that the products of gentle families and of particular schools would be best suited to leadership, irrespective of brain-power and personal worth. Thus, in the age of industrialisation, the public schools upheld aristocracy by mass-producing gentlemen. Instead of the revolutionary replacement of one elite by another, in England aristocrat and bourgeois merged to produce the gentility, a compound of landlords living on rents, a non-landed, *rentier* class living on dividends, and a professional and farming element which gained cohesion only from the uniformity of its outlook and ideals.

This merger altered the character not only of the bourgeoisie but also of the aristocracy. Gentility possessed a strong aristocratic flavour but imparted its own special image, a hybrid of aristocratic and professional values. In subscribing to it, the bourgeois underwent a process of aristocratisation and the aristocracy underwent a process of *embourgeoise-ment*. The development of gentility upheld the aristocracy and contributed to its decline. Responsible for the latter was not only the loss of a ruling function and of privilege but also the abandonment of a distinctive way of life. The aristocracy's subscription to the values of gentility led to a change in life-style and eventually a greater preparedness to pursue professional careers. The aristocratisation of the bourgeoisie, again the product of gentility, also contributed to the decline of aristocracy by creating a competition for popular deference – evident by 1900 in county council and parliamentary elections – between resembling bourgeois gentlemen and aristocratic gentlemen. A crucial stage in the aristocracy's decline as a political elite was reached when non-aristocrats became popularly regarded as the upholders of traditional England and could act as replacements for aristocrats in the fulfilment of this historic task. In permitting non-aristocrats to qualify for such a role, the development of gentility dealt the aristocracy a mortal blow.

(d) Government policy

The survival of nobility owed much to the government's willingness to accept it. In England popular pressures failed in the revolutionary era to alter the government's basic attitude towards aristocracy; and there was no question of governments being driven to make radical concessions in order to withstand revolution. Yet, notably in the late nineteenth and early twentieth centuries, government policy contributed to the aristocracy's decline.

In proceeding against the aristocratic interest, the government was partly moved by professional considerations to regard the traditional aristocracy as a source of political inefficiency and quite inadequate for meeting the needs of the modern state. Thus, from the 1820s pressure was successfully brought on the peerage to place its appellate jurisdiction in the hands of legal experts. Moreover, in accordance with the Northcote – Trevelyan report of 1854, the civil service was eventually reformed, with open competition rather than patronage acting as the means of admission. First implemented in 1870, by 1918 it had been applied to all branches of the civil service. To promote efficiency, proprietary commissions in the army were abolished in 1871. In the following year, the secret ballot was introduced to safeguard democracy from aristocratic intimidation and manipulation. In the 1880s the parliamentary system was made to rest upon a manhood franchise, a reform which a century earlier had been generally regarded as totally alien to a civilised state, and the administration of county government was taken out of the hands of the JP, traditionally an aristocrat, and awarded to the elected councillor and professional administrator. Earlier reforms had upheld the JP's importance. They had established a variety of elected boards upon which the magistrate was allowed *ex-officio* membership. The same arrangement was proposed for the county councils but rejected. The exclusion of the JP from local administration by the County Councils Act of 1888 was consolidated by the Rural District and Parish Councils Act of 1894. A further blow to the aristocracy's influence in local government came in 1910 when lord lieutenants lost their right to nominate JPs. Another blow was delivered in 1911 with the reform of the house of lords. The introduction of salaries for MPs and the establishment of reasonable salaries for civil servants and army officers in the early twentieth century worked against the aristocratic interest and in favour of the professional person. This particular reform broke with the traditional belief that it was best for those in positions of public responsibility to enjoy the independence of a private income, a belief closely connected with the traditional concept of the aristocracy as a political elite.

Governments not only helped to dispose of the aristocracy as a ruling class; especially in the twentieth century they also proceeded against its economic interests, moved by the practical needs to tax its wealth more appropriately, to offer greater protection to the tenant, to gain control of mineral resources such as coal and iron and to improve urban conditions. This led to the introduction and enlargement of taxes on capital: principally the benevolent estate duty with its built-in opportunities for tax avoidance, the capital gains tax of 1965 also blessed with escape hatches, and then in 1976 the more rigorous capital transfer tax which closed up most of the tax avoidance opportunities permitted by the earlier taxes. Wealth taxes were accompanied by the severe taxation of unearned, as opposed to earned, income. These measures encouraged bourgeoisification. To qualify for tax relief, aristocrats took farms in hand. To pay the taxes on capital, land was sold.

Tenant right legislation enfranchised copyholders, the lord receiving compensation for the loss of manorial incidents (in 1841, 1852, 1887 and 1922), and in 1967 enfranchised long-lease property. The latter, however, did not affect agricultural holdings since they were excepted from its terms. Between 1875 and 1976 a succession of agricultural holdings acts increased the tenant farmer's security of tenure, endowing him in 1976 with virtually hereditary possession. In 1906, 1908, 1910, 1923, 1947 and 1948, they awarded him the right to compensation for improvements and for the termination of tenancy. In addition, from 1908 a series of town and country planning acts (notably those of 1947 and 1974) gave local authorities powers of compulsory acquisition to land required for development. Apart from the nationalisation of coal and iron (1945 and 1947), possibly the most oppressive and damaging measures were the security of tenure granted to leaseholders in 1976, which seriously handicapped landlords wishing to convert themselves from landlords to farmers, and the capital transfer tax of 1976. Much of this action was the work of Labour governments. Conservative administrations often legislated in the landlord's favour, as in 1934 when the 1931 provisions for a national land valuation and a land value tax were abrogated; in 1954 and 1958 when the Labour tenant right legislation of 1947 and 1948 was amended; in 1970 when the Heath government abolished the Land Commission established in 1967; in the amendments made by the Thatcher government to the Agriculture (Miscellaneous Provisions) Act of 1976 so as to weaken the tenant's security of tenure, and to the Finance Act of 1976, making it easier for aristocrats to claim public funds for the maintenance of their country seats. The general, long-term effect of all this legislation was not to impoverish the aristocracy but to force upon it changes in character, principally the abandonment of lordship through either the sale or the direct exploitation of its estates.

Governments also abused the aristocracy by changing their policy towards entitlement. Breaking with tradition, governments came to dispense titles as a reward for the successful rather than as a special honour conferred upon those who had already attained aristocratic status. The Liberal governments of the 1890s and the early twentieth century freely granted peerages to men without land. In the twentieth century both Conservative and Labour governments did likewise. The outcome was the development, for the first time, of a substantial non-landed element in the peerage, the baronetcy and the knighthood. The establishment of the life peerage in 1958 carried the policy a stage further. The Peerage Act of 1958 allowed peers to exist in large numbers who lacked estates and hereditary nobility. Thereafter, not only did governments offer titles mainly to commoners but they also virtually stopped the creation of hereditary titles. This final insult was delivered in the late twentieth century. Until 1945 baronetcies were awarded with greater frequency than any other hereditary title. However, the Labour governments of 1945 to 1951 and of 1964 to 1970 created none at all. The intervening conservative administration in compensation created 106 but then the governments of the 1970s all desisted. As a result of this change in policy, the baronetcy's survival has become wholly dependent upon the ability of its member families to avoid extinction. Hereditary peerages continued to be granted, but by the 1960s they had been largely replaced by the life peerage as the highest form of government patronage. From 1964 to 1983 the hereditary peerage was confined, in the early medieval manner, to the royal family. Over the centuries the aristocracy was maintained by the willingness of governments to grant titles to men with the inclination and resources to follow an aristocratic way of life. Now in the twentieth century, government policy in the bestowal of honours seriously affected the baronetcy and the peerage, encouraging landlessness and discouraging hereditary right.

On the other hand, the aristocracy continued to receive a great deal of tolerance from governments of all hues. Proposed anti-aristocratic reforms, notably land nationalisation, and the abolition of the house of lords were never implemented. Some, like the land duties introduced in 1909, were shortlived. Others were applied decades after their initial acceptance. This was the case with civil service reform, leaseholder enfranchisement, the compulsory purchase of urban property and the nationalisation of the coal industry. A further category of anti-aristocratic measures permitted escape hatches for the aristocracy: thus, estate duty legislation permitted landowners to claim forty-five per cent tax relief on farm land and enabled them to avoid the tax completely by transferring the legal ownership of the estate at least seven years prior to the original owner's death. Some measures worked for, as well as against aristocracy, as with the establishment of the National Trust (1907), a gobbler of aristocratic estates with 400,000 acres in its custody by 1968, but also a body which upheld aristocracy through a system of dual ownership and public funding. None of the enacted reforms designed to annihilate the aristocratic interest. Traditionalism, fear of the state and the practical consideration that there were other matters with greater popular appeal, and therefore more deserving of redress, upheld aristocracy.

The Labour Party did not offer much scope for aristocratic MPs and, when in power in the 1960s, it initiated a new attitude towards hereditary titles.[2] By developing the welfare state, Labour also removed one of the major justifications for aristocracy, its role as a dispenser of charity. Its contribution to tenant right, the taxing of capital assets and the nationalisation of mineral resources were all damaging blows. But in power Labour failed to fulfil its socialist pledges, permitting the aristocracy to retain privileges and estates. Prior to the establishment of the life barony, the Labour government even proved capable of creating hereditary peerages in its attempt to establish support in the house of lords. Labour has also tolerated the aristocracy's modern stepping stones to positions of power, influence and prestige, the public school and Oxford/Cambridge.

Liberal and Conservative governments served the aristocratic cause much as one would expect: creating hereditary titles in profusion; allowing aristocrats access to the Commons as MPs and, in the Conservative case, allowing the formation of cabinets with a disproportionately high aristocratic membership. On the other hand, both parties also made vital contributions to the aristocracy's decline: the Liberals with their measures of social welfare in 1909, their reform of the house of lords in 1911 and by increasing the aristocracy's fiscal liability; the Conservative Party with the Life Peerage Act of 1958 – one of the most damaging measures to be taken by any government against the aristocracy, and only equalled in the nineteenth century by the extension of the franchise in 1867 and the County Councils Act of 1888, both of them Conservative measures – and the willingness to forego the creation of hereditary titles in the 1970s.

On the Continent the abolition of nobility usually accompanied the end of kingship.[3] Nobility and monarchy, the two main components of the old order, were very much alike because of their expected ruling function, their juridical privileges and the fact that, in both cases, privileges and function were conferred by birth. Having upheld each other, they tended to disappear together. In this respect, the survival of aristocracy in England is connected with the retention of monarchy and the Crown's unwillingness to propose the aristocracy's removal. The Crown's reverence for rank based on birth, together with the deference or indifference of society, and the inability of radical governments to abolish large estates and the house of lords, kept aristocracy very much alive.

(e) Aristocratic retirement

With neither the state nor society capable of repudiating aristocracy, its survival as a political elite depended upon its members' willingness to soldier on. Its decline was, to some extent, a withdrawal from politics, a retreat from the apparent messiness, inconvenience and answerability of democracy. In parliamentary and local elections, aristocrats often had no difficulty in securing a majority. This was even evident in the local elections immediately following the Municipal Corporations Act of 1835: fifty-one per cent of municipal councillors were of the gentry, and still as much as twenty-four per cent forty years later. It was also evident after the County Councils Act of 1888 and the extension of the parliamentary franchise in 1867 and 1884. Half of the county councillors elected in 1888, for example, were the old nominated magistrates. By the close of the century industrial and traditional towns had no qualms about electing aristocratic lord mayors.

Enraged groups of smallholders, as in the Fens, could vote successfully against the squire; and in counties containing or close to a high degree of urbanisation, such as Cheshire, life was made less easy for the aristocracy by the competition for the Conservative or Liberal vote offered by prosperous professional or businessmen, essentially commuters working in the town but living in the countryside and very keen to adopt the aristocratic role of exercising public responsibility; and in parts of Wales a Liberal nonconformist vote could defeat the Conservative, anglican aristocracy in their bid for local, elected office or parliamentary seats. Yet for aristocrats in many parts of the country, their election to parliament and local government remained a simple consequence of standing.

Prior to the democratisation of national and local government there was little evidence of an aristocratic retreat, apart from the magnates' abdication in the early nineteenth century of their former oligarchic role. For the aristocracy as a whole a resurgence seemed to be taking place. With the decline of oligarchy, the gentry found a renewed interest in local government. Earlier, the county magistracy was tending to fall into clerical hands so much so that in 1832 at least one quarter of acting JPs were clergy. The resurgence was so great that by the 1880s aristocracy almost monopolised the commissions of the peace. It was not simply a case of more aristocrats becoming JPs but of more of them taking the oath to qualify as acting JPs. In Cheshire, for example, the number of aristocrats taking the oath doubled between 1846 and 1886.

But in a democratic world, aristocrats lacked staying power. Besides the increase in the work involved, deterring aristocratic participation was answerability to the electorate and the control exerted by party machines.

Both developed in the 1870s and 1880s in response to the establishment of manhood suffrage. Reflecting the problems which even an aristocratically respectful democracy created for the old order, William Brodrick, son of a viscount and MP for West Surrey, commented in 1883:

> the House of Commons has lost much of its old attractiveness. The duties of a member become yearly more engrossing. It is not only that the hours of work are longer than they were and attendance more trying, but constituencies are much more exacting. The recess is far from being a holiday.

A career in politics was ceasing to be a congenial hobby which could be carried out comfortably between periods dedicated to the full-time task of hunting and socialising.

The demands of political life called for greater professionalisation. Some aristocrats adapted, became professional politicians, and made politics their career. But many were persuaded to retire from public life: some to the Riviera to gamble, some to Kenya to farm and many to their country seats in order to concentrate upon revivifying their dwindling fortunes. But for aristocrats who could cope with democracy, the opportunities and pickings were there for the taking – because of the leeway allowed a lord. This was as true of 1980 as of 1880. On the other hand, with the exception of peers in receipt of lord lieutenancies, chancellorships of universities and a seat in the house of lords, the political role of the aristocrat became indistinguishable from that of the commoners in the public service. In this respect, the bulk of the aristocracy suffered death by bourgeoisification. If the aristocratisation of the bourgeoisie had helped to uphold aristocracy as a political elite, the aristocracy's *embourgeoisement* brought it to an end.

Notes to Chapter 9

1. In 1939 it stood at sixty per cent and in 1972 at seventy-five per cent.
2. The Attlee government refused to create baronets; the Wilson governments desisted from creating hereditary peerages.
3. See Bush, *Noble Privilege*, ch. I (3).

PART THREE

IMPACT

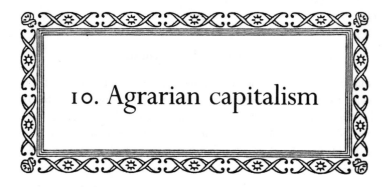

10. Agrarian capitalism

The commercial propensities of the English aristocracy require careful qualification (for reference and reading, see bibliography, sections X and XI). Although a recognised leadership elite, in matters of trade it lacked initiative. Commercial innovation and entrepreneurial dynamism were usually the work of commoners. Furthermore, while fully appreciative of the profitability of commercial activity, the aristocracy shunned direct involvement. In fact, its persistent refusal to farm, trade and manufacture made laws of derogation unnecessary. The huge financial resources of its members were largely dedicated to maintaining an appropriate life-style. The bulk of aristocratic revenues went in current rather than capital expenditure; and the aristocrat's capital spending and credit resources were mostly devoted to the payment of annuities, doweries, portions, the building and rebuilding of family seats, landscaping, estate accumulation, imparking and other non-productive ventures. Because of its immense financial resources and its wasteful manner of spending them, the aristocracy was responsible for diverting large amounts of capital from production, even more so since its example was compulsively followed by commercially and professionally successful commoners.

Nevertheless, in the development of both agrarian and industrial capitalism, the English aristocracy was neither a passive onlooker nor simply a stubborn opposition. Its political dominance, wealth and landownership gave it a vital part to play in the process. Both, in some respects, were a product of its enduring ascendancy rather than a consequence of its decline.

(a) The agrarian revolution

Long before industrialisation, the structure of English society became decidedly peculiar. Urbanisation was not wholly responsible: by 1800 three quarters of the population remained rural. Essentially, its oddity came of a restructured rural community. This was partly due to the long-term development of rural industries which removed a large proportion of the rural population from farming (by 1688 it was calculated by Gregory King that three-fifths of families, and in 1760 by Joseph Massie that over half the families, were not engaged in agriculture), but it was also due to the replacement of the traditional peasant society by a class-divided society of landless, wage-earning farmhands and large-scale commercial farmers. Whereas the medieval farm labourer had tended to work for a relative, now, by the eighteenth century, farm labourer and farmer, in all likelihood, would have no kinship bond. Whereas the farm-holding families had once contained the majority of the farming population, now the farm labourers easily outnumbered the farmers. In place of the traditional two-tiered society of landlord and tenant was a three-tiered society of landlord, tenant and farmhand. These changes seriously affected social relationships: on the one hand, largely healing the traditional break between landlord and tenant; on the other, creating a class conflict between a rural proletariat of landless farmhands and their employers, a middle class of commercial farmers.

The effects of the change can be measured by comparing the rural disturbances of the late middle ages and those of the early nineteenth century. In the former, the grievance was either government policy or harsh landlordship. The complaint against the landlord concerned seigneurial dues, serfdom, rents and rights of common. In the nineteenth century the grievance was predominantly against the employer. Low wages and unemployment were the grounds for complaint. In the medieval revolts hostility focused upon the landlords who, apart from the church, Oxbridge colleges and the Crown, were the peers and the gentry. In the rural revolts of the nineteenth century, the enemy was the farmers who were usually commoners. In this sense a conflict of estates gave way to a conflict of classes. Yet this did not mean the complete replacement of an estates by a class society. As the aristocrats remained the owners of most private land until after the first world war and the commercial farmers remained their tenants, the transformation of rural society simply accentuated the existence of class within the traditional estates society.

The transformation of rural society profoundly affected the character of English farming. Eventually, it became highly efficient and innovative. Dominated by commercial farmers capable of generating and applying capital rather than by peasants prone to subsistence farming, agriculture in England became better equipped for high productivity than that of the many European societies which remained, into the twentieth century, stolidly peasant, undercapitalised, traditionalist, with a high land/labour ratio and a low physical yield. The same social transformation also affected the development of industrial capitalism, creating capital and shedding labour for industrial use, and upholding society's purchasing power for manufactured goods by maintaining a supply of cheap food in a period of rapid population growth. It had important political repercussions. Absent in England by the late eighteenth century was an embittered peasantry with a special loathing of landlords, one of the crucial components of popular revolution. An agrarian revolution thus worked against the possibility of a political revolution and, in the absence of the latter, the aristocracy's decline took the form of a gradual evaporation rather than a sudden repudiation.

Responsible for the social reorganisation of the countryside was the development of the large holding and the withering of the seigneurial system. To both developments the aristocracy made a significant contribution.

(b) The engrossment of farms

In 1974 the average size of farm in England was 112 acres, that is, three times the average in the EEC countries. Considerable engrossment occurred in the course of the twentieth century, but much predated it: even in 1911 seventy-two per cent of cultivated land had lain in holdings of over one hundred acres. The process of engrossment reached back to the middle ages. Engrossment in the fourteenth and fifteenth centuries, however, had not affected the social structure. The farming community had remained peasant, largely composed of family farms bent upon survival rather than capital accumulation. Engrossment merely slotted into the gaps left by depopulation. It co-existed with peasant farming, neither undermining nor replacing it. This was no longer the case in 1700. Smallholdings still persisted in profusion but farming overall was characterised by large-scale operations. Since farms of fifty acres or less occupied no more than one quarter of England and Wales, most of the land was farmed by men who needed to employ wage labour. Peasants continued to exist but, because of the rise of the large farm, peasant farming no longer dominated agricultural production.

In England, the enlargement of farms cannot be wholly attributed to the aristocracy. In much of eastern Europe, where noble and agrarian capitalist were the same person, large-scale farming was a noble creation. In England, however, aristocrats rarely farmed on a commercial basis and the agrarian capitalist was usually a commoner.

The rise of the large farm in England resulted from a variety of conditions. One factor was the land market for tenures, envigorated in the fourteenth and fifteenth centuries by the land glut resulting from the Black Death, and upheld in the sixteenth and early seventeenth centuries by the profitability of farming which prevented the land hunger caused by rapid population growth from pricing tenures out of the market. Another condition was the cost advantages enjoyed by large-scale over small-scale farming. This never applied to dairying, hop growing and market gardening, but it did to sheep-farming, stock-rearing and corn. Engrossment was originally associated with pastoral farming: sheep-farming in the fifteenth and early sixteenth centuries and stock-rearing in the sixteenth and seventeenth centuries. But from the late sixteenth century engrossment also became associated with arable farming. In the course of the late sixteenth and early seventeenth centuries large areas of pastoral England were, for the first time, ploughed. These regions were light soil regions of chalk, limestone and sand: the Wiltshire Downs, the Chilterns, the Cotswolds, the Yorkshire and Lincolnshire Wolds and the sandy lowlands of the north east and of north Norfolk. Instead of a switch from one monoculture to another, they were subjected to a combination of sheep and corn which was termed convertible husbandry. Essential to the success of this system was the use of artificial grasses, legumes and root fodder crops which maintained large numbers of livestock in conjunction with a fair proportion of arable. Convertible husbandry, with its necessarily large outlay of capital, tended to lead to a farming community of large holders and landless farmhands in place of the traditional community of small holders. In addition the extensive land reclamation of the period 1550–1650, mainly in regions of fen and marsh, produced large ranch-type organisations. The capital accumulated from large-scale farming, and the use that was made of it not only to extend the operation but also to set up younger sons with cash rather than land, worked against the subdivision of farms to which peasant communities were notably prone.

Encouraging the process of engrossment was not only the success of large-scale farming but also the failings of small-scale farming. In periods of rapid population growth small holdings multiplied as tenures fragmented. This was as true of the late eighteenth and early nineteenth centuries as it was of the thirteenth and sixteenth centuries. Yet the small holdings rather than the large holdings were subdivided. The survival of the small holding depended upon types of farming which permitted viable, small-scale, commercial operations, as with hop-growing and market gardening, or upon the slow regional development of agrarian capitalism, a distinctive feature, for example, of Cumberland, Westmorland and parts of north Lancashire. It also depended upon the tenant's possession of communal rights and opportunities for off-farm work, notably in the textile industry. But the process of enclosure tended to eradicate common rights and industrialisation eventually destroyed the domestic industries. Furthermore, small holdings were less capable of surviving agricultural depressions than large holdings, as was shown in the late seventeenth and early eighteenth centuries, in the 1820s and 1830s, in the 1880s and 1890s and in the 1920s and 1930s. The introduction of chemical fertilisers and of agricultural machinery in the nineteenth and twentieth centuries also worked against the small hold by increasing the capital outlay of farming and by adding further advantages, especially in the cost of production, to those which the large farmer had enjoyed over the small farmer ever since the introduction of convertible husbandry.

The cost advantages of large-scale farming, the greed of peasants, the vigorous market for tenancies and the profitability of commercial farming all promoted engrossment. Yet in the process the aristocrat was also distinctly present. Contributing to engrossment was the aristocracy's

abandonment of demesne farming in the fourteenth and fifteenth
centuries, their encouragement of leasehold in place of customary or
freehold tenures in the sixteenth and seventeenth centuries, their
appreciation of estates that consisted of a few large holders rather than
many small holders – a fashionable preference of estate management in the
seventeenth and eighteenth centuries – their support for the development
of enclosure between the sixteenth and eighteenth centuries, and their
inability to restore peasant farming in the late nineteenth century, a time
when the failings of large-scale tenant farming forced them to reconsider
the virtues of a peasantry.

Following the spectacular depopulation of the fourteenth century,
demesne cultivation collapsed and thereafter the aristocracy remained
largely withdrawn from farming until the twentieth century. Their policy
of leasing the whole demesne increased the amount of land available for
engrossment, land, moreover, which was annexed by the wealthier
farmers since, unlike the tenures, it was not withheld from the land market
by family inheritance rights and, subject to revisable rather than fixed
rents, it was beyond the reach of the poorer farmers. The termination of
demesne farming also led to the virtual disappearance of labour services.
This also encouraged engrossment by removing a traditional objection.
When labour services were the main obligation of the tenures, the
acquisition by one family of multiple holdings could be opposed as harmful
to their performance. However, when the tenurial obligation consisted
only of rents and dues this objection was not so easily sustained.

The aristocracy's retreat from farming left it largely dependent upon its
tenantry for revenue. This, in conjunction with the extensive depopulation
of the fourteenth and fifteenth centuries, placed the free peasant in a
favourable position for negotiating generous terms with his landlord. The
period therefore saw not only a commutation of labour services but also a
reduction in seigneurial exactions. The latter enabled the peasant to
accumulate capital. Where the landlord's seigneurial rights remained fixed
by custom, and because of the glut of land and the profitability of sheep-
farming in the fifteenth century and the inflation of farm products in the
sixteenth century, the peasant was nicely placed to extend his farming
operations. Whilst the commutation of services allowed the lord to
tolerate more readily the engrossment of holdings, the reduction of
seigneurial dues provided the farmer with the resources to engross.

(c) **Enclosing**

Enclosures were often a consequence, not a cause, of engrossment. On the chalk downs of Wiltshire, for example, the replacement of peasant farms by large-scale commercial operations was well underway by the mid-seventeenth century. In fact, when enclosure came in the late eighteenth century, it merely added the finishing touch to an already transformed society. The same was true of Cardington in Bedfordshire, Chippenham in Cambridgeshire and Wigston Magna in Leicestershire. Quite frequently, moreover, enclosures upheld the small holding. In the butter and cheese region of Wiltshire, the family farm survived in conjunction with enclosure. This was also the case in parts of Devon, Cornwall, Kent, Sussex, Essex, east Suffolk, east Norfolk and the north-west. Furthermore, rather than creating large farms, some enclosure, especially associated with the creation of parks, only reduced the area of cultivation. Yet, true to its reputation, enclosure could cause the enlargement of farms. Engrossing enclosures were frequently the lord's responsibility. For example, when brought about by the lord's arbitrary action, the general enclosure of an estate led in the fifteenth century to the development of large-scale pastoral farming at the expense of small-scale arable farming, especially in the Midlands. General enclosures had the same engrossing effect when they were introduced in the early seventeenth century to the lowlands of Northumberland and the Durham Palatinate. A decisive factor in the process was the insecurity of tenant rights. Where freeholders and copyholders for lives prevailed, enclosure could only take place by agreement with the tenants; and such agreement was usually reached after engrossment had occurred. Furthermore, the general enclosure of an estate could lead to higher rents, a frequent occurrence in the late eighteenth and early nineteenth centuries, which could crush the smaller farmers out of existence; but again, the engrossing effect of enclosure depended upon the tenants' security. Piecemeal enclosure assisted engrossment when applied to the demesne or to the waste. Reclaiming land for cultivation, a traditional function of piecemeal enclosure, was a major cause of engrossment when there was no population pressure to enforce the creation of more small holdings or when there were expansive commercial farmers ready to grab whatever came onto the market. Finally, both general and piecemeal enclosure promoted engrossment by denying small holders the rights of common upon which their survival as farmers could depend.

Enclosure was not totally the work of the aristocrat as landlord. But as a source of permission, promotion and capital, he was an essential agent in the process. In all forms of legitimate enclosure this permission was necessary. This even applied to the parliamentary enclosures of the late eighteenth and early nineteenth centuries when not all proprietorial tenants were required to assent but the lord of the manor's concurrence was inescapable. Aristocrats over the centuries frequently advocated and promoted enclosure because of its evident profitability. Thus, in the sixteenth and seventeenth centuries, it could extend the area of cultivation at the expense of the waste and in this way enlarge the proportion of the manor subjected to rent; and in the eighteenth and nineteenth centuries, it not only expanded the area of cultivation but also modernised the estate and therefore justified an enlargement of its rents. With such profits in mind, aristocrats were not averse to financing the establishment of enclosures.

(d)   The development of leasehold

Aristocrats also assisted the process of engrossment by converting the traditional tenures to leaseholds. If customary and freehold tenures maintained the small holding, the development of leasehold promoted the rise of the large farm. Leasing, either by verbal agreement or by indenture, had a very long history. Originally it was confined to the demesne and also to the subletting activities of customary tenants and freeholders. In fact, most of the manorial estate was traditionally held on other terms of tenancy. Essentially, these terms were customary tenure which imparted to the tenant proprietorial rights to a fixed rent and hereditary possession, and freehold tenure which awarded perpetual possession and the minimum of obligation. Responsible for converting these tenures to leasehold was the lord of the manor. He did it by incorporating the tenure within the demesne. It is not surprising that the start of the conversion coincided with the lord's decision to cease farming the demesne. Earlier, tenures that fell vacant were normally preserved as customary or freehold tenancies; now in the late fourteenth and fifteenth centuries, some were turned into demesne leaseholds. The process of conversion quickened and culminated in the course of the seventeenth and eighteenth centuries.

Leaseholds came in a variety of forms. By 1700 they tended to be short-term and rack-rent. However, those formed from the conversion of tenures had tended, initially, to preserve something of the tenure and featured beneficial rents, arbitrary entry fines and tenancy for life. Yet, no matter what their character, all leases were more subject than the tenures to landlord control. Compelling conversion were the proprietorial rights of the tenure-holders and the pressures (brought by depopulation in the late middle ages and rapid inflation in the sixteenth century) upon lords to counteract the fall in value of their landed incomes. Leasehold was achieved not so much by expropriation as by the lord's ability to persuade tenants to become leaseholders, and by his reclamation of tenures through the tenant family's extinction, the tenant's failure to fulfil his tenurial obligations or straight purchase. The process of conversion was near completion in 1780 when ninety per cent of rented land was leased, but it was well under way by 1688 when Gregory King estimated that there were 180,000 families of freeholders (a category in which he also placed copyholders for life or lives and leaseholders for life) against 150,000 families of leaseholders for years.

In the late sixteenth and early seventeenth centuries lords tended to convert the tenures into long-term beneficial leases with attached entry fines; whereas in the course of the seventeenth and eighteenth centuries, the beneficial lease was often replaced by a lease short in term, subjected to an economic rent and freed of the entry fine. The whole development eliminated the restrictions which the seigneurial system had imposed upon lord and tenant. It made tenancy more flexible and competitive. With commercial farmers eager to extend their operations, the conversion to leasehold promoted engrossment. Because of the shortness of the leasehold, much more land became available for renting; because of rack-renting, the small tenant was offered little protection. The prevalence of leasehold released the tenancy market from the constraints of kinship and created a competition for tenancies which the wealthier farmer was bound to win simply because he could pay the higher rent. Moreover, freed of inheritance rights, the leasehold escaped the process of subdivision which the system of partible inheritance had imposed upon the tenures. Leasehold also influenced the lord's attitude towards engrossment. Under the seigneurial system, a populous tenantry seemed more in the lord's interest especially since his landed income was heavily dependent upon casualties, the incidence of which increased in proportion to the tenantry's size. But once capable of exacting a revisable rent, the lord could seriously consider reducing his tenantry to a minimum on the assumption that what was lost in seigneurial dues could be recouped in rent.

The engrossment of farms, then, owed something to changes in the nature of tenancy. For these changes the lord and his agents were wholly responsible. Yet engrossment essentially occurred because the tenantry was capable of appreciating its advantages and possessed the resources to rent and operate large farms. Vital to the enlargement of farms was the willingness of the tenants who had accumulated multiple tenancies to farm them directly rather than to adopt the stance of aristocrats and to sublet. Furthermore, engrossment was not an inevitable consequence of leasing. In parts of south-west France the tenures were incorporated in the demesne and the leasehold reigned supreme in the early modern period, but the conversion simply proliferated small holdings. Instead of producing the agrarian capitalist sitting on his large farm, it produced the abject sharecropper subsisting on a minute holding. This suggests that the amalgamation of holdings and changes in the nature of tenure are only part of the explanation. An essential ingredient in the emergence of large-scale farming was the economic conditions favouring the rise of the agrarian capitalist. The aristocrat's contribution to engrossment as a landlord basically depended upon this fact. Thus engrossment was assisted by lords who espied advantages in converting their estates into a composition of large rather than small farms. Enabling them to appreciate the large farm was their capacity to regard an estate in economic rather than political terms, as a source of income rather than of following, and to realise the administrative convenience of having fewer rents to collect, and the economy of fewer farmsteads to maintain. However, his response depended upon finding tenants to take on large farms. Such tenants were the fruits of agrarian capitalism. The aristocracy's contribution was merely to encourage engrossment. This they did by failing to use their authority as landlords to defend the interest of the small holder. Even in the sixteenth century when statutes and proclamations exhorted them to save the sturdy yeoman from extinction, they made no constructive response, either as magistrates responsible for enforcing the tillage laws or as landlords.

Having allowed the destruction of the peasantry, the aristocracy did little to resuscitate it. In the late nineteenth century, as tenant farming failed under the competition of foreign meat and corn, a policy developed, both public and private, popular and aristocratic, to revive the smallholding. But this latter-day appreciation of the peasant failed to alter the basic nature of rural society. True, small holdings remained in large numbers: in 1900 thirty per cent of holdings were under five acres. Yet by this time only six per cent of farmland was cultivated in units of less than twenty acres, whilst three quarters was farmed in units of over one hundred acres and in certain regions, notably parts of Northumberland, Norfolk and the southern chalklands, farms of at least five hundred acres prevailed. A rural society of this type was both a far cry from the England of 1300 when all but one per cent of farms were sixty acres or less, and very different from much of the Continent where average farm size in 1900 was at least one half, and frequently one quarter, that of the standard English farm.

(e)   The decline of seigneurialism

The transformation of the agrarian structure saw not only the emergence of the large farm but also a radical change in the landlord–tenant relationship. In England the seigneurial system was largely demolished by the aristocracy, not by a government seeking to implement or withstand revolution. The process of demolition reached back to the middle ages when, to cope with depopulation, lords abandoned demesne farming and the labour services associated with it, emancipated serfs in order to raise revenue from manumission and, in a bid to attract and to retain tenants, reduced their demands on the free tenantry. However, to cope with the rapid inflation of the sixteenth century, lords remained heavily dependent upon the seigneurial system. In a bid to maintain the real values of their landed revenues they relied upon the seigneurial dues which were not fixed by custom and therefore could be raised. Stopped by peasant revolt and swayed by changing fashions in estate management, lords, by the early seventeenth century, were prepared to counter the effects of inflation by disposing of all seigneurial rights but for those of justice and toll. The adoption of the rack-rent lease not only promoted engrossment but it also emancipated the aristocrat from the seigneurial system. Formerly seigneurial dues had been invaluable as a compensation for the lowness of the rent on customary tenures. With the introduction of the revisable rent, they became redundant as a means of extracting revenue from the tenantry. Moreover, the short-term lease was a better means of tenant control than seigneurial rights. The threat of eviction and a negotiable rent ensured tenant respect. Whereas engrossment transformed the relationship between farmer and farm-hand, the decay of the seigneurial system transformed the relationship between landlord and farmer. Depopulation in the fifteenth century and inflation in the sixteenth century had left the lord at the mercy of his tenants; and the lords' attempts to maintain their landed revenues by exploiting the seigneurial system met with resistance and revolt. But conversion to leasehold left the tenant at the mercy of the lord. It reversed the relationship, creating a subservience of farmer to lord and established between the two a harmony which only emerged on the Continent after revolution had driven governments to abolish the seigneurial system.

In the farming operation, the essential role of the lord was to provide the fixed capital. The working capital was the responsibility of the tenant. In this respect, farming was very much dependent upon the latter's resources as well as upon his inventiveness. Enlightened lords experimented on the home farm, allowed arrearages of rent in periods of depression, founded or encouraged agricultural societies, promoted branch railway lines to improve the marketing of farm produce, maintained and extended farm buildings, provided the capital for enclosures and drainage and sided with the agrarian capitalist. On the other hand, many lords were inflexible, regressive and mean, ploughing little back, promoting hunting and shooting at the expense of agriculture, and in periods of depression draining farming of capital by a pig-headed insistence upon high rents. Furthermore, no matter how enlightened the lord, in comparison with the commercial farmer, his importance in developing a productive and progressive agriculture was negligible.

The process of engrossment was frequently spontaneous, the result of large farmers swallowing their smaller brethren; and enabling the seigneurial system to wither was the capacity of farmers to pay high rents. Nonetheless, agrarian capitalism was promoted not only by commercial farmers but also by the aristocracy's estate management. By encouraging the development of leaseholds and enclosure, by preferring large to small farms, the aristocrat played his part in realising an agrarian revolution.

(f) The role of a ruling class

The aristocrat, arguably, contributed more positively to the development of commercial farming as a landlord than as a ruler. The corn laws of the late middle ages, the tillage legislation of the Tudors and the fiscal system developed in the seventeenth and eighteenth centuries worked against the interest of commercial farming. In the interests of the consumer and at the producer's expense, the medieval corn laws banned the export of corn. The aim of the tillage laws was to prevent engrossment and the decay of peasant farming. Although government measures, they were enacted by aristocratic parliaments. Only by ensuring, in their capacity as magistrates, that the tillage laws went unenforced did the aristocracy come to the aid of agrarian capitalism as a ruling class. Both tillage and corn laws were repealed in the seventeenth century. By the late eighteenth century enclosure was being promoted by statutes privately brought and speedily expedited; and instead of banning exported corn, a system now encouraged exports and forbade imports. Thus, by this time, legislation on enclosure and the traffic of corn favoured the commercial farmer rather than peasant or consumer. This reversal of policy was the fruit of the aristocracy's dominance of the Crown. Prior to the twentieth century, little legislation positively assisted farming. Reclamation schemes were enacted in the early seventeenth century and government loans for land drainage were dispensed from the mid-nineteenth century. In 1889 a board of agriculture was established; and in 1896 agricultural land was derated by one half. On the other hand, a fiscal system was allowed to develop which fell heavily upon agriculture in the form of a land tax and taxes on consumption, and which, in the late nineteenth century, anomalously granted relief on undeveloped land but not on developed land.

A more benevolent policy towards agriculture emerged as the aristocracy's domination of parliament and the cabinet slipped away. Apart from the short-lived Corn Law of 1815 and the rate support system introduced in 1849 in compensation for its repeal, the aristocracy offered little defence of the agrarian interest in an alien, industrialising world. Notably in the depression of the 1880s and 1890s the case for restrictions on food imports was weakly presented. Although successfully established in continental countries, government protection of farming hardly existed in Great Britain prior to the 1930s. Farmers required protection not only from foreign products but also against fluctuating prices. Apart from a short period during the first world war, prices guaranteed by government subsidies were not introduced until the 1930s and not substantially established until after the second world war.

Dissuading the aristocrat from using his political authority to protect and promote farming was his own short-term interests as a landlord, his fear of state intrusion, and the fact that, prior to the twentieth century, he chose not to farm. The interests of landlord and farmer were not identical. The aristocracy's incentive to produce a government policy in favour of farming was not as powerful as it would have been if its members had farmed. In fact, the eventual emergence of government protection can be seen, to some extent, as a repercussion of the aristocracy's conversion from landlord to farmer.

11. Industrialisation

(a) The aristocratic contribution

English aristocrats contributed to industrialisation partly by providing capital and entrepreneurial initiative – that is, in ways indistinguishable from those of commoners – and partly in a special aristocratic manner: that is, as a political elite, as landlords and as creators of an ethos which prejudiced society's attitude towards commercial activity (for reference and further reading, see bibliography, section XI). In the main, they neither directly promoted new techniques of production nor provided fixed or working capital for the manufacturing process. In the latter respect, they were even more removed from industrial, than from agricultural, production. Nonetheless, by promoting transport facilities and urban growth, and by making available a glut of capital, cheap food and minerals, they helped to construct a conducive infrastructure. Their landownership, wealth and political pre-eminence placed them in a commanding position to control the emergence of this infrastructure. By actively promoting it, they created a favourable situation for new techniques of production to flourish and take root.

Some historians have regarded the aristocracy's industrial role as so important that the differences between the character of the aristocracies of the British Isles and of the continental nobilities – especially the openness and absolute property rights of the English aristocracy – are seen as determining the location of the first industrial revolution. However, these identified differences are illusions, essentially created by an ignorance of the continental nobilities. For example, there is no good reason to regard the English aristocracy as comparatively more accessible. If it possessed an unusual feature it was not its 'two-way flow' but a downward flow and an upward dribble. Arguable a much better case could be made to show that the English aristocracy was more closed to aspiring commoners than its continental counterparts. Furthermore, the causal connection established between its alleged accessibility and industrial growth is highly questionable. Did social promotion significantly encourage industrial development by creating room for newcomers within the industrialists' ranks and by preserving political stability? And did an increase in demand for industrial products significantly depend upon an emulative spending spree caused by the accessibility of aristocratic status? At both stages, the argument is too far-fetched to carry conviction. Furthermore, the proprietorial rights eventually secured by the English aristocracy were far from unique. Many continental landlords had as much control of the subsoil and tenantry, and as much immunity from state interference. And there is no good reason to believe that mineral resources were more easily released for industrial purposes when owned by the aristocracy than when owned by the state. A second line of argument, that certain peculiarities in its character gave the English aristocracy greater reasons for commercial involvement, tends again to create a false dichotomy, one which underestimates the commercial inclination of continental nobilities and grossly overestimates the commercial inclinations of an aristocracy which rigidly divorced itself from direct production, preferred the *rentier* role and participated in little more than mining, transport and merchant banking. Nevertheless, while its peculiarities do not seem to possess much industrial significance, its very political power, capital resources and landownership ensured that its attitude towards industrialisation contributed importantly to the latter's development; and the profits which it drew from industrial development ensured that this attitude was progressive and promotional rather than reactionary and restrictive.

(b)   **The role of estate management**

(i)   *Farming*

The estate management of the English aristocracy was especially important to industrialisation, partly for encouraging the development of capitalist farming, partly for promoting the mining of minerals and partly for permitting the growth of industrial townships.

The rise of agrarian capitalism, promoted by aristocrats to maximise their landed incomes, served industrialisation as a source of labour, cheap food and capital. Between 1700 and 1830 the rural work force remained roughly constant in spite of the enormous growth of population. This was due partly to emigration, both abroad and to the towns, but also to the re-organisation of the rural community which, no longer dominated by peasant farming, lacked the latter's capacity to maintain surplus labour. As a result, the increase in the labour supply, having been placed wholly at the disposal of urban industry, helped to keep down the cost of industrial production. Furthermore, the improved performance of farming, a direct consequence of the re-structuring of rural society, helped to sustain a favourable balance of trade. It allowed for the export of farm products and made the country in the early stages of industrialisation largely self-sufficient for its food. Although the population more than doubled in the late eighteenth and early nineteenth centuries, the coincidental increase in agricultural production allowed British farming, as late as 1830, to provide ninety per cent of the food consumed in Britain. Such was the efficiency of farming that, in the circumstances of a rapidly rising population and a virtual independence of food imports, a supply of cheap food was maintained for the home market which upheld a vigorous home demand for manufactured goods. Finally, the profitability of farming increased the purchasing power of rural society for industrial goods; and the capital accruing to aristocrats from raised farm rents enabled them to finance improvements in transport. The role of agrarian capitalism as a pre-condition of industrialisation, and the part played by the lord in replacing peasant with commercial farming, renders the estate management of the aristocracy a vital factor in the industrial revolution.

(ii)   *Mining*
The importance of minerals to industrialisation lay not only in their native abundance but also in their availability. In the course of the sixteenth and seventeenth centuries the English aristocracy acquired full ownership of these resources, largely by defeating the proprietorial claims of the Crown. Thus, the landlord's right to the non-metallic minerals of his estate was established by a judgement of the courts in 1569; and his right to the metals upon his estate, apart from gold and silver, was enacted in 1689. Some aristocrats disallowed the mining of mineral deposits. The seventh duke of Bedford, for example, prevented the mining of iron stone upon his

Midland estates simply because he felt that it would deface the countryside. In view of his overall wealth, he could afford to be fastidious. In practice, a huge amount of minerals was released. Some were mined directly by aristocrats, either working their own mines or by leasing the rights of other proprietors. However, by the late eighteenth century lords more commonly leased out their mineral rights than operated them directly. True to form, the aristocracy established a rentier relationship with mining similar to that which it had with farming. The only difference was that the lord's profit from mining derived not simply from a rent but also from a royalty determined by the marketable value of the product. Cornish tin and copper were mined principally by leasees who paid for the right with a royalty. In this case the aristocracy's capital was not normally involved. The same was largely true of lead, chiefly mined in the northern counties. Aristocrats were more directly involved in the mining of iron, although by the late eighteenth century they were more inclined to lease, than to operate, their mines. The mining of iron ore led to an aristocratic involvement in the processing of it: prior to the eighteenth century landed capital was the only means, usually, of providing furnaces and forges. Probably the greatest degree of owner operation occurred in coal mining; but the aristocrat's inclination was again to eschew direct involvement, notably with the discovery in 1784 of Cort's process of puddling and rolling iron. Thereafter the capital of ironmasters came to be invested heavily in the coal industry. With the emergence of entrepreneurs prepared to pay high rents and to risk their own capital, and as pits deepened and therefore involved a much greater capital outlay, aristocrats, with some notable exceptions, were easily persuaded to back out. For this reason their involvement was far more considerable in the seventeenth and early eighteenth centuries than in the nineteenth century. The obvious dependence of industrialisation upon the exploitation of the country's mineral wealth and the latter's ownership by an aristocracy which readily permitted it to be mined and even provided capital for the mining operation, presents a firm, close connection between industrialisation and estate management.

(iii) *Urban development*

Urban development was another product of the aristocracy's estate management. As landlords, the English aristocracy was not averse to encouraging, or at least tolerating, the growth of industrial towns. Again, the persuasive factor was profit. And yet again the aristocrat sought to preserve for himself the role of rentier. Some sold land for urban development, but an overriding tendency was to lease land to developers and builders while retaining the freehold both of the site and of any buildings constructed upon it. Little aristocratic capital was risked in the operation. Urbanisation was a clear response to population growth and the employment opportunities provided by urban industries, but vital to the development was the aristocracy's willingness to sell land to developers and to permit large numbers of houses to be built upon its land. The growth of Liverpool owed something to the estate management of the earls of Sefton and Derby, the development of Tyneside was dependent upon the duke of Northumberland and the earl of Durham. Manchester's emergence as an industrial city was influenced by the estate policy of the Mosleys and the earl of Wilton; Sheffield's by that of the dukes of Norfolk. The umbilical connection between aristocracy and urbanisation is evident in the fact that, of the 261 provincial towns surveyed by a royal commission in 1886, 103 were largely owned by lords. Stamford remained a small market town because of the marquis of Exeter's antipathy to its expansion; and the history of Nottingham was seriously affected by the restrictive estate management of the duke of Newcastle. However, in numerous instances the prospect of profit persuaded lords not to impede the builders. Besides granting leases to developers, aristocrats supplied them with building materials from their quarries. As the owners of much of this material, their open attitude to urban growth was of prime importance in the emergence of large towns. Another contribution was to prepare the site by establishing the roads, sewers and water-works, although their capital investment in the construction of industrial towns tended to go no further than this infrastructural stage.

Frequently, as seigneurs, they owned the market rights of a town and its development depended upon how they exercised them. A Royal Commission on market rights and tolls found, in the 1880s, that of the 531 urban markets in England and Wales situated outside London, 128 were owned and managed by private persons and a further forty-one privately-owned markets were leased by municipal corporations. In the course of the nineteenth century urban markets mostly fell under municipal control but in a number of instances the seigneur continued to hold sway, having the sole right to maintain a public market and drawing large takings from stall rents and sales taxes. In Sheffield, for example, the main markets of the town remained under seigneurial control until 1899.

Occasionally aristocrats created towns by sinking capital in the construction of harbours, docks and transport systems: thus, the Curwens created Whitehaven, the Cavendishes created Barrow-on-Furness and Seaham was founded by the marquis of Londonderry. Moreover, occasionally, their invested capital played a vital part in transforming a town, as with the docks built by the earls of Bute in Cardiff and by the Russells at Rotherhithe.

(c) The contribution of a ruling class

(i) *Transport*

Because of their association with mining, urban development and commercial farming, some aristocrats acquired a progressive attitude towards improving the transport system. For the development of an industrialised society, an effective transport system was a necessary precondition. As members of parliament prepared to pass private bills for the establishment of turnpike trusts and navigation (both river and canal) and railway companies, as leaders of local communities setting an example of sympathy rather than opposition, as investors of capital and even as promoters of schemes, aristocrats made their contribution. Aristocratic opposition was strongly voiced against improving the navigability of certain rivers in the late seventeenth and early eighteenth centuries, largely because, by raising the river level, it threatened meadow land, weirs and watermills; and in the late eighteenth and early nineteenth centuries opposition to canal and railway schemes came from aristocrats already committed to transport improvement ventures. Thus investors in turnpike trusts opposed canals, and investors in canals opposed railways. Improved transport could open up new markets but could also create competition. The latter occasionally served as grounds for aristocratic objection: thus the plan to connect Leicester with the Loughborough canal was initially opposed by local landlords who felt that it would destroy their monopoly in supplying the town with coal and lime.

Aristocrats became involved in the promotion of transport improvements either as an interest or as individuals, not as an order. The contribution made by the duke of Bridgewater to the development of the canal system in the 1760s, the contributions of the earl of Durham, the duke of Norfolk and the duke of Sutherland to the development of the railways in the 1820s and 1830s was that of exceptional individuals rather than typical aristocrats. River and road improvements and the construction of canals and railways all benefited from aristocratic capital but the amount invested was not disproportionate to the aristocracy's wealth and was dwarfed by the considerable investments made by other sections of society, notably the commercial and industrial capitalists of the provincial towns. Arguably the duke of Sutherland's investment of £100,000 in the Liverpool–Manchester railway company in 1825 was a significant moment in railway history; but the railway system was very quickly flooded with capital. Both turnpike trusts and canals engaged aristocratic wealth, but were also sustained by the financial backing of businessmen. In the early stages of each of these developments, aristocratic capital played a significant role, especially as a confidence-inspirer in an apparently risky venture, but once underway and once the profitability was proven, it became redundant.

Probably of greater value in the establishment of a transport system was the aristocracy's willingness to sell at reasonable prices land for canal and railway development and the attitude which aristocrats adopted as members of parliament. Manufacturing was initially financed through the plough-back of profits. Unable to rely upon this device, transport improvements were necessarily dependent, in the absence of state support, upon publicly-raised capital. Since the law of the time generally forbad corporate capitalism, public capital could only be raised through companies specifically authorised by act of parliament. For this reason, and because of the need of canal and railway companies to make compulsory purchases of land, the whole programme of transport improvement depended upon the willingness of parliament to enact the private bills promoting it. Some were successfully opposed, but many were passed. The aristocracy's domination of both house of parliament gave it a decisive voice in their enactment. In this respect, the establishment of an effective transport system was vitally dependent upon aristocratic support: support which was inspired and sustained by considerations of profit, a sense of local responsibility and the political need to conserve the respect and allegiance of wealthy commoners.

(ii)   *Fiscal aid*

As a ruling class, the aristocracy also promoted industrialisation by preserving a primitive, regressive tax system which ensured that the profits of trade and industry mostly went untaxed. With customs and excise duties acting as the main source of fiscal revenue and with direct taxation confined, except for the period 1799–1816 and after 1842, to landed incomes and generally levied at a very low rate, taxation placed little restraint on the accumulation of capital. But this was the extent of the aristocracy's contribution as a ruling class. Directed by the aristocratic interest in parliament, the development of the political system and of government policies worked against, rather than in favour of, industrialisation. The determination to safeguard wealth from heavy taxation left the government reliant upon public loans and consumption taxes for its revenue. The former side-tracked capital from industry, the more effectively because, until 1832, the usury laws limited the interest on commercial and industrial investments but failed to restrain the interest on government stock. The taxes on consumption, moreover, restricted the purchasing power of the masses, countering the productive effects of cheap food; and the heavy duties upon imported timber between 1800 and 1840 added to the cost of industrial production.

(iii)   *Industry and the state*

Industrialisation in Great Britain owed next to nothing to state planning and government spending. For the most part, the government intervened in economic matters only to promote foreign trade and agriculture. It shied away from direct involvement in industry. Government spending was largely devoted to paying interest on the national debt which, in peace time, consumed at least half of it, and to meeting the cost of the military which accounted for one-third of its revenues in peace time and two-thirds in time of war. Moreover, capital could only be raised for manufacturing purposes through family concerns or partnerships, not by public subscription. Public funds were raised by special statutes but their province was confined to transport and enclosure and commerce. The law also limited the size of banks and therefore placed a limit upon another obvious source of capital. Relief only came in 1825 with the repeal of the Bubble Act which in 1720 had prohibited incorporation, and when the Limited Liability Act was passed in 1856. Industrialisation thus occurred in the absence of state promotion and in spite of the restraints which company law placed upon publicly-raised capital.

(d) The contempt for trade

Whilst responsible for creating certain circumstances which were highly sympathetic of industrialisation, the English aristocracy also helped to preserve and create some highly antipathetic conditions. The latter stunted industrialisation in its long-term development, eventually leaving it undercapitalised, old fashioned and bereft of entrepreneurial dynamism. The aristocratic habit of non-involvement in commercial activity was contracted both by the government and the bourgeoisie. A legacy of aristocracy was the strongly-held belief that this non-involvement was a virtue. Another potent legacy was the belief that social superiority was a matter of status rather than of wealth. Under aristocratic influence, tradition and amateurism became thoroughly appreciated, and innovation and the specialist deeply suspect. In spite of industrialisation, pre-industrial values held sway, some in an exaggerated form. In the sixteenth and seventeenth centuries the aristocracy had only considered it improper for aristocrats to participate in business. Aristocratic contempt for trade had been confined to the commercial involvement of its members coupled with the belief that those with an expected political function, the aristocracy, were naturally superior to those with an economic function, the commonalty. Trade itself was respected as a social and political necessity. However, in reaction to industrialisation and its social consequences, the aristocracy became less directly involved than ever before. Moreover, moved by social ambition, the bourgeoisie sought to detach itself from commercial activity. As a result, the bourgeois ideal became not that of the businessman but of the professional man aspiring to attain to aristocratic status through the assumption of gentility.

In the period of industrialisation damage to the economy was not committed by a flight of capital from commerce to landownership: industrialists and merchants bought estates in the time-honoured manner, but not on a massive scale. It was rather inflicted by the bourgeoisie's adoption of a life-style and outlook which involved the inculcation of non-commercial and non-material values, and by the proliferation of academic establishments which attempted to produce not entrepreneurs but gentlemen.

Although the custom of non-involvement in trade was longstanding, it acquired a stronger hold upon the aristocracy in the course of the nineteenth century when the need of its members to preserve social identity in the face of the erosion of privilege, a decline in living standards and a loss of landownership gave it a special meaning. As for the bourgeoisie, a contempt for trade became an essential mark of gentle status since its members were landless and unprivileged. The divorce of the bourgeoisie from trade was a consequence of its rise into the gentility. It was also due to the preservation of an estates society in England, modified to make the line separating chivalry from commonalty a means not of distinguishing aristocrat from bourgeois but of including both within the same order. However, this rise of the bourgeoisie was determined by the survival of aristocracy as a social elite and by the durability of its values. If industrial backwardness was a consequence of the bourgeoisie's social elevation, it was because aristocratic values became objects of reverence, rather than of contempt, for its members.

For the most part, the English aristocracy remained aloof from industrial production, seeking rigorously to maintain the role of rentier and determined to receive its income in the form of rents, royalties and dividends rather than of a directly earned profit or salary. Generally, its adaptability to economic change was sluggish. As a promoter of innovation, its record was poor. On the other hand, its political power, capital resources and proprietorial rights gave special significance to its readiness to accept industrialisation.

The importance of its contribution to the process of industrialisation depends upon the value one attaches to the construction of a transport system, urban development, the extensive mining of minerals and the production of cheap food, and to the aristocracy's role in promoting these conducive infrastructural developments. The existence of such an infrastructure seems incontestably essential; but how important, for example, was aristocratic initiative and capital in the development of the transport system? Perhaps not decisive. Could agrarian capitalism have developed without aristocratic support? Conceivably. On the other hand, both mining and urban development seem crucially dependent upon aristocratic backing since, except by an act of dispossession, neither could have happened without the landlord's consent.

In certain respects, the social and political dominance of the aristocracy created alien circumstances for industrial development. Throughout the nineteenth century the attitude of the government and of society's wealthy element remained unfavourable to industry. The dynamism of the industrial sector had rendered the government's stand-offishness of little significance but society's prevailing contempt for trade, a legacy of aristocratic values travestied by bourgeois imitation, placed a brake upon industrial evolution, eventually producing a new form of economic primitiveness. This existed in spite of industrialisation rather than because industrialisation had yet to occur. In the history of industrialisation, the English aristocracy helped to produce not only the first industrial nation but also the first example of a backward industrial economy.

12. Political impact

Over the centuries the English aristocracy was strongly placed to determine the degree of political stability and government policy. In addition to its influence upon day-to-day politics, it helped to shape and make distinctive the state's long-term development (for reference and further reading, see bibliography, section XII). The traditional importance of parliament, the early achievement of representative government and the belated establishment of numerical democracy reflected the aristocracy's success in opposing the Crown and avoiding revolutionary overthrow. The enduring primitiveness of the bureaucratic, military and fiscal system can be explained in the same way. So, to some extent, can the paradox of a state with a low level of political intrusiveness coupled with a high degree of centralisation. On the Continent state control and centralisation were the work of royal absolutism confirmed by revolution. In defeating royal absolutism and avoiding popular revolution, the English aristocracy preserved a political system in which the presence of the state was weakly felt. A growing intrusiveness, in fact, only came with the aristocracy's decline. On the other hand, centralisation in England was the result of the early extension of royal justice and the aristocracy's willingness to serve, in the absence of a sufficient bureaucracy, as its instrument.

The aristocracy's contribution to the development of the English state, then, was both progressive and reactionary. Modernisation was promoted by the aristocracy's defence and promotion of parliament and retarded by the aristocracy's antipathy towards universal suffrage, bureaucracy and a progressive fiscal system.

(a) **Representation**

According to Barrington Moore's *Social Origins of Dictatorship and Democracy*, 'English parliamentary democracy (was) very largely the creation of' the aristocracy. Unfortunately, his elaboration of the point contradicts this statement. Essentially he asserts that the establishment of a stable democracy is the work of an independent bourgeoisie, realised either by its rejection of the old order or by its ability to direct the old order's decisions. Thus, in France democracy came of bourgeois revolution, whereas in England it resulted from the rise of a capitalist middle class whom the aristocracy had to accommodate. Nonetheless, he usefully emphasises a causal connection between aristocracy and the development of representative government and focuses upon the relationship between the Crown and the aristocracy as one of its major determinants. His basic mistake was to run together the several stages of development and to provide one explanation for the whole process. Since the explanation for the development of a system of representative government fails to account for the establishment of democracy, the several stages of development need to be segregated. Moreover, the aristocracy's specific contribution to each of them needs to be defined and assessed as positive and promotional or passive and permissive.

The present system of representative government derived from (1) the emergence of parliament as a basic part of the constitution; (2) the development of parliament as a necessary part of everyday government and (3) the extension of the franchise to make parliament directly representative of the whole nation. In stages one and two, the aristocracy had a clearly creative role, whereas its contribution to stage three was merely to shelve die-hard opposition to democracy and instead to seek a limit upon its operation.

Its positive contribution stemmed from a basic interest in upholding parliament and its effectiveness in resisting the Crown. Its commitment to parliament came of the fact that for most of its history it lacked the privilege of fiscal exemption, its domination of the Commons as well as the Lords, and parliament's long-held right to grant all taxes and to make and repeal all laws enforceable in the courts of common law. Established by the mid-fourteenth century, these parliamentary powers were thereafter zealously and successfully defended by its largely aristocratic membership.

The aristocracy's early take-over of the third estate gave parliament a social unity which allowed the Crown no chance to divide and rule. The aristocracy's opposition to the attempted establishment of royal absolutism in the seventeenth century was only the culmination of a tradition in which, to defend English liberties against the encroachments of the Crown, the aristocracy had established and enlarged the authority of parliament. Following the revolutionary events of 1688 and 1689 the function of parliament became so elevated that it ceased to be an occasional body, summoned only if new taxes were required or if the law needed alteration, and became a body in regular session which, because of the answerability of the executive, exercised control over the making of policy and the operation of everyday government. In the development of parliament, the aristocracy's capacity to take charge of the third estate and to oppose royal absolutism was of outstanding importance; and the outcome of aristocratic revolt in seventeenth-century England was that, in a period when the powers of continental parliaments were contracting or disappearing under the weight of royal absolutism, in England the contrary occurred.

The aristocracy had everything to gain from a form of government in which the state was ruled by a noble-dominated parliament. For this reason parliamentary government was highly valued by aristocracy. But its attitude towards parliament was heavily reliant upon its capacity to control it. Parliament had traditionally safeguarded the aristocratic interest against royal aggrandisement but because it also opened the prospect of domination by the people, the aristocracy could only appreciate a parliamentary system with an extremely limited electorate. The aristocracy was no intrinsic friend of democracy. The idea went completely counter to its basic beliefs in birthright and ascriptive authority. By protecting and promoting parliament, the aristocracy helped to establish a form of government which was responsible to the subjects of the realm as well as to its hereditary ruler, but this was the extent of their positive contribution to the creation of a system of government dependent upon popular rather than royal sovereignty. The aristocracy was amenable to the idea of rule by parliament but deeply hostile to the idea of rule by the people. Through parliament, its aim was to preserve liberty, not to implement equality. The aristocracy instinctively feared two tyrannies: on the one hand, royal despotism; on the other, the tyranny of the multitude.

Parliament could safeguard against the designs of the Crown but, if unchecked, it could easily generate a popular tyranny, especially through the system of democracy. To prevent the latter, the aristocracy accepted that both the size and character of the electorate needed careful restriction. Aristocrats felt that only men of property could act responsibly, basically because they had something to lose. It was therefore vital that the vote should not extend to the propertyless. In 1430 an act narrowly restricted the country franchise to the freeholder with property worth at least 40/- p.a. Its explicit aim was to deny the vote to persons 'of small substance and of no value'. However, as inflation increased land values the electorate grew, notably in the course of the sixteenth and early seventeenth centuries. In reaction, aristocrats planned an increase in the property qualification. Between 1654 and 1660 a £200 property franchise operated which Lord Shaftesbury sought to re-introduce in 1679. A logical extension of the aristocracy's association of property with responsibility was the creation of a property qualification for MPs: in 1711 it was enacted that knights of the shire must own landed property worth £600 p.a. and that burgesses must own landed property worth £300 p.a. They sought to control the electorate in other ways: the Last Determination Act of 1696 placed a restriction on the size of borough electorates and encouraged the keeping of a record of how the electorate voted in the form of poll books. Aristocrats were found advocating a widening of the franchise in the seventeenth century in reaction to the court party's wish to restrict it and in the late eighteenth and early nineteenth centuries in reaction to oligarchy, but only mavericks among these parliamentary reformers backed manhood suffrage. The idea remained anathema to aristocracy, whether it was expressed by the Levellers in the 1640s, the corresponding societies of the 1790s, the Hampden clubs of the early nineteenth century or the Chartists of the 1830s and 1840s.

An outstanding feature of the English state was that, whereas parliamentary government was established by revolution, a fully democratic parliament was realised by constitutional means. The former clearly owed much to the effectiveness of the aristocracy's opposition to the Crown; the latter clearly owed something to the aristocracy's compliancy with the commonalty's demands for parliamentary reform. This compliancy was not enforced. It largely happened because parliamentary reform occurred slowly, in several stages and over a relatively long period; and because at each stage, even that of 1884, the old order could persuade itself that what was retained compensated for what reform had taken away. For example, not until 1911 was the house of lords' traditional authority severely reduced. Democracy was acceptable in the late nineteenth century because a crucial part of the legislative process remained completely free of democratic control. Furthermore not until 1918 was manhood suffrage – theoretically introduced in 1884 – freed of petty exclusions from the franchise (e.g. resident domestic servants, sons living with parents, soldiers in barracks) and of registration regulations which, between them, denied the vote to forty per cent of the male population. Not until 1911 was provision made for the payment of MPs; and not until 1858 was the MP's property qualification abolished. In 1867 the franchise was widened considerably but, at the time, the system of open ballot was retained (until 1872) and before 1883 the bribery of electors was perfectly legitimate.

Parts of the reform of parliament, notably the acts of 1832 and 1867, happened when the aristocracy still dominated the Commons as well as the Lords. Convincing aristocrats of the need for parliamentary reform was the malfunctioning of the old system with urban voters threatening the sway of the aristocracy in county elections. The Reform Act of 1832 responded in the aristocracy's favour by awarding towns their own seats, thereby depriving the inhabitants of their county votes. There was also the feeling, both in 1832 and in 1867, that an extension of the franchise would restore what was thought to be the social harmony of the old estates society. On both occasions, parliament was influenced by the strength of feeling outside parliament, but the aristocracy's acceptance of reform, while activated by the fear of revolution, was not simply a surrender. From the aristocracy's point of view, reform was a strategic shift aimed at upholding the landed order as a political force in a society transformed by industrialisation. The stand taken by Lord John Russell from 1819 to the 1860s aimed to restore rather than to cede influence; and it was not untypical. Also moving aristocrats to accept reform was the party struggle for political power. Reform appeared essential for securing political dominance: for the Whigs under Lord Grey in the 1830s and for the Tories under the direction of Disraeli in 1867. The mixture of losses and gains realised by each act helped to make reform acceptable. Thus, the 1832 act created, alongside sixty-four new borough seats, sixty-two county seats, as well as restricting the working-class vote in a number of towns with a traditionally wide franchise. Then, in 1867 there was a further increase of county seats, from 144 to 172, whilst boroughs seats were reduced from 323 to 286. Finally, in spite of the two reforms, many of the seats continued to belong to very small boroughs which, like the counties, were amenable to aristocratic control.

The later parliamentary reforms occurred after the aristocracy had ceased to occupy the majority of Commons seats. In fact, the establishment of full democracy in England succeeded only after the political ascendancy of the aristocracy had gone. These later reforms also followed a course of piecemeal concession, partly because of the enduring presence of aristocrats in the Lords and Commons but also because large sections of the bourgeoisie found full democracy equally distasteful. The tortuous and belated establishment of democracy in England, then, cannot be attributed wholly to the aristocracy. But their responsibility for retarding its development is expressed by the slow response of the political system to the economic and social changes which demanded parliamentary reform in the period when the aristocracy retained firm control of the legislative process; and by the persistence of the house of lords in impeding electoral reform between 1884 and 1914.

(b)   State apparatus

Paradoxically, the revolutions of the seventeenth century not only awarded the English aristocracy a part in the modernisation of the state by establishing a system of parliamentary government based upon contract rather than divine right, but also gave it a reactionary role to play in the state's long-term development since they excluded the apparatus of royal absolutism, as well as royal domination. On the Continent, a process of political modernisation, closely linked with royal absolutism, featured the establishment of large national armies and extensive bureaucracies, each run by a professional elite subjected to a career structure determined by experience and merit. In England the reaction against royal absolutism was also a revulsion against everything that it stood for. The conciliar developments of the Tudors, having been used as an instrument of early Stuart absolutism, were dismantled never to be replaced. In their stead the JP ruled, freed of bureaucratic restraints and subjected only to the supervision and selection of the lord lieutenant. Chosen for office because of the local standing imparted by their landownership, both JPs and lord lieutenants operated as a service elite but in an aristocratic, not a professional capacity.

Throughout the eighteenth century the state remained administratively primitive with a professional bureaucracy exiguous in the provinces and underdeveloped even at Westminster, with the possible exception of the treasury, the war office and the admiralty. This left the government heavily dependent upon the untrained, unpaid aristocrat for the enforcement of policy and the maintenance of law and order. Centuries earlier, the willingness of the aristocracy to fulfil this task had allowed a centralised state to develop without an extensive bureaucracy for its operation. In this sense, a traditional role of the English aristocracy was to act as a substitute for bureaucracy. Throughout much of the medieval period, a range of European nobilities exercised the same function. Yet in the modern period many of them adapted to royal absolutism and aided the development of professional bureaucracies by serving as their personnel. In contrast, in England the aristocracy continued to serve the government in the traditional manner. Delayed by aristocratic resistance and service, a modern professional bureaucracy struggled into being only in the nineteenth century, a response to the social problems of industrialisation rather than, in the earlier continental manner, to the financial problems of the Crown.

Its emergence was directed by the aristocratic presence. Prior to the acts of 1888 and 1894 establishing elected county and parish councils, local government came to consist of a complication of elected boards whose coherence and coordination depended upon the *ex officio* membership of the aristocratic JP. Furthermore, the reform of the civil service, making it patronage free and giving it a professional career structure, was a painfully slow process, in spite of the momentum provided by the reaction against the corruption of oligarchic rule. This was largely because the aristocracy used the civil service as 'a sort of Foundling Hospital', in the words of Sir Charles Trevelyan, for its less well-off members. The Tomlin Commission of 1929 implied that patronage was no longer exercised in the civil service, but the scouring out process was a long one. The meritocratic proposals of the Northcote–Trevelyan report of 1853 were not fully implemented fifty years later. Only in 1870 did an order-in-council subject all vacancies to open competition and even then, many posts remained in practice reserved for nomination by heads of departments; and excluded from the 1870 order was a section of the service with strong aristocratic connections, the foreign office, which was only brought into line in 1912. Furthermore, as the MacDonnell Commission of 1913 revealed, the examination syllabus for admission to the civil service favoured candidates from Oxford and Cambridge, thus allowing aristocrats to benefit from the easy access which their background gave them to these ancient seats of learning. Also favouring aristocrats in the civil service was the survival of low salaries which necessitated the supplement of a private income.

A modern bureaucratic system developed much later in Great Britain than in many continental states. Party responsible was the aristocracy's inability to accept royal absolutism and its earlier co-operation with the Crown which enabled a constitutional rather than a bureaucratic form of political centralisation to take place. Moreover when bureaucratisation became inevitable, the aristocracy impeded the establishment of a fully professionalised service by upholding the patronage and status elements of the old system.

The aristocratic reaction against royal absolutism also marred the development of a regular army and a sophisticated tax system. In the course of the late seventeenth century a standing army emerged, originally founded by the parliamentarians in the civil war and developed by Charles II and James II to bolster their political position. Its development was restricted in two respects. To prevent it from serving as the instrument of royal absolutism, especially after James II's expansion of the force, an aristocratic parliament insisted upon regulating it by means of Mutiny Acts and expenditure controls. It also determined that, while the king should have sole command, the army should be subjected to a system of proprietary office. Proprietary office was part of the state apparatus of French absolutism and in the standing armies of Russian and Prussian absolutism the membership of the officer corps was determined by a strong preference for the noble-born. But alongside the proprietary *officier* in France was the appointed *commissaire*; and in the non-venal Russian and Prussian armies noble domination of the officer corps was not at the expense of professionalisation. In England, the regular army's command remained largely outside the Crown's control, distinctly aristocratic and persistently non-professional. There was no equivalent of the *commissaire*:

until 1871 all commissions up to lieutenant-colonel were normally purchased. There was, moreover, no career structure allowing promotion to result naturally from merit or experience. Money and patronage secured office and promotion. Also working against professionalisation was the level of pay. As with office in the civil service, the low pay of army commissions was determined not simply by considerations of economy but by the desire to exclude men without private means. Reacting against the threat of professionalisation, originally posed by the military innovations of royal absolutism and later by the rise of the middle class, the aristocracy sought to maintain the regular commission as the preserve of the amateur gentleman. It succeeded in this aim until the early 1870s. Throughout the eighteenth and early nineteenth centuries the higher commands in the militia were also preserved for the aristocracy with a similar low level of efficiency in the leadership.

(c) Taxation

Until at least the late seventeenth century, the fiscal system in England remained unsophisticated and inadequate, especially in comparison with the other states of western Europe. Much of the responsibility for its backwardness lay with the aristocracy's ability to oppose the wishes of the government. From the Conquest to the fourteenth century government was largely financed from taxation. In the fourteenth century, however, a product of aristocratic resistance was the theory that the king should live of his own: that is, that ordinary government should be financed out of the king's private resources and that, apart from customs dues, taxes should only meet the cost of extraordinary expenditure such as war. This theory, and its implication that direct taxation was an extraordinary levy which in normal circumstances could be dispensed with, prevailed for centuries, in spite of the dwindling private resources of the Crown and its consequent increasing dependence upon parliamentary supplies. Its effect in retarding the development of an adequate fiscal system is evident in the fact that no system of regular direct taxation was established until 1692, although France and Spain had possessed one since the fifteenth century. In England direct taxation could only be levied in the circumstances of emergency. Moreover, each levy required parliamentary consent. By maintaining this system, the aristocracy compensated for the absence of fiscal exemption among its privileges. Moreover, since the system of indirect taxation also remained comparatively underdeveloped until the late seventeenth century, the government for much of the medieval and early modern periods remained heavily dependent on parliamentary supplies: absent were the permanent sales taxes which on the Continent left government finances relatively free of parliamentary consent.

In England a system of regular direct taxation finally came with the Glorious Revolution but, from the government's point of view, its operation was severely restricted by the Commons' right to appoint tax commissioners and to determine its appropriation. Although the regular land tax initially fell heavily upon the aristocracy, it soon ceased to be oppressive because the aristocracy's domination of parliament ensured that no reassessment of landed incomes occurred. Moreover, its introduction was accompanied by the development of other sources of revenue, especially indirect taxes on consumption and also the national debt which made direct taxation a minor source of government funds. Before the twentieth century, attempts to enlarge the contribution of direct taxation and to tax wealth appropriately failed.

Thus, the aristocracy used its control of the political system to postpone the introduction of regular direct taxation. Moreover, when admitted, it was quickly replaced by sources of revenue which fell heavily upon the poor. Not only did the aristocracy protect itself by restricting taxes on income but also by holding off the imposition of taxes on capital. In both respects the tax system remained primitive and prejudicial until the establishment of wealth taxes and high rates of income tax in the twentieth century.

At the heart of the English aristocracy's contribution to the development of the state was its relationship to revolution. The fact that it committed a revolution in the seventeenth century and avoided one in the nineteenth and twentieth centuries gave it a decisive impact. Absolutism and its trappings were repudiated and democracy was slowly but peacefully realised. Yet the aristocracy's contribution reached much further back in time. Arousing the Stuarts' attempts at royal absolutism was the limited, constitutional monarchy already in existence. This polity, with its law-making parliament, its meagre state apparatus, its inadequate tax system, was a legacy of the medieval aristocracy which had kept the royal prerogative in its place by acts of resistance and had permitted, by acts of co-operation with the Crown, a remarkably centralised political system to function with the minimum of state interference and exaction.

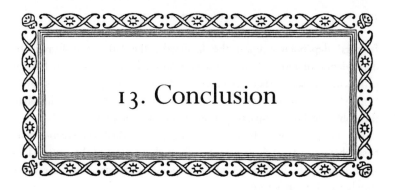

13. Conclusion

Viewed in the long term, certain periods in the history of the English aristocracy seem especially prominent. Apart from the formative century after the Conquest and the destructive last hundred years, the fourteenth and seventeenth centuries stand out as significant turning points. In the fourteenth century, the aristocracy acquired its distinctive features: the conjunction of an overprivileged peerage with an underprivileged gentry, its essential political functions, imparted by the emergence of parliament and the creation of the commission of the peace, and, with the decline of serfdom, a landlord–tenant relationship featuring few seigneurial rights. In the seventeenth century, a tradition of aristocratic revolt came to successful fruition, severely reducing the powers of the Crown by elevating those of an aristocratic parliament, and awarding the aristocracy a control of the state which formerly it had only exercised when permitted by royal minority or the personal insufficiency of the monarch. The effect of aristocratic revolt in the seventeenth century is measurable in the contrasting polities of the Tudors and Hanoverians. Quite apart from revolt, the development of the lord lieutenancy in the seventeenth century, established as the leading office in county government with the charge of nominating the JPs and bestowing leases on Crown lands, ensured that the aristocratic control of the shires should rest with the territorial magnates, the natural recipients of the office. Coincidental with the political changes, a process of estate management, underway in earlier centuries and extended in later ones, transformed the relationship between aristocracy and people, removing traditional tenant rights by converting customary and freehold tenures to leaseholds, and promoting capitalist, at the expense of peasant, farming. The former increased the farmers' dependency upon the landlords; the latter transferred the dependency of most of the rural population from landlord to farmer, producing social conflicts, essentially between employer and employee, from which the aristocracy was safeguarded by virtue of its subscription to the noble ideal of non-participation in commercial activity.

On the other hand, these two turning points failed to disturb certain basic characteristics which persisted throughout most of the order's life-span, notably the inadequacy of its corporate privileges and the relative simplicity of its structure.

In England, there was no *noblesse de robe*. The aristocracy's response to royal absolutism and the prospect of bureaucratisation was not to become professionalised as a political elite, in the manner of the Danish, Swedish, Austrian, Bohemian, French, Russian and Prussian nobilities, but, like the Polish and Hungarian nobilities, to preserve by effective armed and parliamentary resistance its traditional functions. Shaped by the early centralisation of the judiciary and its dependence upon commissions of gentlemen rather than trained judges, the early emergence and durability of parliament and the early decay of seigneurial authority, these political functions relied upon appointment or election rather than private ownership, but were clearly non-professional since the aristocrat qualified for office by virtue of his name and landedness. They lasted until the parliamentary and local government reforms of the late nineteenth century produced a system which favoured the professional politician and administrator and from which the aristocrat was inclined to retire. Even in the army professionalisation was held at bay until the late nineteenth century by a system of proprietary office and, within the officer corps, an ingrained amateurism.

The simplicity of structure was upheld by the relative absence of poor and landless nobles. In England poverty tended to denoble, except in the case of peers and baronets whose aristocratic identity was maintained by privilege. For the rest, the few privileges in their possession and the tendency of commoners to assume them without ennoblement made the aristocrat's identity heavily reliant upon his ability to subscribe to the noble ideals. Since these ideals required considerable resources for their fulfilment, poverty left aristocrats with little means of distinguishing themselves from commoners. Limiting the numbers of poor nobles in England was not only the process of social demotion but also the size of the aristocracy in proportion to the whole population, and the predominance of primogeniture in the inheritance of privileges, especially those which escaped commoner assumption. Populous nobilities and large numbers of poor nobles went together, as in Castile, Poland and Hungary. However, England probably possessed a smaller proportion of poor nobles than France even though their nobilities were roughly of equal density. Producing poor nobles in France were the corporate privileges and their inheritance by gavelkind. Such a system continually spawned nobles whose resources were inadequate for maintaining a noble life-style. In England there was much less to sustain the aristocratic status of the younger son who, unless born into the peerage or the baronetcy, tended to sink into the commonalty. Another source of poor nobility was ennobling office: a system whereby commoners, sometimes simply by an act of purchase but often by service, secured noble status as a result of becoming professional administrators and army officers. The limited nature of bureaucracy in England, the tendency of aristocrats to purchase the army offices, the domination of the public services by aristocrats, and the practice of elevating into the aristocracy only the landed, meant that few commoners could attain noble status by way of office. Instead, the way to social promotion was to acquire the trappings of nobility and the resources necessary for maintaining them. On the Continent, the prevalence of poor nobles meant that the noble order frequently contained the whole social spectrum, its members in large numbers following commoner, as well as noble, occupations. In England, with the rare exception, this was not the case prior to the twentieth century.

The English aristocracy remained closely attached to land until the final decades of the nineteenth century. For the gentry, the connection was a vital source of identity; for the peerage and baronetcy the connection was firmly upheld by the application of primogeniture to both privileges and land and by the government's policy of only elevating subjects who had already attained the credential of landownership. On the Continent, the landless noble was a common feature not only of the populous nobilities but also of small nobilities subjected to royal absolutism or other forms of bureaucratic monarchy since the generous ennobling policies of their rulers created nobles in large numbers who lacked the means to purchase an estate: as in eighteenth-century Denmark, Sweden, France and Russia. In England the landed connection was upheld by the limited access of landless commoners to aristocratic status and the ease with which landless aristocrats underwent social demotion. In England the aristocracy's coherence was imparted not only by landedness but also by its stolidly rentier character. To fulfil the aristocratic ideal of landownership, it was important that the estate was both substantial – preferably several thousand acres – and well tenanted. In a manner typical of western Europe, the latter consideration combined with a contempt for trade to persuade aristocrats to let, rather than to farm, their estates.

Thus, preserving a coherence of membership was not an abundance of corporate privileges but the inclination of aristocrats, whether gentry or peers, to possess the resources necessary for following a way of life centring upon the belief that for aristocrats public service was a duty rather than a means of subsistence, and that the latter should be unearned, take in the form of rent and stem from landownership.

The English aristocracy's ideals closely resembled those of the continental noble orders, apart from the nobles of Poland, Prussia and Hungary who farmed without ignobility. Hereditary, and conferring political power as well as honorific distinction, its privileges also followed the continental pattern. In the continental manner all English aristocrats possessed some privilege – in this respect the gentry was a lesser nobility – while some privileges were confined to a part of the aristocracy. Its composition was akin to that of the continental nobilities: a class not a caste, with membership determined by promotion as well as birth. In the traditional continental manner, its landownership gave it a special role to play in the running of the state. What made it unusual was the relative absence of members with commoner occupations, the degree of denoblement, the limited nature of its corporate privileges and its seigneurial rights coupled with the abundance of rank privileges, and its ability to resist the government both in parliament and by armed revolt, the latter preserving its traditional public function until the late nineteenth century.

In England the aristocracy protected its identity as a ruling class by rejecting royal absolutism. Continental nobilities preserved their aristocratic identity in other ways: submitting to professionalisation but possessing proprietary offices as in France; exercising seigneurial authority as in France, Russia, Prussia, Austria and Bohemia; and valuing offices which were diet-elected rather than government-appointed, as in nineteenth-century Prussia and Russia. In England the rejection of royal absolutism excluded the extensive, professional public services associated with it. In place of the *intendant* was the lord lieutenant, his appointment determined by a local ascendancy based upon extensive landownership. In the absence of alternative means, the English aristocracy's traditional public functions remained irreplaceably relevant well into the nineteenth century.

In England the aristocracy's survival depended not only upon the success of aristocratic revolt but also upon the absence of popular revolution. Ensuring the latter was not so much aristocratic flexibility as the absence of the political and social circumstances normally conducive of revolution. Absent in England was an absolutist, indebted government and the social elements responsible for revolution: an aggrieved professional class and a militant peasantry, both hostile to the nobility, the one because of noble privileges and career opportunities, the other because of seigneurial rights. Directed by industrial and commercial capitalism, popular hostility in England failed to beam specifically upon an injustice which the aristocracy could be presented as the embodiment. In the absence of popular or government rejection, the English aristocracy suffered the slow erosion of power and privilege that came of government malevolence, public indifference and commoner assumption. Destroying the corporate privileges as noble rights and the aristocracy's political ascendancy was the commoners' adoption of coats of arms and aristocratic forms of address, and their usurpation of its role as conservers of traditional England. On the other hand, it survived, if in a transformed state, largely because governments could not use the abolition of the house of lords or land nationalisation to win public support. In the circumstances, its political decline was a matter of choice rather than compulsion. Thus some aristocrats retained public functions, mainly as professional administrators, soldiers and politicians, whilst the rest withdrew. Except for the peerage, no matter how aristocrats chose, they suffered loss: the ones retaining a political function, as civil servants and MPs, became professionalised; whilst those retaining a clear aristocratic identity through rentier landownership and by avoiding professionalisation became a social rather than a political elite. Only the peers preserved a political function that was indisputably aristocratic, a consequence of their hereditary or life membership of the house of lords and the survival of their service as lord lieutenants.

In a typical continental manner, the English aristocracy weathered, over the centuries, a succession of crises in landownership and then was downed, but not terminated, by a long-drawn-out slump in rents and land values that lasted from the 1870s to the 1960s. The gentry was badly affected. Moreover, with other opportunities for investment and a need to contain extravagance, the aristocracy generally was driven to change its ways. In this period land sales no longer merely transferred land from sinking aristocrats to rising aristocrats, preserving it as an aristocratic possession, but passed the ownership to farmers, the state and financial institutions. Nevertheless, whilst landlessness developed within the English aristocracy on an unprecedented scale, converting it, through decimating the gentry, into an order which for the first time predominantly consisted of peers and baronets, a close connection with landownership remained; and salvation for landowners came in the late twentieth century when land values made a spectacular recovery.

The English aristocracy's antipathy towards commercial activity was a constant characteristic from the thirteenth to the twentieth centuries, stoutly maintained by its members in spite of the temptations which the profitability of agrarian and industrial capitalism offered. Nonetheless, contempt for trade did not prevent aristocrats from promoting it. The contempt only related to direct involvement. If carried out by commoners and if it enhanced rents, aristocrats tended to be tolerant and sympathetic. Even though they eschewed farming, providing no more than its fixed capital as landlords, and chose not to own factories or workshops nor to invest at all in manufacturing, and set an example whereby capital was withdrawn from production and sunk in social status, aristocrats, as landlords and parliamentarians, helped to promote both commercial farming and industrialisation. In some respects their contribution was not specifically aristocratic: like commoners, they invested in communications, commerce and finance. In some respects their contribution was hardly decisive: railways and canals would have developed anyway, as would agrarian capitalism; and industrialisation did not occur earlier in Great Britain than elsewhere because of the English aristocracy's peculiarity. Yet in determining parliamentary business, and as owners of most privately owned land and its resources which included minerals, they made a special aristocratic contribution. As approvers of acts for enclosure and transport improvements, and as landlords permitting commercial farming, the exploitation of their mineral resources, and the growth of manufacturing towns upon their lands, they had a clear hand in modernising the economy.

In spite of its need to uphold traditional ways, its postponement of a professional bureaucracy through acting as an alternative instrument of government and through soundly defeating royal absolutism; and in spite of retarding the development of a regular system of direct taxation and opposing universal suffrage, the English aristocracy also had a hand in the modernisation of the state, especially in enabling the Crown to centralise it from the twelfth century in the absence of an extensive bureaucracy, and by maintaining and extending the political function of parliament. Numerical democracy was ceded by the aristocracy in the face of popular pressure rather than naturally endorsed; but it was constructed on a system of parliamentary government developed by aristocrats who, lacking the privilege of fiscal exemption, had traditionally valued parliament because of its tax-granting powers and who raised its importance, at a time when representative assemblies were falling victim to the Crown, by successfully opposing the absolutist ambitions of the Stuarts. In view of the aristocracy's long-term role as a substitute instrument of government for bureaucracy, its involvement with parliament and its effectiveness in resisting government innovation, the features peculiar to the development of the English state – notably a low level of state control coupled with a high level of centralisation, a strong parliament and a feeble professional bureaucracy – owed much to the aristocratic presence.

Like the rest of rural society, the English aristocracy has suffered from the historian's tendency to conceive it as highly individualistic (see bibliography, section I (b)). Comparisons with continental nobilities are inclined to stress its differences and to overlook the similarities. But no two European nobilities were alike. In this sense, the oddities of the English aristocracy do not make it automatically atypical. The strong and obvious affinities, in fact, render the differences matters of detail rather than of kind. Landed, rentier, privileged, hereditary, composed of an upper and lower strata delineated by privilege and wealth, revering birthright but prepared to admit commoners-born, imbued with the belief that it had, like the Crown, a special role to play in the running of the state, it was sustained, shaped and stunted by the basic traits, habits and prejudices of the European nobility.

Bibliography

This is a selection, rather than a comprehensive statement, of the works consulted. Its aim is to provide basic reference and to suggest further reading. Within each section the works are arranged, wherever possible, in chronological order.

I Introduction

(a) *Definition and terminology*

N. Saul, *Knights and Esquires: the Gloucestershire Gentry in the Fourteenth Century* (Oxford, 1981), chs. 1 and 7

A. B. Ferguson, *The Indian Summer of English Chivalry* (Duke University, 1960)

D. Cressy, 'Describing the social order of Elizabethan and Stuart England', *Literature and History*, III (1976)

P. Zagorin, *The Court and the Country, the Beginning of the English Revolution* (London, 1969), ch. 2

K. Wrightson, *English Society, 1580–1680* (London, 1982), ch. 1

L. Stone, 'Social mobility in England, 1500–1700', *Past and Present*, XXXII (1966)

P. Laslett, *The World We Have Lost* (London, 1965)

L. P. Labatut, *Les noblesses européennes de la fin du XVe siècle à la fin du XVIIIe siècle* (Paris, 1978), ch. 2 (3)

(b) *Peculiarity*

M. Bloch, *Feudal Society* (English translation, London, 1961), ch. 24

S. J. Woolf, 'The Aristocracy in transition: a continental comparison', *Economic History Review*, 2nd series, XXIII (1970)

R. Forster and R. B. Litchfield, 'Four nobilities of the Ancien Regime', *Comparative Studies in Society and History*, VII (1965)

H. J. Habakkuk, 'England', in *The European Nobility in the Eighteenth Century*, ed. A. Goodwin (London, 1953)

G. E. Mingay, *English Landed Society in the Eighteenth Century* (London, 1963), ch. 11

B. Behrens, 'Nobles, privileges and taxes in France at the end of the Ancien Regime', *Economic History Review*, 2nd series, XV (1963)

H. J. Perkin, 'The social causes of the British industrial revolution', *Transactions of the Royal Historical Society*, 5th series, XVIII (1968)

Barrington Moore, *Social Origins of Dictatorship and Democracy* (London, 1967), chs. 1 and 2

II   Privileges

(a)   *Noble privileges*

M. L. Bush, *Noble Privilege* (Manchester, 1983)

N. Denholm-Young, *The County Gentry in the Fourteenth Century* (Oxford, 1969), chs. 1 and 2

L. G. Pine, *The Story of Heraldry* (Vermont, 1963), chs. 7 and 10

G. D. Squibb, *Precedence in England and Wales* (Oxford, 1981)

A. R. Wagner, *English Genealogy* (Oxford, 1960)

K. S. Van Eerde, 'The Jacobean baronets: an Issue between king and parliament', *Journal of Modern History*, XXXIII (1961)

N. B. Harte, 'State control of dress and social change in pre-industrial England', in *Trade, Government and Economy in Pre-Industrial England*, ed. D. C. Coleman and A. H. John (London, 1976)

M. Graves, 'Freedom of peers from arrest', *American Journal of Legal History*, XXI (1977)

J. C. Lassiter, 'Defamation of peers: the rise and decline of the action of Scandalum Magnatum, 1497–1773', *ibid.*, XXII (1978)

E. Chamberlayne, *Angliae Notitia* (London, 1700 ed.)

P. B. Munsche, *Gentlemen and Poachers, the English Game Laws, 1671–1831* (Cambridge, 1981), ch. 1

L. O. Pike, *A Constitutional History of the House of Lords* (London, 1884), ch. 12

F. B. Palmer, *Peerage Law in England* (London, 1907)

R. Stevens, *Law and Politics, The House of Lords as a Judicial Body, 1800–1976* (London, 1979)

P. A. Bromhead, *The House of Lords and Contemporary Politics, 1911–1957* (London, 1958)

E. Lyon and A. Wigram, *The House of Lords* (London, 1977), part 1

(b)   *Seigneurial rights*

M. Bloch, *Seigneurie française et manoir anglais* (Paris, 1960)

E. Miller and J. Hatcher, *Medieval England: Rural Society and Economic Change, 1086–1348* (London, 1978), chs. 5–8

J. L. Bolton, *The Medieval English Economy, 1150–1500* (London, 1980), chs. 1 and 7

E. Searle, 'Seigneurial control of womens' marriage: the antecedents and functions of merchet in England', *Past and Present*, LXXXII (1979)

E. B. Dewindt, *Land and People at Holywell-cum-Needingworth 1252–1457* (Toronto, 1972)

L. Stone, *The Crisis of the Aristocracy* (Oxford, 1965), ch. 6

W. O. Ault, *Private Jurisdiction in England* (New Haven, 1923)

J. P. Dawson, *A History of Lay Judges* (Cambridge, Mass., 1960), ch. 4

S. and B. Webb, *English Local Government* (London, 1908), II, chs. 1 and 2

III Composition

G. E. Mingay, *The Gentry* (London, 1976)

K. B. McFarlane, *The Nobility of Later Medieval England* (Oxford, 1973), chs. 1, 2 and 8

T. B. Pugh, 'The magnates, knights and gentry', in *Fifteenth-Century England, 1399–1509*, ed. S. B. Chrimes (Manchester, 1972)

N. Saul, *Knights and Esquires: the Gloucestershire Gentry in the Fourteenth Century* (Oxford, 1981)

L. Stone, *The Crisis of the Aristocracy* (Oxford, 1965), chs. 2 and 3

J. S. Morrill, 'The northern gentry and the Great Rebellion', *Northern History*, XV (1979)

J. T. Cliffe, *The Yorkshire Gentry from the Reformation to the Civil War* (London, 1969)

B. G. Blackwood, *The Lancashire Gentry and the Great Rebellion, 1640–60* (Manchester, 1978)

A. Fletcher, *A County Community in Peace and War, Sussex 1600–1660* (London, 1975)

J. P. Cooper, 'The counting of manors', *Economic History Review*, 2nd series, VIII (1956)

J. H. Hexter, 'Storm over the gentry', in his *Reappraisals in History* (London, 1961)

K. S. Van Eerde, 'The creation of the baronetage in England', *Huntington Library Quarterly*, XXII (1959)

—— 'The Jacobean baronets: an issue between king and parliament', *Journal of Modern History*, XXXIII (1961)

K. W. Wachter and P. Laslett, 'Measuring patriline extinction for modeling social mobility in the past', in *Statistical Studies of Historical Social Structure*, ed. K. W. Wachter (New York, 1978)

F. M. L. Thompson, 'The social distribution of landed property in England since the sixteenth century', *Economic History Review*, 2nd series, XIX (1966)

H. J. Habakkuk, 'England' in *The European Nobility in the Eighteenth Century*, ed. A. Goodwin (London, 1953)

—— 'English landownership, 1680–1740', *Economic History Review*, 2nd series, X (1940) and his 'The English land market in the eighteenth century', in *Britain and the Netherlands*, I, ed. J. S. Bromley and E. H. Kossmann (London, 1960). But also see the criticism of this thesis by J. V. Beckett in *Economic History Review*, 2nd series, XXX (1977), C. Clay, *op. cit.*, XXVII (1974) and B. A. Holderness, *ibid.* and L. Bonfield in his *Marriage Settlements 1601–1740* (Cambridge, 1983), ch. 6

M. W. McCahill, 'Peerage creations and the changing character of the British nobility, 1750–1830', *English Historical Review*, XCVI (1981)

F. M. L. Thompson, *English Landed Society in the Nineteenth Century* (London, 1963), chs. 2, 11 and 12

A. Sampson, *The Anatomy of Britain Today* (London, 1965), ch. 1

The Economist, 21 and 28 July 1956

J. P. Morgan, *The House of Lords and the Labour Government, 1964–1970* (Oxford, 1975)

IV   Political function and power

H. M. Jewell, *English Local Administration in the Middle Ages* (Newton Abbot, 1972)

M. Powicke, *Military Obligation in Medieval England* (Oxford, 1962)

G. O. Sayles, *The King's Parliament of England* (London, 1975)

W. O. Ault, *Private Jurisdiction in England* (New Haven, 1923)

R. R. Reid, 'Barony and thanage', *English Historical Review*, XXXV (1920)

R. R. Davies, *Lordship and Society in the Marches of Wales, 1282–1400* (Oxford, 1978)

H. Cam, 'The decline and fall of English feudalism', *History*, XXV (1940)

G. A. Holmes, *The Estates of the Higher Nobility in Fourteenth-Century England* (Cambridge, 1957), chs. 1 and 3

J. R. Maddicott, 'Law and lordship: royal justices as retainers in thirteenth- and fourteenth-century England', *Past and Present*, supplement 4 (1978)

W. H. Dunham, 'Lord Hastings' indentured retainers, 1461–1483', *Connecticut Academy of Arts and Sciences, Transactions*, XXXIX (1955)

M. E. James, 'Change and continuity in the Tudor north', *Borthwick Papers,* XXVII (1965)

—— 'A Tudor Magnate and the Tudor State', *Borthwick Papers*, XXX (1966)

B. Coward, *The Stanleys, 1395–1672* (Manchester, 1983), chs. 7, 8 and 10

P. Williams, *The Tudor Regime* (Oxford, 1979), part 1

J. Cornwall, 'The early Tudor gentry', *Economic History Review*, 2nd series, XVII (1965)

J. P. Dawson, *A History of Lay Judges* (Cambridge, Mass., 1960)

J. Hurstfield, 'County government, 1530–1660', *Victoria County History, Wiltshire*, V (London, 1957)

L. Stone, *The Crisis of the Aristocracy* (Oxford, 1965), chs. 5 and 8

J. H. Hexter, *Reappraisals in History* (London, 1961), chs. 2 and 6

J. C. Sainty, 'Lieutenants of counties, 1585–1642', *Bulletin of the Institute of Historical Research*, special supplement 8 (1970)

R. Ashton, 'The aristocracy in transition', *Economic History Review*, 2nd series, XXII (1969)

G. E. Mingay, *English Landed Society in the Eighteenth Century* (London, 1963), chs. 5 and 6

F. M. L. Thompson, *English Landed Society in the Nineteenth Century* (London, 1963), ch. 3

F. L. Guttsman, *The British Political Elite* (London, 1963)

C. H. E. Zangerl, 'The social composition of the county magistracy in England and Wales, 1831–1887', *Journal of British Studies*, XI (1971)

E. M. Spiers, *The Army and Society, 1815–1914* (London, 1980), ch. 1

V Wealth

E. Miller and J. Hatcher, *Medieval England, 1086–1348* (London, 1978), chs. 7 and 8

N. Saul, *Knights and Esquires* (Oxford, 1981), ch. 6

K. B. McFarlane, *The Nobility of Later Medieval England* (Oxford, 1973), chs. 1 and 3

G. A. Holmes, *The Estates of the Higher Nobility in Fourteenth-Century England* (Cambridge, 1957)

L. Stone, *The Crisis of the Aristocracy* (Oxford, 1965), part 2

T. K. Rabb, *Enterprise and Empire: Merchant and Gentry Investment in the Expansion of England, 1575–1630* (Harvard, 1967)

P. Roebuck, *Yorkshire Baronets, 1640–1760*, ch. 1

C. Shrimpton, *The Landed Society and the Farming Community of Essex in the late Eighteenth and early Nineteenth Centuries* (New York, 1977)

R. A. Kelch, *Newcastle, a Duke without Money* (London, 1974)

H. J. Habakkuk, 'The rise and fall of English landed families, 1600–1800', *Transactions of the Royal Historical Society*, 5th series, XXIX (1979)

E. Richards, *The Leviathan of Wealth, the Sutherland Fortune in the Industrial Revolution* (London, 1973)

D. Spring, 'English landowners and nineteenth-century industrialism', in *Land and Industry*, ed. J. T. Ward and R. G. Wilson (Newton Abbot, 1971)

—— *The English Landed Estate in the Nineteenth Century: its Administration* (Baltimore, 1963)

C. W. Chalklin, *The Provincial Towns of Georgian England, A Study of the Building Process, 1740–1820* (London, 1974)

S. W. Martins, *A Great Estate at Work: the Holkham Estate and its Inhabitants in the Nineteenth Century* (Cambridge, 1980)

D. Cannadine, 'Aristocratic indebtedness in the nineteenth century: the case re-opened', *Economic History Review*, 2nd series, XXX (1977)

W. O. Rubinstein, *Men of Property, the Very Wealthy in Britain since the Industrial Revolution* (London, 1981)

F. Bedarida, *A Social History of England, 1851–1975* (English translation, London, 1979), ch. 8

VI Ethos

K. B. McFarlane, *The Nobility of Later Medieval England* (Oxford, 1973), ch. 6

A. B. Ferguson, *The Indian Summer of English Chivalry* (Duke University, 1960)

Fritz Caspari, *Humanism and the Social Order in Tudor England* (New York, 1968)

H. V. Kearney, *Gentlemen and Scholars, Universities and Society in Pre-Industrial Britain, 1500–1700* (London, 1970)

M. E. James, 'English politics and the concept of honour, 1485–1642', *Past and Present*, supplement 3 (1978)

L. Stone, *The Crisis of the Aristocracy* (Oxford, 1965), chs. 6, 7 and 12

B. A Holderness, *Pre-Industrial England* (London, 1976), ch. 3

H. J. Habakkuk, 'The economic functions of English landowners in the seventeenth and eighteenth centuries', *Essays in Agrarian History*, I, ed. W. E. Minchinton (Newton Abbot, 1968)

D. Spring, 'Aristocracy, social structure and religion in the early Victorian period', *Victorian Studies*, VI (1962–3)

W. L. Arnstein, 'The survival of the Victorian aristocracy', in *The Rich, the Well Born and the Powerful*, ed. F. C. Jaher (Urbana, 1973)

F. M. L. Thompson, *English Landed Society in the Nineteenth Century* (London, 1963), ch. 4

D. C. Itzkowitz, *Peculiar Privilege, A Social History of English Fox-hunting, 1753–1885* (Harvard, 1977)

M. H. Wiener, *English Culture and the Decline of the Industrial Spirit, 1850–1980* (Cambridge, 1981)

M. Girouard, *Life in the English Country House* (New Haven and London, 1978)
—— *The Return to Camelot, Chivalry and the English Gentleman* (New Haven and London, 1981)

Clive Aslet, *The Last Country Houses* (New Haven and London, 1983)

VII Formation

H. M. Chadwick, *Studies in Anglo-Saxon Institutions* (Cambridge, 1905), pp. 378–83

E. John, 'English feudalism and the structure of Anglo-Saxon society', in *Orbis Britanniae and other Studies* (Leicester, 1960)

R. H. Loyn, *Anglo-Saxon England and the Norman Conquest* (London, 1962)

T. H. Aston, 'The origins of the manor in England', *Transactions of the Royal Historical Society*, 5th series, VIII (1958)

C. Warren Hollister, *Military Organisation of Norman England* (Oxford, 1965), ch. 2

F. Stenton, 'The changing feudalism of the Middle Ages', *History*, XIX (1935)

M. Bloch, *Feudal Society* (London, 1961), ch. 24

J. C. Holt, 'Politics and property in early medieval England', *Past and Present*, LVII (1972)

E. King, 'Large and small landowners in thirteenth-century England', *Past and Present*, XLVII (1970)

S. Harvey, 'The knight and the knight's fee in England', *Past and Present*, XLIX (1970)

J. M. W. Bean, *The Decline of English Feudalism, 1215–1540* (Manchester, 1968)

K. B. McFarlane, *The Nobility of Later Medieval England* (Oxford, 1973), chs. 1 (App. A), 2 and 8

T. B. Pugh, 'The magnates, knights and gentry', in *Fifteenth-Century England*, ed. S. B. Chrimes (Manchester, 1972)

N. Saul, *Knights and Esquires* (Oxford, 1981), chs. 1 and 7

J. L. Bolton, *The Medieval English Economy, 1150–1500* (London, 1980), chs. 1 and 7

VIII   The ascendancy of aristocracy

(a)   *The appreciation of the Crown*

K. B. McFarlane, *The Nobility of Later Medieval England* (Oxford, 1973), chs. 7 and 8

G. A. Holmes, *The Estates of the Higher Nobility in Fourteenth-Century England*, ch. 1

A. Tuck, *Richard II and the English Nobility* (London, 1973), ch. 1

T. B. Pugh, 'The magnates, knights and gentry', in *The Fifteenth Century*, ed. S. B. Chrimes (Manchester, 1972)

J. R. Lander, *Crown and Nobility, 1450–1509* (Oxford, 1976), chs. 1, 2, 5 and 11

T. B. Pugh, 'The ending of the middle ages, 1485–1536', in *Glamorgan County History* (Cardiff, 1971), III, ch. 11

M. L. Bush, 'The Tudors and the royal race', *History*, LV (1970)

—— 'The problem of the far north', *Northern History*, VI (1971)

W. T. MacCaffrey, 'England: the Crown and the new aristocracy, 1540–1600', *Past and Present*, XXX (1965)

D. Willen, 'Lord Russell and the western counties, 1539–1553', *Journal of British Studies*, XV (1975)

B. Coward, *The Stanleys* (Manchester, 1983), chs. 1 and 10

L. Stone, *The Crisis of the Aristocracy* (Oxford, 1965), chs. 5 and 8

(b)   *Aristocratic revolt*

H. Cam, *England before Elizabeth* (London, 1950), chs. 6, 8, 9, 12 and 13

F. Stenton, 'The changing feudalism of the middle ages', *History*, XIX (1935)

J. C. Holt, *Magna Carta* (Cambridge, 1965)

—— *The Northerners, a Study in the Reign of King John* (Oxford, 1961)

G. O. Sayles, *The King's Parliament of England* (London, 1975), ch. 4

G. A. Holmes, *The Later Middle Ages* (London, 1962), ch. 6

J. R. Maddicott, *Thomas of Lancaster, 1307–1322* (Oxford, 1970)

A. Tuck, *Richard II and the English Nobility* (London, 1973)

W. H. Dunham and Charles T. Wood, 'The right to rule in England: depositions and the kingdom's authority, 1327–1485', *American Historical Review*, LXXXI (1976)

C. Ross, *The Wars of the Roses* (London, 1976)

M. E. James, 'English politics and the concept of honour, 1485–1642', *Past and Present*, supplement 3 (1978)

J. S. Morrill, *The Revolt of the Provinces: Conservatives and Radicals in the English Civil War, 1630–1650* (London, 1976)

L. Stone, *The Causes of the English Revolution, 1529–1642* (London, 1972)

P. Christianson, 'The causes of the English revolution: a reappraisal', *Journal of British Studies*, XV (1976)

—— 'The peers, the people and parliamentary management in the first sixth months of the Long Parliament', *Journal of Modern History*, XLIX (1977)

C. Roberts, 'The Earl of Bedford and the coming of the English revolution', in *ibid.*

B. S. Manning, 'The aristocracy and the downfall of Charles I', in his *Politics, Religion and the English Civil War* (London, 1973)

P. Zagorin, *The Court and the Country, the Beginning of the English Revolution* (London, 1969), chs. 2, 3 and 4

J. R. Jones, *The Revolution of 1688 in England* (London, 1972)

J. P. Kenyon, *The Nobility and the Revolution of 1688* (Hull, 1963)

—— *Revolution Principles, the Politics of Party, 1688–1720* (Cambridge, 1977)

J. H. Plumb, *The Growth of Political Stability, 1675–1725* (London, 1967), chs. 1 and 2

L. Colley, *In Defiance of Oligarchy: the Tory Party 1714–1760* (Cambridge, 1982), part 1

(c)   *Aristocratic dominance*

R. Grassby, 'English merchant capitalism in the late seventeenth century', *Past and Present*, LXVII (1970)

P. Borsay, 'The English urban renaissance: the development of provincial urban culture, *c.* 1680–1760', *Social History*, V (1977)

P. B. Munsche, *Gentlemen and poachers, the English Game Laws, 1671–1831* (Cambridge, 1981), chs. 1, 4 and 5

L. Stone, 'Social mobility in England, 1500–1700', *Past and Present*, XXXIII (1966)

J. R. Jones, *The Revolution of 1688 in England* (London, 1972)

A. McInnes, 'The revolution and the people', in *Britain after the Glorious Revolution, 1688–1744*, ed. G. Holmes (London, 1969)

L. Colley, *In Defiance of Oligarchy* (Cambridge, 1982)

J. H. Plumb, *The Growth of Political Stability* (London, 1967)

E. P. Thompson, 'Patrician society, plebian culture', *Journal of Social History*, VII (1973–4)

H. J. Habakkuk, 'England', in *The European Nobility in the Eighteenth Century*, ed. A. Goodwin (Oxford, 1953)

D. C. Itzkowitz, *Peculiar Privilege* (Harvard, 1977), chs. 8, 9 and 10

H. Perkin, *The Origins of Modern English Society, 1780–1880* (London, 1969), ch. 2

(d)   *Anti-aristocratic sentiment*

R. Hilton, *The English Peasantry in the Later Middle Ages* (Oxford, 1975), ch. 4

R. Owst, *Preaching in Medieval England* (Cambridge, 1926)

H. C. White, *Social Criticism in Popular Religious Literature of the Sixteenth Century* (New York, 1944)

M. L. Bush, *The Government Policy of Protector Somerset* (London, 1975), ch. 4

L. Stone, *The Crisis of the Aristocracy*, chs. 2 and 14

R. B. Manning, 'Violence and social conflict in mid-Tudor rebellions', *Journal of British Studies*, XVI (1977)

A. Charlesworth, *An Atlas of Rural Protest in Britain, 1548–1900* (London, 1982)

B. S. Manning, *The English People and the English Revolution* (London, 1976), ch. 7

A. L. Morton, *The World of the Ranters* (London, 1970)

C. Hill, *The World Turned Upside Down: Radical Ideas during the English Revolution* (London, 1972)

D. Veall, *The Popular Movement for Law Reform, 1640–1660* (Oxford, 1970), chs. 5, 8 and 10

B. S. Capp, *The Fifth Monarchy Men, a Study in Seventeenth-Century English Millenarianism* (London, 1972), ch. 6

C. Hill, 'From Lollards to Levellers', in *Rebels and their Causes*, ed. M. Cornforth (London, 1978)

W. H. G. Armytage, *Heavens Below, Utopian Experiments in England, 1560–1960* (London, 1961)

J. Cannon, *Parliamentary Reform, 1640–1832* (Cambridge, 1972)

C. C. Weston, *English Constitutional Theory and the House of Lords, 1556–1832* (Oxford, 1965), chs. 2, 5 and 6

J. H. Plumb, 'Politcal man', in *Man Versus Society in Eighteenth-Century Britain*, ed. J. L. Clifford (Cambridge, 1968)

J. Stevenson, *Popular Disturbances in England, 1700–1870* (London, 1979)

E. P. Thompson, 'Eighteenth-century English society: class struggle without class', *Social History*, III (1978)

—— *The Making of the English Working Class* (London, 1963)

I. Prothero, *Artisans and Politics in early Nineteenth-Century London* (London, 1979)

E. J. Hobsbawm and G. Rudé, *Captain Swing* (London, 1969), parts 1 and 3

R. W. Davis, *Political Change and Continuity, 1760–1885, a Buckinghamshire Study* (Newton Abbot, 1972)

R. Douglas, *Land, People and Politics, a History of the Land Question in the United Kingdom, 1878–1952* (London, 1976)

A . Offer, *Land and Politics* (Cambridge, 1982), chs. 12 and 19–22

IX Decline and survival

A. S. Turberville, 'Aristocracy and revolution, the British peerage, 1789–1832', *History*, XXVI (1942)

Barrington Moore, *Social Origins of Dictatorship and Democracy* (London, 1967), chs. 1 and 2

T. Skocpol, *States and Social Revolutions* (Cambridge, 1979)

H. J. Perkin, *The Origins of Modern English Society* (London, 1969), ch. 6

G. Best, *Mid-Victorian Britain, 1851–1875* (London, 1971), ch. 4

R. Quinault, 'The Warwickshire county magistracy and public order, c. 1830–

1870', in *Popular Protest and Public Order*, ed. J. Stevenson and R. Quinault (London, 1974)

C. H. E. Zangerl, 'The social composition of the county magistracy in England and Wales, 1831–1887', *Journal of British Studies*, XI (1971)

W. L. Arnstein, 'The survival of the Victorian aristocracy', in *The Rich, the Well Born and the Powerful*, ed. F. C. Jaher (Urbana, 1973)

D. Spring, 'The role of the aristocracy in the late nineteenth century', *Victorian Studies*, IV (1960)

R. W. Davis, *Political Change and Continuity, 1760–1885, a Buckinghamshire Study* (Newton Abbot, 1972)

J. P. D. Dunbabin, 'Expectations of the new county councils and their realisation', *Historical Journal*, VIII (1965)

J. M. Lee, *Social Leaders and Public Persons, a Study of County Government in Cheshire since 1888* (Oxford, 1963)

D. Cannadine, *Lords and Landlords, the Aristocracy and the Towns, 1774–1967* (Leicester, 1980) ch. 1

H. Newby et al., *Property, Paternalism and Power: Class and Control in Rural England* (London, 1978)

W. L. Guttsman, *The British Political Elite* (London, 1963), chs. 4 and 5

H. J. Hanham, *Elections and Party Management* (London, 1959)

P. A. Bromhead, *The House of Lords and Contemporary Politics, 1911–1957* (London, 1958)

J. P. Cornford, 'The parliamentary foundations of the Hotel Cecil', in R. Robson (ed.), *Ideas and Institutions of Victorian Britain* (London, 1967)

R. A. Chapman and J. R. Greenaway, *The Dynamics of Administrative Reform* (London, 1980)

D. H. J. Morgan, 'The social and educational background of Anglican bishops', *British Journal of Sociology*, XX (1969)

C. B. Otley, 'The social origins of British army officers', *The Sociological Review*, new series, XVIII (1970)

E. M. Spiers, *The Army and Society, 1815–1914* (London, 1980), ch. 1

D. Cannadine, 'Aristocratic indebtedness in the nineteenth century: the case re-opened', *Economic History Review*, 2nd series, XXX (1977)

—— 'The theory and practice of the English leisure classes', *Historical Journal*, XXI (1978)

F. M. L. Thompson, *English Landed Society in the Nineteenth Century* (London, 1963), chs. 10–12

W. D. Rubinstein, *Men of Property* (London, 1981)

A. Sampson, *Anatomy of Britain Today* (London, 1965), ch. 1

The Economist, 21 and 28 July 1956

S. Glover, 'The Old Rich', *The Spectator*, January 1977

M. J. Wiener, *English Culture and the Decline of the Industrial Spirit, 1850–1980* (Cambridge, 1981)

F. Bederida, *A Social History of England, 1851–1975* (London, 1979), chs. 2, 5, 8, 9 and 11

R. Douglas, *Land, People and Politics, a History of the Land Question in the United Kingdom, 1878–1952* (London, 1976)

Clive Aslet, *The Last Country Houses* (New Haven and London, 1982)

H. A. Clemenson, *English Country Houses and Landed Estates* (London, 1982)

X Agrarian capitalism

B. A. Holderness, *Pre-Industrial England* (London, 1976), ch. 3

A. B. Appleby, 'Agrarian capitalism or seigneurial reaction', *American Historical Review*, LXXX (1975)

E. Kerridge, 'Agriculture, 1500–1793', *Victorian County History, Wiltshire*, IV (London, 1959)

L. Stone, *The Crisis of the Aristocracy* (Oxford, 1965), chs. 6 and 7

R. Brenner, 'Agrarian class structure and economic development in pre-industrial Europe', *Past and Present*, LXX (1976)

J. P. Cooper, 'In search of agrarian capitalism', in *ibid.*, LXXX (1978)

K. Wrightson, 'Aspects of social differentiation in rural England, c. 1580–1660', *Journal of Peasant Studies*, V (1977)

E. P. Thompson, 'Patrician society, plebian culture', *Journal of Social History*, VII (1973–4)

E. L. Jones, *Agriculture and the Industrial Revolution* (Oxford, 1974), chs. 2, 3 and 4

G. E. Mingay, 'The size of farms in the eighteenth century', *Economic History Review*, XIV (1962)

B. Sexauer, 'English and French agriculture in the late eighteenth century', *Agricultural History*, XXX (1976)

P. O'Brien and C. Keyder, *Economic Growth in Britain and France, 1780–1914* (London, 1978), ch. 5

S. W. Martins, *A Great Estate at Work: the Holkham Estate and its Inhabitants in the Nineteenth Century* (Cambridge, 1980)

F. M. L. Thompson, 'English great estates in the nineteenth century, 1790–1914', *Contributions to the First International Conference of Economic History* (Stockholm, 1960)

J. Blum, 'English parliamentary enclosure', *Journal of Modern History*, LIII (1981)

D. R. Mills, *Lord and Peasant in Nineteenth-Century Britain* (London, 1980)

R. Perren, 'The landlord and agricultural transformation, 1870–1900', in *British Agriculture, 1875–1914*, ed. P. J. Perry (London, 1973)

XI Industrialisation

H. J. Habakkuk, 'Economic functions of English landowners in the seventeenth and eighteenth centuries', in *Essays in Agrarian History*, I, ed. W. E. Minchinton (Newton Abbot, 1965)

——— 'Historical experience of economic development', in *Problems in Economic*

Development, ed. E. A. G. Robinson (Proceedings of a Conference held by the International Economists' Association, 1965)

J. T. Ward and R. G. Wilson (eds.), *Land and Industry* (Newton Abbot, 1971)

H. J. Perkin, 'The social causes of the British industrial revolution', *Transactions of the Royal Historical Society*, 5th series, XVIII (1968)

M. W. McCahill, 'Peers, patronage and the industrial revolution, 1760–1800', *Journal of British Studies*, XVI (1976)

E. Richards, *The Leviathan of Wealth, the Sutherland Fortune in the Industrial Revolution* (London, 1973)

D. Cannadine, 'The landowner as millionaire: the finances of the Dukes of Devonshire, *c.* 1800 to *c.* 1926', *Agricultural History Review*, XXV (1977)

T. S. Willan, *River Navigation in England, 1600–1750* (London, 1936), chs. 3 and 4

J. R. Ward, *The Finance of Canal Building in Eighteenth-Century England* (Oxford, 1974)

P. Mathias, *The First Industrial Nation* (London, 1969), ch. 3

M. W. Flinn, *The Origins of the Industrial Revolution* (London, 1966), ch. 3

D. C. Coleman, 'Gentlemen and players', *Economic History Review*, 2nd series, XXVI (1973)

M. J. Wiener, *English Culture and the Decline of the Industrial Spirit, 1850–1980* (Cambridge, 1981)

XII   Political impact

Barrington Moore, *Social Origins of Dictatorship and Democracy* (London, 1967), chs. 1, 7, 8 and epilogue

G. O. Sayles, *The King's Parliament of England* (London, 1975)

G. R. Elton, 'The body of the whole realm: parliament and representation in medieval and Tudor England', *Studies in Tudor and Stuart Politics and Government* (Cambridge, 1974), II, ch. 22

J. S. Roskell, 'Perspectives in English parliamentary history', *Bulletin of the John Rylands Library*, XLVI (1963–4)

B. P. Wolffe, *The Crown Lands, 1461 to 1536* (London, 1969), ch. 1

J. R. Jones, *The Revolution of 1688 in England* (London, 1972)

L. Stone, 'The results of the English revolutions of the seventeenth century', in *Three British Revolutions*, ed. J. G. A. Pocock (Princeton 1980)

W. R. Ward, *The Land Tax in the Eighteenth Century* (Oxford, 1953)

B. Behrens, 'Nobles, privileges and taxes in France at the end of the Ancien Regime', *Economic History Review*, 2nd series, XV (1963)

P. Mathias and P. O'Brien, 'Taxation in Britain and France, 1715–1810', *Journal of European Economic History*, V (1976)

J. Cannon, *Parliamentary Reform, 1640–1832* (Cambridge, 1972)

D. C. Moore, *The Politics of Deference* (Hassocks, 1976)

H. J. Hanham, *Elections and Party Management* (London, 1959)

N. Blewett, 'The franchise in the United Kingdom, 1885–1918', *Past and Present*, XXXII (1965)

R. A. Chapman and J. R. Greenaway, *The Dynamics of Administrative Reform* (London, 1980)

E. M. Spiers, *The Army and Society, 1815–1914* (London, 1980)

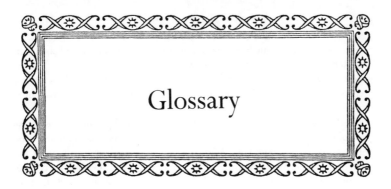

Glossary

ALECONNER an inspector responsible for upholding the regulations applying to the brewing and sale of ale

ALLOD an estate held in absolute ownership and completely free of the conditions of tenancy appertaining to fiefs and tenures

BANALITIES seigneurial monopoly rights over baking, brewing, milling etc.

BOOKLAND land and lordship granted by charter and mostly free of the obligations and proprietorial limitations of folkland

BURGBRYCE a compensatory fine payable by a convicted housebreaker to the owner of the house he has violated, and graduated in accordance with the status of the victim

BYRNIE a coat of mail

CEORL a freeman without noble status

CHAMPART a seigneurial due exacted annually and paid in kind

CHEVAGE a seigneurial tax levied on serfs

COPYHOLD a customary tenure recorded on the manor court roll

DANEGELD a royal land tax of the tenth and eleventh centuries

ESCHEATOR a royal official appointed to administer the property and goods forfeited by subjects to the Crown

FIEF an estate originally held on condition of military service to a feudal overlord

FOLKLAND land distributed by the ruler to subjects and held not in perpetuity but terminally, under obligation of military and civil service and without the immunities from royal government associated with bookland

FRANKPLEDGE a system of law and order whereby every member of a Tithing (a subdivision of a Hundred) was held responsible for the conduct of the other members. View of frankpledge was the royal sheriff's right of adjudication over such a system, a right which could become the property of subjects through alienation or usurpation

FYRD a royal army consisting of subjects under obligation of military service to the king

GAVELKIND the equal inheritance of a man's status or property by his sons; the opposite of primogeniture

GRESSOM a seigneurial due liable for payment on the renegotiation of the terms of a tenure, and a synonym for entry fine

HERIOT a seigneurial due, originally the best beast payable to the lord upon a tenant's death and later commuted to a sum of money or a lesser payment in kind

LEET a seigneurial court which, unlike the court baron, had powers of jurisdiction and officer appointment beyond the making, enforcement and administration of manorial regulations. These powers included the public jurisdictional and officer-appointing functions originally exercised by royal sheriffs, especially in connection with the view of frankpledge and the assize of bread and ale. They fell into the hands of lords of the manor by a process of alienation or usurpation

LERYWITE a fine imposed in the manor court for immorality

MERCHET a licence fee paid by serfs to their lord in order to secure his permission for the marriage of their daughters

MUNDBRYCE a compensatory fine payable by a criminal to a man whose protection he has offended by committing an act of violence in his company or household, and graduated in accordance with the status of the offended party

OYER AND TERMINER a royal commission appointed to judge matters criminal

PRIMOGENITURE the sole inheritance of a man's status or property by his eldest, surviving son; the opposite of gavelkind

RACK-RENT a revisable, economic rent, rather than one fixed by custom

RITTERSGUT an estate endowed, like the fief, with the privileges and obligations of knighthood

SAKE AND SOKE, TOLL AND TEAM, AND INFANGTHEF seigneurial rights of jurisdiction and taxation, limited by the fact that they did not include pleas of the Crown or exclude royal taxes

TAILLE a royal tax, direct and regular

TALLAGE a seigneurial tax levied upon free and unfree tenants

THEGN noble

TITHINGMAN originally, the chief man of a Tithing, and later a parish official with constabulary duties

VAVASOUR vassal of a vassal; a sub-vassal

WERGELD a compensatory fine, in the nature of blood money, paid by a convicted murderer to his victim's family, and graduated in accordance with the status of the victim

WITES judicial fines

Index

abbots, *see* spiritual peers
absolute monarchy, 11–12, 35, 48–50, 53, 58, 75, 95, 99, 115–16, 119, 121–24, 127, 134, 159–60, 198, 200, 203–5
address, forms of, 23–4
admiralty, 204
African kingdoms, 5
agricultural depression, 130, 147, 155–7, 177, 214
agricultural holdings acts, 164–5
Agricultural (Miscellaneous Provisions) Act (1976), 165
agricultural societies, 62
agriculture, *see* farming
aleconners, 53 and glossary
allod, 88 and glossary
amateurism, cult of, 73, 75, 162, 195
American revolution, 143, 145
American wheat, import of, 65, 155
Anabaptists, 142
Angevin dynasty, 86, 113–14
Anglo-Saxons, 19, 71, 81–4, 86–7, 144
Anjou, duchy of, 114
Anne, Queen, 48
annuitants, annuities, 41, 56, 94, 106
Antinomians, 142
apparel
   privileges, 17, 23–4, 27
   statutes restricting, 23

Appellate Jurisdiction Act (1876), 36
appellate jurisdiction of house of lords, 96, 126, 154, 163
Apprenticeship Act (1563), 27, 141–2
apprenticeships, 74–5
Aragon, nobles of, 57
armies
   national, 51, 69, 203, 205–6
   private, 50–1, 56, 104, 107–8, 122–3
armorial bearings, *see* coats of arms
armouries, private, 104
arms-bearing privilege, 87
arrest, immunity from, 20–1
artisans, 139–42
Arundel
   Richard FitzAlan, 4th earl of, 117
   house of, 92
assessment tax privilege, 22
assize judges, 90
assize of bread and ale, 51, 53
attainder, acts of, 100–1
Attlee, Clement, 1st earl, 169, n. 2
Australian wool, 65, 155
Austria, nobles of, 35, 210, 212

bailiffs, 53
Ball, John, 132
banalities, 97 and glossary
banking, 66–7, 69, 156, 188
Baptists, 142
barbed wire fences, 147

Barmby, Goodwyn, 130
bastard feudalism, see retaining system
baronetcy, baronet, 2, 4–8, 18, 24–5, 28,
    36–7, 40, 44–7, 61, 151–4, 156–8,
    165–6
barony, baron
    by patent, 23, 88, 91–2
    tenurial, 2, 85, 89, 91, 95; see also
        tenants-in-chief
    see also life barony
barony, franchise of, 52, 55, 88, 93
Barrow-on-Furness, 192
Bath, 64
Bayonne, 114
Beadles, 53
Beauchamp family, 118; see also War-
    wick, earl of
Becon, Thomas, 133, 135–6
Bedford
    Francis Russell, 4th earl of, and
        William Russell, 5th earl of, 122
    Francis Russell, 7th duke of, 189–90
benefit of clergy, peerage privilege, 20
Bentham, Jeremy, 145
Beowulf, 83
Berkshire farming, 62
Bill of Rights (1689), 112, 121
Birmingham, 64
birthright
    of the aristocracy, 4–5, 11, 13, 40, 73,
        75, 81–3, 200
    of the Crown, 115
    of the tenures, 33, 178, 180–1
bishops, see spiritual peers
Black Death (1349), 96–7
board of agriculture, 185
boards of guardians, 55
Bodmin, 132
Bohemia, nobles of, 210, 212
Boleyn, Mary and Anne, 103
Book of Saint Albans, 3
bookland, 19, 22, 82–3 and glossary
boon work, 32
Bordeaux, 114

boroughs, 122, 202–3
Bourbons, ruling dynasty of, 39
bourgeois, bourgeoisie, 73–7, 130,
    138–40, 146, 151–2, 155, 161–4,
    169, 195–6, 199
Brandenburg-Prussia, see Prussia
Brandon
    Charles, 1st duke of Suffolk, 101,
        104–5
    family of, 110
breach of promise, manorial jurisdic-
    tion in, 53
bread weighers, 53
brewing, 67–8
Bridgewater, Francis Egerton, 3rd
    duke of, 193
Bristol, 64
Brittany, duchy and province of
    loss of, 114
    nobles of, 7
Brodrick, W. St. John, 9th viscount
    Midleton and 1st earl of Midle-
    ton, 169
Bromyard, Thomas, 133
Brooke, Robert Greville, 2nd baron,
    122
Bubble Act (1720), repeal of (1825), 194
Buckingham, Edward Stafford, 3rd
    duke of, 107–8
Buckinghamshire gentry, 54
bureaucracy, 11–12, 49, 59, 90, 99, 160,
    203–5
burgbryce, 82 and glossary
Burghley, William Cecil, 1st baron, 118
Burke's General Armoury, 26
Burke's Landed Gentry, 26, 67, 157
businessmen, 73–4, 76, 152, 168, 193,
    195
Bute, earls of, 192

cabinet, 124, 150, 152, 167
Caird, James, 3
Calais, 114
Calvinism, 142

Cambridge University, 158, 167, 205
Campbell-Bannerman, Sir Henry, 148
canals, 68, 74, 192–3
capital gains tax, 164
capital transfer tax, 164–5
capitalism
    agrarian, 9–13, 29–31, 59–60, 72–4,
    128, 139–40, 161, 173, 175, 188–9,
    196 and ch. 10
    industrial, 9–13, 59–62, 72–4,
    139–40, 146, 161, 173, 193, 213
    and ch. 11
Cardiff, 192
Cardington, Bedfordshire, 179
Carrington, Peter Carington, 6th bar-
    on, 152
Carteret family, 68
Cartwright, Major John, 145
castellany, 51
Castile, nobles of, 7, 35, 211
castles, 71–2, 104
casualties, 31–2, 182
Catholic emancipation, 58
Catholicism, 119–20
Cavendish family, 68, 192; see also
    Devonshire
Caxton, William, 2
ceorl, 82–3 and glossary
Chamberlain, Joseph, 148
Chamberlayne, Edward, 3, 27
champart, 31 and glossary
chantries, dissolution of, 39, 42, 102–3
charity, 4, 69, 75–6, 135, 166
Charles I, 37, 119, 121–2, 126
Charles II, 121, 123, 126, 205
Charter of the Forest (1217), 112
Chartist movement, 145, 201
Cherbourg, 114
Cheshire aristocracy, 45, 168
Chester, palatinate of, 93
chevage, 97 and glossary
Chilterns, 176
Chippenham, Cambridgeshire, 179
chivalry

code, 71–2
    term, 8–9
christianity, conversion to, 71–2
Churchill, Sir Winston, 152
Cicero, 71
civil service, servants, 54–5, 69, 72,
    149–50, 163–4, 166, 204–6; see
    also noblesse de robe
civil war in England, 89, 105; see also
    Wars of the Roses; English Civil
    War; revolt, aristocratic
Clapham sect, 72
clergy, 36, 110, 113, 136, 150, 158,
    168, 174
clientage, 41
Clifford
    family of, 55
    Margaret, wife of 4th earl of Der-
    by, 106
    see also Cumberland, earl of
coats of arms, 8, 18, 24–8, 38–40, 45,
    91, 95, 110–11, 151
Cokes of Holkham, 66–7
collateral descent, 44
College of Heralds, 26, 45, 157
Colmore estate, 64
Colquhoun, Patrick, 138
Combination Acts (1799 and 1800),
    141
commercial activity, aristocratic atti-
    tude to, 4, 7, 9, 68–9, 74, 156,
    173, 214
commission of gaol delivery, 53, 90
commission of oyer and terminer, 90;
    see glossary (under Oyer and
    terminer)
commission of the peace, see justices
    of the peace
common, rights of, 134, 136–7, 140,
    145, 174, 177
commoners, commonalty, 4–6, 8–9,
    13, 17–18, 23, 25–8, 39–40,
    45–6, 59–60, 73–7, 151–3, 173,
    201, 213

commons, house of, 3, 5, 20, 22, 26–7, 43, 49, 55, 96, 23–4, 141, 145, 150–2, 159–60, 169, 199, 202–3, 207
communism, 131, 145
conciliar developments, see regional councils
conquest, see Norman conquest
Conservatives, see Tories
constables
    peerage privilege, 21
    seigneurial right to appoint, 53
constitutional monarchy, 11–12, 113, 121–2, 207–8
consumption, taxes on, 22, 127, 156, 185, 194, 207
convertible husbandry, 176–7
co-operative farms, 145
Coppe, Abiezer, 134
copyhold, see glossary; customary tenures
corn laws, 58, 126, 139, 141, 146, 148, 185
Cornwall, 104, 179, 190
coronation oath, 115, 118
coroner, 90
corporal punishment, immunity from, 21
corresponding societies, 201
Cort's process, 190
Cotswolds, 176
Council of the North, see regional councils
Council of the Welsh Marches, see regional councils
count, office and title of, 51, 84
county councils, 54–5, 162–4, 204
County Councils Act (1888), 54, 164, 167–8, 204
county courts, see shire courts
court baron, 51, 53
court leet, 21, 29, 51, 53–4; see glossary (under Leet)
court, royal, 43, 94, 106–8, 114, 116, 118, 120
court of chivalry, 26
court of conscience, 54
court of delegates, 149 n. 1
court of requests, 54
Courtenay
    family, 100–1, 103–4
    William, 9th earl of Devon, 105
Crimean war, 51
Cromwell, Thomas, 1st earl of Essex, 118
crossbow, use of, 17, 23
Crown, 4, 8–9, 11–13, 18, 23, 26, 28–9, 37–8, 41–5, 48–52, 56–9, 67, 81–2, 85–6, 88–90, 92–4, 99–109, 111–24, 126–7, 167, 189, 198–201, 205–8
Cumberland
    Henry Clifford, 1st earl of, 108
    Henry Clifford, 2nd earl of, 105
Cumberland farming, 177
Curwen family, 192
customary tenures, 11, 32–3, 53, 63, 97–8, 127–8, 137, 161, 164, 178–80, 184
customs dues, 68, 194, 206

Dacre family, 55
Danby, Thomas Osborne, 1st earl of, 123
danegeld, 19, 22, 87, 92 and glossary
Davenport, Allen, 130
death duties, see estate duty
debt
    indemnity from imprisonment for, 17, 20–1
    seigneurial jurisdiction in, 53
deference, popular, 4, 59–60, 66, 128–9, 132, 140, 144, 146, 161–3, 167, 184
Delamere, Henry Booth, 2nd baron, and 1st earl of Warrington, 123
de la Pole family, 105–6
demesne
    farming, 30–2, 62, 66, 178–83

management of, 63, 97, 179–80
democracy, 11–12, 55, 133, 139, 141,
    144–6, 161, 163, 168–9, 200–2,
    215
Denmark, nobles of, 210–11
deposition, royal, 112, 115, 117–18,
    120
deputy lieutenants, 54–5, 126
Derby, earldom of, 92, 191; see also
    Stanley
derogation, 9–10, 74, 128
Devon, 104, 132, 179
Devonshire, William Cavendish, 1st
    duke of, 123
Diggers, 132–5, 143, 145
dispensing powers, royal, 121
Disraeli, Benjamin 1st earl of Beacons-
    field, 202
dissent, 142–3
docks, 74, 146–7, 192
Dorset, Henry Grey, 3rd marquis of,
    42, 105
Dorset gentry, 45
Douglas, Lady Margaret, countess of
    Lennox, 101
Dudley, Edmund, 2
duel
    aristocratic right, 26
    changing nature, 107
dues, seigneurial, 28–31, 62–3, 65–6,
    74, 96–7, 128, 174, 178, 182–4
dukedom, 23, 47, 51, 84, 91
Durham, earls of, 191, 193
Durham palatinate, 179

earldom, 37, 84, 91–2
East India Company, 67
education, aristocracy and, 71–2, 107,
    109, 129; see also inns of court;
    public schools; universities
Education Act (1870), 55
Education Act (1944), 159
Edward I, 19, 93, 100, 114–15, 117
Edward II, 96, 100, 112–17

Edward III, 38, 91, 92–3, 100, 105,
    114, 121
Edward IV, 93–4, 101, 105–6
Edward VI, 42, 100, 103–4, 106, 136
Elizabeth I, 50, 102, 106, 118
enclosures, 30, 74, 137, 139, 177–80
English Civil War, 112–13, 119–23,
    125, 203, 205
English Revolution, 207; see also Engl-
    ish Civil War; Glorious Revolu-
    tion
engrossment of farms, 60, 63, 66, 74,
    98, 128, 136, 175–84
entry fines, 30–3, 64, 97, 136–7, 181
eolderman, office of, 84
escheators, 90 and glossary
escutcheons, see coats of arms
esquires, 3, 17, 24–6, 28, 38, 91–2
Essex, 44, 66, 179
Essex, Robert Devereux, 3rd earl of,
    122
estate duty, 155–6, 164, 166
Eton school, 76–7
EEC, 175
Evans, Thomas, 130
evil ministers, 113–14, 116, 118
excise, 127, 194; see also consumption,
    taxes on
Exeter, 146–7
Exeter, marquis of
    Courtenay, 105
    Cecil, 191
extinction of families, 43–7

Failing and Perishing, 142
Familists, 142
farming, 4, 10–11, 30, 39–40, 61–3,
    65, 68–9, 73–4, 97–8, 128, 136,
    140, 148, 155–7, 161, 174–86,
    188–9
Feake, Christopher, 134
felony, 20
Fens, 168
feudal host, 50

feudal system, 41, 52, 55–6, 84–5, 88–
    92, 94–5, 99, 101, 106, 109–10,
    115–16, 125–7
fief, fiefholder, 18, 86, 91–2 and
    glossary
Fifth Monarchists, 133–5, 142
Finance Act (1976), 165
first world war, 40, 152–3, 155, 186
fiscal exemption, 6, 17–18, 22, 28, 83,
    86–7, 92, 127, 199
fish ponds, 30
fishing, seigneurial right to, 32
Fitzgerald family, 100–1
Fitzroy, Henry, duke of Richmond, 103
Flanders, 31
Fleming Commission (1944), 158–9
flogging, immunity from, 18
folkland, 82–3 and glossary
foraging rights, 140
foreign office, 205
foreign secretary, 152
forestry, see timber
Forestry Commission, 157
forfeiture of estates and titles, 46, 100–
    2
fox hunting, 72, 76, 128–9, 140
France, 30, 35, 49–50, 57, 67, 84, 87,
    103, 113–14, 121, 138, 140, 143,
    182, 199, 205, 210–12
Franchise of Norfolk, 93–4
franchises, rights of, 29, 51–2, 59, 93–4,
    104, 106, 147
Frankish law, 81
frankpledge, view of, 51, 53 and
    glossary
freeholds, freeholders, 11, 24–5, 32–3,
    38, 64, 128, 153, 161, 178–81, 191,
    201
freemen, 81–2, 87, 96, 115
French revolution (1789), 11–12, 22, 72,
    125, 131–2, 138–40, 143–5
fyrd, 82 and glossary

gallows, seigneurial right of, 53

game laws, 23, 25, 128, 140–1
game reserves, 148
gamekeepers, 25
Gaunt, John of, 2nd duke of Lancaster,
    92–3
gavelkind, 6, 23–4, 26, 28, 155, 181 and
    glossary
gentility, 3, 9, 12, 77, 128–9, 161–3,
    195–6
gentleman, 24, 26–8, 38, 71, 91, 109,
    132–6, 162–3
gentry, 2–6, 18–19, 21, 24–5, 27–8, 36–
    46, 54, 56, 61, 63, 67, 69, 84, 91,
    94–5, 102, 106–11, 122–4, 128,
    139, 152–7, 162, 168
George, Henry, 147
George I, 48
gesith, 84
gifts, seigneurial right to, 31
Gladstone, William, 148
Glastonbury Abbey, 103
Glorious Revolution, (1689), 45, 48, 50,
    112–3, 119–23, 126, 200, 203, 207
Gloucester, Thomas of Woodstock, 1st
    duke of, 117
Godwin, William, 131, 143
Gogol, Nikolai, 154–5
gothic revival, 72
government bonds, 67–8, 129, 156, 194
grammar schools, 71, 76–7
Granville, earls of, see Carteret family
great charter, see Magna Carta
gressoms, see entry fines and glossary
Grey
    Catherine, 101
    Jane, 106, 112
Grey, Charles, 2nd earl, 202
Grindletonians, 142
Grosmont, Henry of, 1st duke of
    Lancaster, 93
Grosvenor family, 47

Haggard, Rider, 69
Hales, John, 136

Halifax, Lord, 152
Hampden clubs, 201
handguns, use of, 17, 23
hanging, immunity from, 18, 21
Hanoverians, 209
Hardwicke, Philip Yorke, 1st earl of, 127
Harrison, William, 3
Hastings family, 123; see also Huntingdon, earl of
hat, refusal to doff, 134, 142
haywards, 53
Heath, Edward, 47, 165
Hebrides, peasant disturbances in, 148
heiresses, aristocratic, 44–5, 101
Henry I, 113
Henry III, 95, 100, 112–13, 115–17, 119, 121
Henry IV, 93, 117
Henry V, 114
Henry VI, 91, 115
Henry VII, 100–2, 105–6
Henry VIII, 19, 23, 50, 52, 100–6
Herbert, William, 1st earl of Pembroke, 103
Herbert family, 123
heriot, 82–3
heriot, the seigneurial right, 31, 97 and glossary
Home, Alexander Douglas-Home, 14th earl of, 152
hon., 23
honorific privileges, 23–4, 151–2
honour, belief in, 75–6
honour, franchise of, 52, 55, 88, 93
Hooper, John, bishop of Gloucester, 136
hospitality, 4, 75–6, 135
houses, households of aristocracy, 40, 55, 71–2, 76, 109, 129, 153–4, 158, 161, 165, 173; see also castles
Howard, Thomas Lord, 101
Howard, Thomas, 3rd duke of Norfolk, 105

Howard family, 104, 110
humanism, 71–2, 135, 162
hundred courts, 51–3, 87
Hungary, nobles of, 7, 21, 35, 57, 210–12
hunting, 32, 128, 136, 140, 169, 184; see also fox hunting; game laws
Huntingdon, Henry Hastings, 3rd earl of, 106; see also Hastings family
husbandry, exemption from, 27
Hyndman, H. M., 130

Iceland, 81
Imperial China, 5
imprisonment, seigneurial right of, 53
imprisonment for debt, see debt
income tax, 155
indentured retaining, see retaining system
Independent Labour Party, 147
industry, industrialisation, 4, 9–10, 12, 63–4, 66, 68–9, 74, 131–2, 138–40, 146–7, 161, 177 and ch. 11
inflation, 29–30, 32, 39, 63, 65–6, 97–8, 107–8, 128, 136, 181, 201
inheritance, see birthright; gavelkind; primogeniture
inns of court, 71, 109
institutional landownership, 157–8
insurance companies, 157
Ireland, peasant disturbances in, 148
Irish Home Rule, 58, 148
Irish peerage, 37
Italian renaissance, 72, 107, 109; see also humanism
Italy
    noble privilege, 21
    seigneurial right, 31

Jacobinism, 131, 138, 143–4, 146
Jacobite uprising (1715), 58
James I, 36–7
James II, 48, 119, 121, 122–3, 205

John, King of England, 95, 112, 114–15, 119, 122
John Reeves' Association, see Reeves, John
judicial indemnity, 87; see also trial by peerage
jury service, exemption from, 21
justices of the peace, 12, 17, 23, 29, 53–5, 69, 90, 95–6, 110, 122, 126–7, 150, 163–4, 168, 203–4

Kent, 66, 179
Kenya, 169
Ket's rebellion, (1549), 30, 137
King, Gregory, 3, 174, 181
king's chapel, exemption from service in, 27
king's great council, 91, 96
knight errantry, 71
knights, knighthood, 2–3, 5, 7–8, 20, 24–8, 38–40, 45, 51, 71, 84–5, 87–90, 92, 153, 157–8, 165

Labour
    governments, 47, 165–6
    Party, 149, 166–7; see also Independent Labour Party
labour services, 37, 96–7, 140, 178
Lacy, Henry de, 3rd earl of Lincoln, 92
Lancashire
    farming, 177
    gentry, 39, 45
    magnates, 100
Lancaster
    earldom, 92
    house of, 100, 117
    palatinate, 93
Lancaster, Thomas, 2nd earl of, 92–3, 112–13, 116–17
Land Commission, 165
land duties, 166
land market, 8, 39, 46, 111, 178
land nationalisation, 130, 145, 147–9, 151, 166–7

Land Nationalisation Society, 130, 147
land reform, 148–9, 151
land tax, 22, 67–8, 124, 185, 207
land value tax, 145, 147, 148, 165
land values, 36, 40, 46, 62, 67, 152–3, 155, 158
landowners, landownership, 3–5, 7–13, 17, 28–33, 35, 37–40, 46, 59–68, 73–4, 82–5, 87–90, 95, 111, 124, 126–30, 133–4, 144–5, 151, 152–3, 156–8, 175, 188–9, 195, 214
Langland, William, 135–6
Last Determination Act (1696), 201
Latimer, Hugh, 135–6
law lords, 36, 154
lawyers, 39
leasehold, 25, 32, 53, 62–6, 97–8, 127, 137, 147, 161, 165, 178, 180–2, 184, 190–1
leasehold enfranchisement, 145, 147, 164–6
Leeds, 64
legal training, 69, 71
Leicester, 64, 192
Leicester, earldom of, 92; see also Montfort, Simon de
Leicestershire gentry, 123
lerywite, 97 and glossary
Levellers, 132–5, 141, 143, 145, 201
Liberals
    governments, 47, 165, 167
    party, 147–9, 168
liberties, 52
licence fees, 32
life barony, 36–8, 47, 153, 165–6
Life Peerage Act (1958), 165, 167
Limited Liability Act (1856), 194
Lincoln, earldom of, 92
Lincolnshire Wolds, farming in, 176
Liverpool, 64, 191
Liverpool–Manchester Railway Company, 193
Lloyd George, David, 1st earl, 148–9

local government, 41, 43, 53–4, 58, 90–1, 95–6, 108–9, 124, 150, 163–5, 168, 204
Lollards, Lollardy, 134, 142
London
  aristocratic residence, 76, 146, 153
  development, 63–4
  wealth, 46, 65
London clubs, 129
Londonderry, marquisate of, 192
lord, title of, 23, 28
lord chancellor, 22
lord high steward, court of, 20
lord lieutenants, 4, 54–6, 94, 108–9, 111, 122, 124, 126–7, 164, 169, 204, 213
lord treasurer, 22
lords, house of, 3–4, 11, 19, 28, 37, 47, 49, 84, 95–6, 124, 126, 130, 133, 141, 145, 147–8, 151, 154, 160, 164, 166–7, 169, 202–3
lords of the manor, 25, 28–33, 51–4, 96–8, 164, 179–80, 191–2; see also seigneurial system
Loughborough canal, 192
Louis XIV, 121, 128
Lovett, William, 138
Low Countries, 87
Lull, Raymond, 2

MacDonald, Ramsay, 152
MacDonnell Commission (1913), 205
Magna Carta (1216), 20, 112–13, 115, 117, 121
magnates, 41–3, 54–6, 58–9, 92–4, 99–109, 111–12, 116–17, 122–4, 168
Manchester, 64, 191
Manchester, Edward Montagu, 2nd earl of, 122
manhood franchise, suffrage, 12, 141, 163, 169, 201–2
manor court rolls, 31–2; see also private justice
manorial lords, see lords of the manor

manors, 17, 21; see also lords of the manor
manufacturing, aristocratic disdain for, see commercial activity
manumission, 22–3, 97, 183
March, earls of, see Mortimer family
marcher lordships of Wales, 52, 107
Market, seigneurial right of, 147, 191–2
marquisate, 23, 47, 84, 91
martial law, 121
Mary I, 100, 106
Mary II, 48
Mary Queen of Scots, 106
Massie, Joseph, 174
mayors, lord, 168
Melton Mowbray, 76
members of parliament, 23, 126, 159, 164, 166–7, 192–3, 201–2
mercenaries, 50
merchet, 97 and glossary
Methodism, 143
military office, 4, 50–1, 93, 110, 150, 205–6
military service
  aristocratic forms of, 50–1, 88, 93
  immunity from, 17–18, 22
militia, 22, 50–1, 108, 206
Militia Act (1757), 22, 127
Mill, James, 130
mill, seigneurial right of, 32
millenarianism, 142
millionaires, 61
minerals tax, 65, 155
mines, minerals, 10–11, 61, 63–5, 68–9, 74, 146–7, 188–90, 196–7
Moghul India, 5
monasteries, dissolution of, 39, 42, 102–3, 136–7
Monmouth's uprising (1685), 120
Montfort, Simon de, earl of Leicester, 92, 113, 116
Montherlant, Henri de, 154–5
More, Sir Thomas, 132, 135
Morison, Richard, 135

Mortalists, 142

mortgages, 46, 65, 67, 129

Mortimer family, 92

Mosley family, 191

Mowbray family, 93–4

mr., 18, 24–8

Mulcaster, Richard, 3

mundbryce, 82 and glossary

Municipal Corporations Act (1835), 168

mutiny acts, 205

Napoleonic wars, 147

national armies, see armies

national debt, 68, 125, 194, 207

National Trust, 153, 157, 166

nationalisation, 165–7

navigation companies, 192

navy, royal, 51

New Levellers, see Diggers

new model army, 123

New Poor Law (1834), 55, 140–1

Newcastle, Thomas Pelham-Holles, 1st duke of, 191; see also Pelham-Holles

Newcastle Philosophical Society, 129

noble privilege, 4–7, 11, 13, 17–28, 35, 58, 81–3, 85–7, 91, 94–5, 110, 124, 133, 144, 150–2, 155, 159–60, 167, 192; see also address; apparel; arms-bearing; arrest; assessment; baronetcy; barony; benefit of clergy; burgbryce; coats of arms; constables; count; court of chivalry; crossbow; debt; duel; dukedom; earldom; esquires; fiscal exemption; flogging; gentry; gesith; hanging; heriot; hon.; husbandry; jury service; king's chapel; life barony; lord; lord high steward; lords, house of; marquisate; mr.; mundbryce; oath-taking; peers; posse comitatus; precedence; requisitioning; re-served office; scandalum magnatum; state services; striking a gentleman; subpoena; tithingmen; trial by peerage; universities; viscountcy; wergeld; wine imports; wites; witness; writs

noblesse de robe, 35

Norfolk

    farming, 176, 179, 183

    gentry, 41, 67

Norfolk

    dukes of, 191, 193

    Thomas Howard, 3rd duke of, 104

    see also Howard family and Mowbray family

Norman conquest, 6, 19, 22, 52–3, 84–9, 92, 134, 144, 206, 209

Norman monarchy, 84–6, 89–90, 113

Normandy, 89, 113–14

Northamptonshire gentry, 45

Northcote–Trevelyan reforms (1854), 54–5, 148, 163, 204–5

northern revolts

    1536–7: 30, 33, 104, 112, 118, 136–7

    1569: 112, 118

Northumberland

    dukes of, 191

    earls of, see Percy family

Northumberland farming, 179, 183

Norway, nobles of, 151

Norwich, aristocratic residence in, 146

Nottingham, 64, 191

nuisance jurisdiction, 53

oath-taking

    authority of, 82

    immunity from, 20

O'Brien, Bronterre, 130

office, income from, 67–9

Ordinances (1311), 112–13

Ottoman empire, 5

oven, seigneurial right of, 32

Owen, Robert, 130, 145

Oxford University, 24–5, 27–8, 158,

167, 205
Oxfordshire, aristocracy of, 154, 158

Paine, Thomas, 130–1, 138, 143–5
palatinates, see Chester; Durham; West
  March; franchises
parish councils, 29, 164, 204
parish vestries, 54
parks, parkland, 73, 158, 173, 179
parliament, 3, 11, 17, 20, 22, 24, 41,
  48–50, 56–8, 95–6, 112, 114,
  116–9, 123–5, 127, 139, 141–2,
  144–5, 148, 151–2, 162–3, 168–9,
  192–3, 198–203, 206–7
Parliament Act (1858), 23
Parliament Act (1911), 38, 55, 151–2
parliamentary enclosures, 180
Parr
  family, 103
  Katherine, 103
partible inheritance, see gavelkind
particule, 26
Paston family, 41
paternalism, 59, 69, 76, 135, 142
patrician status, 81
patronage, 39, 41–3, 48–9, 57, 94, 99,
  103, 106–10, 119–20, 125–6, 148,
  151, 153, 163, 204–6
peasant revolt, 29–30, 33, 66, 97–8, 132,
  137, 183
peasants, 10–12, 29, 39, 66, 97–8, 107,
  139–40, 160–1, 174–9, 183, 189
Peerage Act (1958), see Life Peerage Act
peers, peerage, 3–8, 17–28, 36–8, 40–7,
  51, 61, 69, 84–5, 87, 89, 91–2, 95,
  102, 130, 151–4, 156–8, 163,
  165–7
Pelham-Holles, Thomas, 68; see also
  Newcastle, duke of
pension funds, 157
people, popular, see commoners
Percy family, 55, 101, 118
Petition of Right (1628), 112
Petrie, George, 130

Piers Plowman tradition, 135–6
Pilgrimage of Grace (1536), 136–7; see
  also northern revolts
Pitt, William, 37
Plato, 71
pleas of the crown, 52
Plumpton family, 41
Poland, nobles of, 7, 21, 35, 57, 210–12
poor nobles, 7, 35–6, 61, 154–5
population
  contraction, 29–31, 62, 65–6, 97,
    176, 178, 181
  growth, 31, 38, 97, 176–7, 189, 191
ports, development of, 68, 74, 76, 192
posse comitatus, exemption from serving
  in, 21
pound keepers, 53
precedence, 18, 23–4, 28
predicates, 26
prescription, 26
Preston, Thomas, 130
price rise, price revolution, see inflation
prime minister
  first landless, 152
  earldom for, 47
primogeniture, 4–7, 18, 23, 27–8, 35,
  45, 65, 145, 155, 210–11 and
  glossary
private jurisdiction, 28–9, 32, 51–5, 83,
  87–8, 93–4, 183
private taxes, 29, 31, 52, 83, 183, 191–2;
  see also chevage; tallage
privateering, 51
privy council, 126
professional, professionalised, 11–12,
  35, 41, 54–5, 69, 72–3, 75, 89–90,
  123, 148, 152, 159–60, 162–3,
  168–9, 195, 203, 205–6
proletariat, 66, 128, 140, 146, 161, 174
proprietary office, 148, 163, 205–6
Protestantism
  aristocratic life-style and, 71
  social criticism generated, 135–6,
    142

Provisions of Oxford (1258), 112, 117
Prussia, nobles of, 35, 49, 57, 205, 210–11
public schools, 55, 76–7, 129, 158–9, 161–2, 167, 196

Quakers, 134, 142–3
quarter-sessions, see justices of the peace
Quia Emptores (1290) statute, 55

rabbit warrens, 30
railways, 67–9, 74, 184, 192–3
ransoms, 67
Ranters, 133–5, 142
rates, local, 148, 185
Redesdale, liberty of, 52
reeves
   royal, 84
   seigneurial, 53
Reeves, John, 144
Reform Act (1832), 146, 202–3
Reform Act (1867), 55, 152, 167, 202–3
Reform Act (1884), 55
Reformation
   opposition to, 137
   social complaint and, 142–3
refrigeration, 155
regional councils, 49, 58, 106, 108, 110, 203–4
register of land titles, 145
relief, seigneurial, 31
religious schism
   aristocratic revolt and, 118–20, 122
   social conflict and, 140
renaissance, see humanism and Italian renaissance
rentier landownership, 5, 9, 11, 36, 40, 61–7, 69, 73–4, 156–7, 190, 196
rents, 11, 29–31, 40, 46, 61–3, 65, 97–8, 127–9, 136–7, 140, 147–9, 151–3, 155–7, 162, 179–82

representative government, aristocratic contribution to, 199–203
republicanism, 143–5
republics, ennobling practices of, 9
requisitioning, immunity from, 27
reserved office, 5–6, 24, 28, 95
retaining system, 23, 25, 41, 55–6, 94, 104, 106–7
revolt
   aristocratic, 111–26, 144
   popular, 30, 126, 132, 134, 136–40, 184; see also peasant revolt
revolution, revolutionaries, 6–7, 9–12, 28–9, 125, 132, 134–5, 143–5, 151, 159–63, 175, 200–3, 207–8, 213; see also American revolution; English civil war; French revolution; Glorious Revolution
Ricardo, David, 130, 147
Richard II, 91–2, 114–15, 117, 119
Richard III, 94
Riche, Richard, 1st baron, 118
Rittersgut, 18 and glossary
river improvements, 192
Riviera, 169
Robin Hood ballads, 137
Rockingham, marquis of, see Watson-Wentworth
Roman occupation, 81
romanticism, 76
Rotherhithe, development of, 192
royal absolutism, see absolute monarchy
royal heralds, 17, 26, 39, 95, 111
royal household, 4, 90, 106, 116
royal justice, 29, 52–3, 87–8, 95–6
royalties, mining, 190, 196
Rural District and Parish Councils Act (1894), 164
Russell, John, 1st earl of Bedford, 103
Russell, John, 1st earl Russell, 202
Russell, Lord William, son of 1st duke of Bedford, 123
Russell, family, 103, 147, 192

Russia
  government, 205
  nobles of, 7, 35, 210–12
Rutland, Henry Manners, 2nd earl of, 42
Rutland gentry, 54

St Simonians, 131, 145
sake and soke, toll and team and infangthef, 52 and glossary
sale of honours, 8, 35, 120
Salisbury, earldom of, 92
Sandemanians, 142–3
Sandhurst college, 51
Saye, William Fiennes, 1st viscount of Saye and of Sele, 122
Saxon, see Anglo-Saxon
scandalum magnatum, 20
Scandinavia, nobles of, 21
Scarborough, Richard Lumley-Saunderson, 4th earl of, 32
school boards, aristocratic membership of, 55
Scotland, 50, 67, 85, 103, 113–15
Scottish Highlands, 68
Scottish peerage, 37
Seaham, development of, 192
seaside resorts, aristocracy and, 63–4
seats, see houses
second world war, 47, 53
Secret Ballot Act (1872), 55, 152, 163, 202
sectarianism, 142–3
Sedition Acts (1792 and 1795), 141
Sefton, earls of, 191
seigneurial system, 6–7, 10–11, 17, 28–33, 51–3, 58, 63, 65–6, 83, 85, 92, 96–100, 147, 151, 160, 175, 178, 180–4, 191–2; see also aleconners; assize of bread and ale; bailiffs; banalities; barony; beadles; boon work; breach of promise; bread weighers; casualties; champart; chevage; constables; court baron; court leet; customary tenures; debt jurisdiction; dues; entry fines; fishing; franchises; frankpledge; freeholds; gallows; gamekeepers; gifts; haywards; heriot; honours; hundred courts; hunting; imprisonment; labour services; lerywite; liberties; licence fees; lords of the manor; market; merchet; mill; nuisance; oven; pound keepers; reeves, relief; sake and soke; serfdom; tallage; tithingmen; tolls; town criers; trespass; week work; weights and measures
senatorial status, 79–83
serfdom, serfs, 29–30, 32–3, 65–6, 97, 127, 136–7, 174, 183
servants, 153–4, 158, 202
Seymour
  Edward, see Somerset, Protector
  Jane, 103
  Thomas, 1st baron Seymour of Sudeley, 42
Seymour family, 103, 123
Shaftesbury, Anthony Ashley Cooper, 1st earl of, 123, 201
sharecroppers, 30, 182
Sheffield, 64, 191–2
Shelley, Percy Bysshe, 131
sheriffs, 17, 21, 51–3
shire courts, 51, 87
shopkeepers, 140
Shrewsbury
  George Talbot, 4th earl of, 104
  Charles Talbot, 12th earl and 1st duke of, 123
Sicily, nobles of, 86
Six Articles Act (1539), 132
slaves, 83
smallholders, smallholdings, 3, 30, 139–40, 168, 176–7, 179–80, 182–3; see also peasants
Smith, James, 131, 145

Smith, Sir Thomas, 2–3
Social Democratic Federation, 130, 147
social mobility
down, 6, 8, 9, 13, 45–6, 61, 155–6
up, 4, 6, 8–9, 13, 37–41, 44–6, 75, 128–9, 155, 187–8
Socinians, 142
Somerset, Protector, 42, 103–4, 110, 132
Spanish Habsburgs, ennoblement by, 35, 39
spas, aristocracy and, 63
Spence, Thomas, 129–30, 134, 143
spiritual peers, 36
Stafford, Bishop, 3
Stafford family, 100; see also Buckingham
Stamford, 191
standing army, see armies
Stanley, Ferdinando, 5th earl of Derby, 106
Stanley family, 100; see also Derby, earldom of
Star Chamber, court of, 20
state services, immunity from, 21–2, 27
Statute of Gloucester (1278), 52–3
Statute of Labourers (1563), see Apprenticeship Act
Statute of Marlborough (1268), 21
Statute of Retainers (1390), 23, 25; see also retaining system
stocks and shares, stock market, 68, 156–7
strict settlements, 46, 64, 145
striking a gentleman, 27
Stuarts, 58, 102, 112, 118–23, 126–7, 147, 203, 207
subinfeudation, 55, 85, 88–90, 94, 99
subpoena, immunity from, 20
subservience, see deference
subsidy, special assessment right, 22
subsistence farming, 10, 30
Suffolk, duke of, see Brandon, Charles
Suffolk farming, 179

Suffolk gentry, 45, 54
supertax, 156
suspending powers, royal, 121
Sussex farming, 179
Sussex gentry, 54
Sutherland, George Leveson-Gower, 1st duke of, 68, 193
Sweden, nobles of, 35, 210–11
sword-wearing privilege, 17

tallage, 31, 97 and glossary
tax on wool, 117
taxation, 22–3, 40, 49–50, 58, 62, 68, 86–7, 96, 114, 117, 125, 127, 137, 147, 153, 155–6, 164–5, 185, 194, 206–8; see also consumption; excise; land tax; private taxes; wealth taxes
tenant right, 137, 164–6, 179
tenantry, 10–11, 30–3, 40–1, 62–3, 65–6, 127–8, 135–7, 156–7, 161, 164–5, 181–4
tenants-in-chief, 19, 22, 52, 56, 84–7, 89, 91, 96, 101, 109–10, 116; see also barony, tenurial
Thatcher, Margaret, 152, 165
thegns, 73, 84–5 and glossary
Thompson, Flora, 154, 158
'thouing', 134, 142
tillage legislation, 126, 136–7, 147–8, 182, 185
timber, 61, 63, 69
tithes, 140, 147
tithingmen
immunity from serving as, 21
seigneurial appointment of, 53
see glossary
tolls, 29, 31, 191
Tomlin Commission (1929), 204
Tories
government, 47, 165–7
Party, 124–5, 127, 168, 202
town and country planning acts, 164–6
town criers, 53

towns
and electoral reform, 202–3
aristocratic residence in, 76, 146,
153
aristocratic development of, 190–2
opposition to aristocracy, 139–40,
147
support for aristocracy, 168
see also urban development
trading companies, joint-stock, 67
transport improvements, 10, 68, 74,
188, 192–3, 196
treason, 20, 52, 89, 93, 101
treasury, 204
trespass, seigneurial jurisdiction in, 53
Trevelyan, Sir Charles, see Northcote
–Trevelyan reforms
trial by peerage, 20–1
Tudor, Jasper, earl of Pembroke and
duke of Bedford, 100
Tudor, Mary, daughter of Henry VIII,
105
Tudors, 42–3, 49, 55, 57–9, 94, 100–12,
118, 120, 123, 126–7, 147, 162,
203, 209
turnpike trusts, 192–3
Tyler, Wat, 132
Tyndale, William, 136
Tyndale, liberty of, 52

unit trusts, 157
universities
education, 71, 109, 159
privilege, 23–5, 27
see also Oxford University, Cambridge University
urban development, 10–11, 61, 63–4,
190–2, 196–7
Uses, 109
usury laws, 194
utilitarianism, 131

vassals, 41
vavasours, 56, 84, 89, 95 and glossary

Verga, Giovanni, 154–5
viscountcy
office, 51
title, 23, 84, 91
visitations of heralds, 26, 29
vocation, neglect of, 136
Volney, Comte de, 138

wages, 140–1, 148, 161, 174
Wales, 40, 85, 114, 168
Wallace, Alfred Russel, 130, 147
Walpole, Robert, 1st earl of Oxford,
127
Wantage, Robert Loyd-Lindsay, 1st
baron, 62–3
war of the Spanish succession, 121
war office, 204
wardship, 24, 89
Wars of the Roses, 41–2, 105, 107, 114
Warwick
Thomas de Beauchamp, 12th earl of,
117
Robert Rich, 2nd earl of, 122
waterworks, 147, 191
Watson-Wentworth family, 68
wealth taxes, 207; see also estate duty;
capital gains tax; capital transfer
tax
Wear, river, 32
weights and measures, seigneurial right
over, 53
welfare state, 150, 166–7
Welles, John, 10th baron and 1st
viscount, 105
wergeld, 19, 81–2, 94–5 and glossary
West March, palatinate of, 94
Westminster, 43, 90, 204
Westmorland farming, 177
Wharton, Philip, 4th baron, 122
Whigs, 124–5, 202
Whitehaven, development of, 192
Wigston Magna, Leicestershire, 179
William I, 85
William III, 48, 121, 123

Wills, Statute of (1540), 109–10
Wilson, James Harold, Baron Wilson of Rievaulx, 169 n. 2
Wilson, Thomas, 3
Wilton, earls of, 191
Wiltshire farming, 176, 179
Wiltshire gentry, 123
Winchelsey, Robert, archbishop of Canterbury, 117
Winchester school, 76–7
wine imports, 22
Winstanley, Gerard, 133–4
wire fences, 147

wites, 82 and glossary
witness, immunity from service as, 21
writs, immunity from, 20
Wyatt's rebellion (1554), 112
Wycliffe, John, 136

yeomanry, 39, 42
York, aristocratic residence in, 146
Yorkists, 42, 58, 102
Yorkshire
  farming, 176
  gentry, 41, 46
  revolt, 132